POTTERY AND PORCELAIN

A Dictionary of Terms.

POTTERY AND PORCELAIN

A Dictionary of Terms

BERNARD H. CHARLES

HIPPOCRENE
BOOKS, INC.
NEW YORK CITY

Hippocrene Books
171 Madison Avenue
New York, N.Y. 10016

Library of Congress Catalog Card Number 74-81392
ISBN 0-88254-278-8

Printed in Great Britain

CONTENTS

INTRODUCTION

Probably more than most other ancient crafts, that of making pottery and porcelain abounds in a multiplicity of styles and techniques, couched in a language of terminology as diverse as the civilisations which have made it, and as various as the materials used. This dictionary defines and classifies most of the terms in normal usage and to record many which are disappearing or which are already obsolete—the latter being mainly those in the categories of equipment and processes, having been replaced by modern mechanised methods of production.

Being a dictionary, and not an encyclopaedia, the names of localities, factories or individuals are not listed, except where their names have become synonymous with a particular style or technique, eg *Martin ware, Rockingham glaze*. Some terms have several meanings, conversely some processes or styles are known by different names in different localities, or even from one factory to another in the same locality. Wherever alternative information has been found this has been recorded, but the author recognises that many gaps are still left to be filled. Some terms are dealt with at length, for a dictionary, others are necessarily brief. None claim to be anything more than a summary; not authoritative in themselves but based upon authoritative sources—a bibliography is provided. The aims are to provide a companion volume to most other ceramic publications; a related technical guide for the connoisseur, private collector and art historian; a historical outline for the technical ceramist; a general introduction for the student, craftsman, those engaged in the retail trade, amateur potters and others who derive pleasure as laymen.

Throughout the text, alternative terminology is indicated by quotation marks, and italics denote entries under which additional related information may be found. The cross reference thus obtained will provide a trail of related information. This is supported by a classified list of entries which affords a possible reference approach when perhaps the principle of a style or technique is known but its actual name is not. The classification is broad so that some entries are to be found listed under more than one heading. Initial reference under the appropriate heading may bring to mind two or three possible terms, one of which through the cross reference of italics may lead the reader to the information required.

B.C.

GLOSSARY OF TERMS

Accouchment set or vasi puerperali composite piece comprising a broth basin, a shallow dish, a cup and a salt-cellar with cover; the whole nesting together to form a large impressive vase. Probably originated in Italy during the Renaissance but made in various forms throughout Europe. Made as presentation pieces, frequently for ladies in confinement.

Achette Scottish word for a dish. From the French—'assiette'.

Acid etch or acid gold decoration gold relief decoration introduced during the nineteenth century and still used today. Intricate patterns are etched into the glazed *whiteware*, banded with 'best gold' (cf *burnished gold*) and burnished. The gold on the low-lying areas of the relief burnishes to a lesser degree than that on the upstanding areas, thus serving to emphasise the pattern of the relief.

Acid-proof ware ware which is inert to most acids (except hydrofluoric acid) and is used to contain them. It is made in the form of jars, tanks, bottles etc. Acid-proof wares are made of vitreous *stoneware* and *porcelain*.

Acetabula small Roman bowl, corresponding to the Greek *bell krater*.

Ackey resist substance used in conjunction with *sheet-pattern* transfers. It is applied to such areas of the ware as are to be left plain, to prevent the transfer sticking in these areas. Also used as an expedient for fitting a transfer to a shape for which it is not specifically designed, so as to prevent overlap on to areas to be left plain.

Adobe   sandy, surface clay used by primitive peoples for making sun-dried bricks.

Aeolian clay   formation of clay transported by wind action.

Aerography or aerograph decoration   method of decoration or glazing using compressed air and a spray gun. The colour or *glaze* is finely ground and suspended in a thin medium of water or oil. Extensively used for glazing, but for decorating it is usually reserved for the paler colours. Speedier than *groundlay* but not so suitable for strong colour requiring depth.

1   *Staffordshire agate-ware tea-pot c 1750 (Victoria & Albert Museum)*

Agate   (1) technique simulating veined agate stone. Alternate slices of clay of differing colours, but of otherwise similar firing characteristics, are laid upon each other and kneaded together. After *throwing* and *turning* the agate quality is revealed (see ill 1). Sometimes referred to as 'onyx ware' or 'pebble ware', or in

10

the USA as *scroddled ware* or 'lava ware'; (2) pointed stone used for burnishing *best gold* in deeply embossed areas. Particularly important when burnishing a *scratch-edge*.

Ageing storage of a prepared clay or *body* in a moist condition to improve plasticity. Also known as 'maturing' or 'souring'. Not to be confused with *weathering*.

Agglomerate clay clay containing a high proportion of rock fragments. Of little use to potters on account of the relatively high cost of cleaning, but it may sometimes be ground and used for brick making, cf *conglomerate clay*; *colluvial clay*.

Ailes de mouches French term for the opalescent fly's wing quality found on some K'ang Hsi (see appendix 1) *apple-green* wares.

Air-drying drying under natural conditions without the use of applied heat, cf *sun pan*.

Ai vakariri Fijian cooking pot, shaped somewhat like a cauldron, occasionally having a pouring lip similar to a *mortar*.

Aka see *boccaro*.

Akaji-kinga popular, red and gold decoration on the Japanese Kaga ware of the late nineteenth century.

Akaraku Japanese—'red raku'; *raku* ware made of a fine red clay; the softest fired of the different types of raku ware, cf *juraku-zuchi*; *kuroraku*.

Alabaster hard translucent form of *gypsum*; used by Bottger in his early *soft-paste* porcelain trials (not to be confused with his later *hard-paste*), and as a flux in Sèvres and other soft-pastes. Used to make pottery moulds before the introduction of *plaster of Paris* (calcined gypsum) in the 1740s.

Alabastron small, narrow-necked Greek bottle with a round base. Used for containing perfumes, cf *Greek vases* (ill 47).

11

Albany slip   slip made from clay found near Albany USA. It is very fine and contains such a high quantity of *flux* that it makes a ready base for stoneware glazes, cf *glaze*.

Albarello   apothecary jar of cylindrical form, waisted about its centre which facilitates easy removal from within a row of similar shapes on a shelf. Made of *maiolica* in Italy as early as the fifteenth century but the shape was made in the East at a much earlier date, it continued in use throughout Europe until the eighteenth century. The Italian jars were usually well decorated with flowing, polychrome brushwork; those of northern Europe and Britain were less profusely decorated and mostly in blue and white, following the Chinese influence. An inscription indicating the contents is usually included in the pattern. Derivation of the term is thought either to be a diminutive of the Italian for 'a little tree', or more probably from the Persian—'el barini' meaning a vase for drugs, cf *apothecary jars* (ill 4).

Albite   see *felspar*.

Alcarraza   porous *earthenware* jar used as a water cooler.

Alfardone   Spanish elongated hexagonal tile, often set round a square tile, called a *loseta*, to form an octagon; made in Spain from the fifteenth century (see ill 2).

2   Alfardone

Alginate   marine organic matter obtained from seaweed, used as a suspension agent for *glaze* and *slip* to reduce the tendency to settle out during use. Sometimes known as 'Irish moss', cf *carrageen.*

Alicatados   decorative mosaic panels made in Spain from the thirteenth century onwards.

Aliceras   *tesserae* made by cutting coloured glazed tiles; a technique reaching its peak during the fourteenth century in Spain, to be seen in the mosaics at Alhambra and Seville.

Alkaline glaze   glaze in which the principal flux is alkaline, eg *vegetable ash, calcium oxide, barium oxide.*

Alla castellana ware   see *mezza-maiolica.*

Alla porcelana   Italian term for a style of *maiolica* characterised by designs of foliage with twisted stems; in blue and white after the manner of imported fifteenth-century Chinese *porcelain.*

Alligator's-teeth   see *dog's-teeth.*

Alluvial clays   *secondary clays* of variable composition, formed by settling out in rivers and lakes. Often used in the manufacture of bricks.

Alumina Al_2O_3, aluminium oxide, a highly *refractory* material having a melting temperature in the region of 2,040°C. In glazes it is used to increase the viscosity during the molten period; it gives durability; prevents the formation of crystals during cooling (cf *crystalline glaze*); it may also be used as an opacifier and matting agent if introduced in relatively high proportions. Alumina is usually introduced into a glaze as a constituent of clay, but it also is available in a pure ground state, having been recovered from *bauxite.* It is used in the preparation of *bat wash* and as a *placing sand* for *bone china.* In the field of technology, alumina ceramics have made a significant contribution in the development of a wide range of scientific equipment, from refractories (cf *refractory*), laboratory ware and electronics, to aeronautics and space exploration.

13

Aluminium oxide   see *alumina*.

Amakusa   Japanese felspathic rock or clay; a form of *pegmatite*, so named after the island where it was found. Used by the Arita factories as a constituent of their porcelain body.

Amorini or Amoretti   winged cupids sometimes to be found in Italian *maiolica* painting. Cupids without wings are known as *putti*.

Amphora   Greek shape, a storage jar for wine (see ill 3). The shape often has a pointed base (with or without a foot) designed to concentrate the wine lees, thus facilitating efficient decanting, cf *Greek vases*.

3   *Amphora with black-figure decoration*

Anatase TiO_2; a form of titania, cf *titanium oxide*; *rutile*; *brookite*.

Anglo gum or British gum   gum prepared from dextrine; suitable as an alternative to *gum Arabic*, cf *carrageen*; *gum tragacanth*; *funori*.

An-hua   'secret decoration'; a porcelain technique in which the unfired ware is carved in very slight, almost imperceptible relief. The full effect of the decoration is visible only after firing, when, if a piece is held to the light, the pattern will show as varying degrees of translucency. To be found on Ming wares (see appendix

1), usually white bowls, the pattern often being on the bases. European nineteenth-century equivalents are known as *lithophanes*, or 'Berlin transparencies'.

Aniseed   (oil of aniseed); used in *enamel painting* to keep colour open for a longer period to allow for fine painting, the oils of fennel and lavender may be similarly used.

Anorthite   see *felspar*.

Antikzierat   relief pattern of *fluting* on Berlin *porcelain* tablewares, 1767-8 onwards.

Antimonate of lead Sb_2O_3, a yellow colourant for low-temperature *glazes*; or can be used as a pigment for *underglaze decoration* and *maiolica* painting; otherwise known as 'Naples yellow'.

Antimony   material which, if combined with *lead oxide,* will produce the yellow pigment known as 'Naples yellow', cf *antimonate of lead*.

AO   see *buccaro*.

Apothecary jars or drug jars   essentially practical, though highly decorative, sturdy storage pots for dry and liquid drugs; made in Europe since the fifteenth century. The *Hispano-Moresque ware* and Italian *maiolica* examples are particularly colourful and decorative. The principal shapes are the *albarello* and the *baluster* pot for dry powders, pills etc; narrow-necked bottles and full-bellied pots with spouts (the Spanish variety known as *boetja*) for liquids (see ill 4).

Apple green   green transparent *enamel* of the K'ang Hsi period of the Ch'ing dynasty (see appendix 1). Used over a clear or white porcelain glaze as a self colour. Sometimes broken by a *crackle* in the glaze giving an opalescent effect like that of a fly's wing, and known in Europe as *ailes de mouches,* cf *coral red; clair-de-lune; peach bloom; mirror black; kingfisher blue; Nankin yellow; Imperial yellow; sang-de-boeuf; sang-de-pigeon; celadon.*

15

4   *Apothecary jars : 1 albarello ; 2 boetja ; 3, 4 English drug jars for liquid and dry drugs*

Aquamanile jug or water pot made in the form of an animal, or sometimes as a mounted knight.

Arabian lustre see *lustre*.

Arbour group figure group set in a background of foliage.

Argil from the French—'argile' meaning clay; a term used with particular regard to potter's clay.

Arista see *cuenca*.

Ark large vat or tank, usually below floor level, used for mixing and storing *slip*. In the preparation of fine tableware bodies it is usual to process through three arks: (1) the 'dirty ark', for preliminary preparation and storage; (2) the 'mixing ark' for blending wet ingredients; (3) the 'clean ark' for continued blending and storage after the slip has been sieved and passed over magnets to extract iron; (4) another type known as a 'settling ark' is a tank used to settle water-ground materials prior to grading.

Armenian bole ferruginous earth useful as a painting pigment. Its composition is virtually that of *red iron oxide* plus a small amount of clay, cf *iron oxide*.

Armorial ware shields, coats of arms and other such heraldic devices appear on pottery and porcelain from an early date, becoming most popular during the Renaissance. *Hispano-Moresque ware* and Italian *maiolica* were often decorated with the coats of arms of their patrons. Rhenish salt-glazed wares (cf *Rhenish stoneware*), French *faience,* Dutch and English *delftware* all produced armorial ware. Chinese *porcelain,* usually in services and painted with coats of arms, crests or initials, was made to order and imported into Europe during the late seventeenth and eighteenth centuries. Some English factories, notably Worcester, made armorial china and porcelain in the late eighteenth century. Minton, Spode, Wedgwood and other leading factories have continued to make armorial wares (see ill 5), embassy services and commemorative wares (see ill 78). In the nineteenth century

17

the factory of W. H. Goss became almost synonymous with armorial ware, it claims to have supplied appropriate armorial china to every town in England with a coat of arms.

5   *Armorial ware, modern bone-china service produced by Spode for the Bank of London & South America*

Arretine ware   type of Roman pottery first made at Arretine from where it derives its generic name. A *redware* considered as the finest Roman pottery and made from about 155 BC until the end of the first century AD. Because of its smooth shiny surface it is sometimes known as *red-gloss ware*. It is nearly always decorated in *bas relief*.

Aryballos   small Greek oil container, used by athletes at the baths, cf *Greek vases* (see ill 47).

Asbolite   also known as 'gosu'; an impure ore of *cobalt oxide*, used by the early Chinese and Persian potters to obtain mellow blues known as 'Chinese blue' or 'Mohammedan blue'.

Ash   vegetable ashes are a source of *potash* and are widely used by studio potters as a *flux* for *stoneware* glazes, often with most rewarding results. Some of the finest Chinese glazes are of this type. The actual composition of the ashes vary from plant to plant and in relation to the earth upon which the plant grew. Most ashes will be found to contain *potash, lime, alumina* and *silica*, cf *ash glaze*; *chun glaze*.

Ash glaze   when vegetable ash is used as the principal or only *flux* in a *stoneware* glaze it imparts characteristic qualities not otherwise obtainable. The vast range of colour and texture is dependent upon the type of plant from which the ash originates. The choice of fuel used for firing the kiln is also significant. A good basic glaze recipe for comparing the effects of different types of ash is: two parts ash; two parts felspar; one part clay (preferably a relatively iron-free variety, eg china clay or one of the purer ball clays), cf *ash*; *chun glaze*.

Ash marl   variety of *fireclay* used for making *saggars*.

Askos   small Greek flask used for oil or perfume. Usually asymmetrical in shape with an offset neck and handle. Sometimes in the form of stylised birds or boats (see ill 6), cf *Greek vases*.

6   *Askos*

Asparagus holder   flat, trough-shaped container for asparagus; open at each end and tapering towards one end, so that if a number are placed side by side they form a circle. Perhaps designed to fit a large round serving dish for presentation at table, each article containing an individual portion. Many of these pieces were made by Spode and decorated with *engraved decoration* in blue and white.

Aubergine purple purple painting pigment obtained from *manganese oxide*.

Aventurine glaze *crystalline glaze* with a high iron content (up to 10 per cent) and low in *alumina*. Such glazes must be cooled slowly, when the lack of alumina permits some of the iron to crystallise forming brilliant red-gold flecks on the surface of an otherwise deep-black glaze. Crystalline glazes can be achieved using other oxides but the term aventurine properly belongs to those containing iron, cf *devitrification*.

Azulejo general term for a Spanish tile but more correctly refers to the highly decorative tiles made at Seville and Malaga from the fourteenth century. These tiles were decorated by the *cuenca* and *cuerda seca* methods; they measured about 14cm square, cf *olambrilla*; *tablero*.

Bacile a deep, bowl-shaped dish.

Bacile amatori Italian; emblematic love gifts in *maiolica*, cf *coppa d'amore*.

Bacino decorative dish or plaque let into the walls of churches. Originally *lustre* wares from Egypt and Syria, the idea eventually spread to Spain and Italy where it was carried out in *maiolica* and set in mosaic, cf *cachala*.

Back stamp maker's name or trademark as it appears on the back or underside of *ware*. The usual method of application is by rubber stamp (cf *stamping*), either manual or mechanised. Sometimes a small version of the *Murray-curvex machine* is used when justified by long production runs. Better-quality stamps, often including details of the pattern, its reference number etc, are used for more expensive wares and are usually applied by transfer, cf *transfer decoration*.

Backstone circular cast-iron plate with a handle, used by engraved-transfer printers to keep their colour at exactly the right temperature. It rests half on the hot-plate and can be manoeuvered so that the right heat is maintained. Derived from 'bakestone', a one-time household item for baking, cf *engraved decoration*.

Bad bench term used in some factories to describe a bench or table on which non-perfect *ware* is displayed for the management to appraise faults, cf *seconds*; *lump*; *waster*.

Baffle see *bag wall*.

Bag wall *refractory* wall inside a kiln, built to deflect flames and hot gases through the path required and to protect the *ware* from *flashing*. Sometimes referred to as a *flash wall* or 'baffle'.

Bagyne cup *porringer* with two flat *lug handles*, made in *maiolica* from about the sixteenth century.

7 *Devonshire ball-clay pit*

21

Ball clay very plastic *secondary clay* which, compared with most other secondary clays, is relatively free of *iron oxide* and therefore white or cream burning. Used in the preparation of a *body* to impart plasticity and to assist vitrification; in a glaze as a source of *alumina* and as an aid to the suspension of less-plastic materials. The main deposits in England are in Devon (see ill 7) and Dorset; in the USA they are to be found in Tennessee and Kentucky. There are two opinions concerning the origin of the term 'ball' clay. In Devon it is thought to be on account of the fact that at one time the clay was made up into ball-shaped pieces, weighing about 35lb each, to facilitate easy handling. In Dorset there is a strong opinion that the derivation of the term is a contraction of *tubal*, a special adze-like tool used for digging clay, cf *bentonite*.

Balling (1) *casting* fault which occurs if a section of a mould is almost isolated from the rest, connected only by a narrow channel which may have a tendency to fill and thus starve the isolated section of *slip* so that it does not fill; (2) sometimes used to define a glaze fault otherwise known as *crawling* or 'ruckling'; (3) making up of pieces of clay in readiness for use by the thrower or jolley operator, cf *throwing*; *jigger and jolley*.

Ball mill sometimes referred to as a 'pebble mill'; grinding machine consisting of a *porcelain* or granite-lined steel cylinder which is rotated horizontally about its axis. The *charge* of materials to be ground is loaded, together with a quantity of porcelain balls or flint pebbles which create a grinding action against the lining when the mill is in motion. The principle was patented by Alsing in 1867; the first Alsing ball mill was imported into England in 1910.

Baluster vase or jug tall shape with a fullness about the middle, a frequently occurring shape in European medieval wares and Chinese ceramics (see ill 8).

Bamboo ware alternative name for *cane ware*.

22

8 *English medieval baluster
jug*

Band or bont iron band or strap fitted to the outside of a *bottle
oven* (and other kilns) to strengthen the brickwork and prevent
bulging and other similar distortion due to constant firing.

Bander (1) type of pottery-painter's brush or *pencil,* shaped for
the painting of bands of colour on *ware* (see ill 94), cf *pencil*;
lining; (2) an operative employed to apply bands of colour on
ware.

Banding painting bands of colour on *ware*, cf *lining* (3); *banding
wheel*.

Banding wheel pottery-decorator's wheel, a turntable on
which an article to be banded is centred and spun in order to
apply bands, or lines, of colour.

Bank see *pot-bank*.

Banking of clay stacking of clay in heaps exposed to the
elements to 'weather', cf *weathering*.

Barbeaux a French term for cornflowers; a popular motif on
French porcelain of the eighteenth and nineteenth centuries.

Barber's bowl see *bleeding bowl* (ill 15).

Barbman French—*bellarmine*, cf *greybeard*; *bartmannskrug*.

23

Barbotine decoration   use of coloured *slip* applied by painting or *trailing,* often further worked up with the fingers or a spatula, cf *impasto ware*; *slipware.*

Bar crusher   crushing machine in which loosely fitting bars (which act as hammers) are mounted on a rotating drum. The drum rotates at high speed causing the bars to strike the material being processed as it is fed from an inclined hopper. Also known as a 'hammer mill' or 'cage mill'.

Barium carbonate $BaCo_3$, occurs naturally as *witherite* or is obtained from *barium sulphate (barytes)*; it is the usual source of barium oxide in glazes. Barium carbonate can be used as a *flux* in high-temperature glazes when its presence encourages the development of colour. When used in larger quantities it produces *matt glaze.* As an additive to clays, barium carbonate prevents *scumming,* this is particularly applicable in the manufacture of bricks and other *redware* and *red heavy-clay ware,* when it is normally introduced as *barytes* or in some instances, as 'black ash' *(barium sulphide)*, cf *Canton blue.*

Barium oxide   BaO, see *barium carbonate.*

Barium sulphate $BaSO_4$, also known as 'barytes' or 'heavy spar', cf *barium carbonate.*

Barium sulphide   commonly known as 'black ash', cf *barium carbonate.*

Bartmannskrug   sixteenth-century German, Rhenish salt-glazed *bellarmine,* cf *bellarmine*; *greybeard*; *barbmann*; *Rhenish stoneware*; *salt glaze* (see ill 115).

Barytes $BaSO_4$, *barium sulphate,* cf *caulk stone.*

Basalt ware   black *vitreous* ware, first made by Josiah Wedgwood in the mid-eighteenth century and still in current production. Named after the rock, the body is stained with *iron oxide* and *manganese oxide,* it is unglazed externally and frequently decorated in relief, though recent pieces have been decorated in gold lustre, cf *liquid lustre*. Sometimes erroneously referred to as *Egyptian Black*.

Basket ware   thin strips of clay are extruded (cf *extrusion*) from a *wad box* and used to construct articles after the fashion of basket work. This is usually carried out in a plaster mould which acts as a former. Sometimes the construction is actually woven, alternatively, as in Beleek ware, the strips are simply laid upon each other with the possible use of *slip* for adhesion.

Bas relief   shallow, low relief, raised above the background and with no undercutting. *Sprigged decoration* on Wedgwood *jasper ware* is an example.

Basse-taille   very subtle *bas relief* decoration glazed with a transparent, coloured glaze. The variation in depth of the modelling causes a corresponding variation in the colour intensity and tonal relationships within the glaze.

Bat   (1) flat slab of clay, sometimes called a 'clot', as beaten out, or 'batted out' (cf *batting out*) either by hand or with a *batting machine*, and used for making *flatware*; (2) flat piece of *plaster of Paris* or board used to place *ware* upon. A kiln bat is a *refractory* shelf used for *placing* ware in the kiln; (3) gelatine pad used in the process of *bat printing*.

Batavian ware   alternative name for the lustrous brown-glazed ware of the K'ang Hsi period of the Ch'ing dynasty (see appendix 1). Sometimes used as a self colour and sometimes as a background to reserved panels in white containing decoration in the *famille verte* style. So called after the Dutch settlement and trading post at Batavia in Java, through which the Dutch East India Company imported these wares.

Batch   the correct amount and proportion of raw materials ready to be loaded, or 'charged' (cf *charge*) into a mill, *frit* kiln, *mixing ark* or other such equipment.

Bat printing   method of reproducing an engraved pattern on ceramic *ware*; introduced into England from the continent of

Europe about 1760 and subsequently developed in Staffordshire by Adams of Cobridge, Baddeley of Shelton, Mintons and Spode of Stoke-on-Trent, also by Worcester, Swansea and the Herculaneum pottery (Liverpool).

The engraving used is finer and shallower than that for the usual printing on tissue (see *engraved decoration*), so much so in fact, that the normal mixture of ceramic colour in oil would nearly all be wiped out of the engraving when the plate is 'scraped' and 'bossed' (cf *scraper*; *boss*). Instead, the engraving is filled with printing oil only, which, after scraping and bossing in the normal way, is printed onto a gelatine pad or *bat*. The bat is then applied to the ware, rather after the manner of *stamping*, causing the oiled image to be transferred to it. This is subsequently dusted with powdered ceramic colour to the decorator's choice, cf *underglaze decoration*; *enamel*.

Batter   slightly domed disc of *plaster of Paris* or wood with a handle on the reverse, used for *batting out* clay (see ill 9).

9   *Presser's batter*

Batting machine   otherwise known as a 'spreader'; machine for making flat slabs of clay used in plate making, saucer making etc. It has a flat *plaster of Paris* turntable onto which a ball of plastic clay is thrown, a flat template is brought into contact with the clay forcing it into a flat *bat*. The thickness of the bat may be varied by adjusting the travel of the template arm, or 'monkey', cf *jigger and jolley*.

Batting out   making flat *bats* of clay suitable for making flatware. This may be achieved by using a wire bow to cut an initial slice and followed by beating and rolling to the required thickness. Such is the hand method as practised by craft potters and until quite recent times still in use by some parts of the industry. Batting out was the principal task of the much joked of *saggar-maker's bottom-knocker*.

Bat wash   *refractory* materials such as *flint*, *alumina* and *china clay* suspended in water to make a milky wash; applied to *kiln furniture* to prevent sticking at high temperatures, cf *stuck ware*; *sucked ware*.

Bauxite   *sedimentary* rock; the raw material from which *alumina* is recovered. It consists of hydrated alumina, *titanium* and *iron oxide*.

Beading   relief decoration using an *embossing wheel* to impress a repeat pattern by rolling it over the surface of the *ware*.

Beaker   basic pottery shape; a drinking vessel, usually tall in relation to its girth, with or without a handle.

Beaker ware   pottery made by an ancient warrior race known as the 'Beaker Folk' on account of the characteristic beaker shapes of their pottery. Made of a pink firing clay, beaker wares are well made and are usually decorated with incised geometric or *cord-mark decoration*.

Bear jug   salt-glazed (cf *salt glaze*) *stoneware* jug and cup in the form of a seated bear, the head of which is detachable and forms the cup. The bear's coat is depicted by small pieces of clay extruded through a coarse sieve (see ill 10). Made in Staffordshire, Chesterfield and Nottingham during the eighteenth century.

10   18th-century Staffordshire bear jug

Beater wooden tool used at one time in the Dorset *ball clay* mines to beat down and compact the surface of the *clay bed*, in readiness to lay a railway track for the clay trucks, cf *packer*; *tubal* (see ill 129).

Bedder placer's tool, cf *placer*; a *plaster of Paris* shape conforming to the ware being placed. When pressed into a bed of *placing sand* a perfect support is made on which the ware may be fired without fear of warping. Essential for the *biscuit firing* of *bone-china flatware*, cf *bedding*; *setter* (see ill 120).

Bedding *setting* of *ware* in a support of *placing sand* or powdered *alumina*, to prevent warping during the *biscuit firing* (see ill 11); particularly important in the production of *bone china*. A number of similar pieces or groups of compatible shapes are 'bedded' together in a *bung* within a *saggar*, as opposed to a single article in a *setter* (see ill 120), cf *setter*; *bedder*; *setting-in*; *'oss*.

11 Bedding

Bekko Japanese tortoise-shell glaze made by the Chosa potters of the Satsuma princedom since the seventeenth century. Other Chosa glazes are *ja katsu, namako, tessha*, also an inlaid decoration called *mishima*.

Bellarmine name given in England to the salt-glazed (cf *salt-glaze*) *stoneware* wine bottles characterised by a bearded mask on the neck (see ill 12). Sometimes called 'greybeards', the name is taken from Cardinal Bellarmine well known at the time for his opposition to the Protestant Church. Made in Germany late in the sixteenth century and copied in England by John Dwight, cf *Cologne ware*; *Rhenish stoneware*; *barbman*; *bartmannskrug*; *d'alva bottle*.

28

*12 German salt-glazed
bellarmine*

Bell krater Greek shape, sometimes incorrectly called 'oxy-baphon'; a bowl for mixing wine and water; bell-shaped body with two handles, cf *Greek vases* (see ill 47).

Benitor container for holy water. Often in the form of an angel or saint holding a shell.

Bentonite sticky volcanic clay used as an additive to other clays to improve their plasticity. It should not be used in excess of 2 per cent otherwise the entire blend will become too sticky and there may be drying problems due to high shrinkage. Also used as a *glaze suspender*, cf *ball clay*.

Berittino *maiolica* technique in which the *tin glaze* is stained blue with *cobalt oxide*, so providing a blue *ground* for painting in place of the conventional white. Originated in Faenza in the early sixteenth century, cf *smaltino*; *smalts*; *bianco-sopra-bianco*; *blanc fixe*; *bleu persan*.

29

Berlin transparency see *lithophane*.

Best gold see *burnished gold*.

Beutelflasche sixteenth-century German *pilgrim bottle* (see ill 115). Also known as a 'krause' or 'costrel', cf *Rhenish stoneware*.

Bianco-sopra-bianco literally translated means, white on white, but more accurately is a technique of painting with a white glaze pigment on a *tin glaze* which has been stained blue or grey. To be found on Italian *maiolica* from the sixteenth century and in northern Europe including the English Lambeth and Bristol wares during the eighteenth century (see ill 13), cf *blanc fixe*; *berittino*; *bleu persan*.

13   Bristol, earthenware plate, blue and opaque white on a pale grey-blue tin glaze (bianco-sopra-bianco) c 1760 (Victoria & Albert Museum)

Biberon Italian drinking vessel, usually having a bulbous body, sometimes on a tall foot, with one or more drinking spouts projecting from the shoulders of the full body shape, cf *cantaros*; *boetja*.

30

Biddy shovel round-ended shovel formerly used in the Dorset ball-clay mines for digging clay out of the *clay beds* after *weathering*, cf *graft*; *skivet*; *tubal* (ill 129).

Bing ore lead ore, formerly used to produce a fine powder known as *smithum* for glazing early *slipware*, cf *smithum*; *galena*.

Biscuit or bisque *ware* which has been fired once and not yet glazed. Both terms are in common usage, biscuit being more common in Britain and bisque favoured in the USA.

Biscuit figure unglazed *porcelain* figures.

Biscuit firing up to the time when wares are first placed in the kiln the clay may be reclaimed for re-use merely by the addition of water. The purpose of the biscuit firing is to bring about a chemical change in the clay which will turn it into a permanent and durable material, unaffected by water, most corrosives or thousands of years of decay other than physical breakage, as is testified by the archaeological remains of early civilisations.

During the firing the clay undergoes a series of complex changes:
0°C–100°C   free water driven off.
400°C–500°C   chemically combined water driven off.
550°C–600°C   alpha quartz (derived from *silica* in the clay) converts to beta quartz.
1,100°C   formation of *mullite* (necessary to prevent *crazing*).
660°C–550°C   (cooling); beta quartz reverts to alpha quartz.
200°C   (cooling); beta *cristobalite* converts to alpha *cristobalite*.

The importance of careful biscuit firing cannot be under-estimated, it is of vital significance in the successful production of tableware and other industrial applications. Nevertheless the procedure is a relatively simple one which can be competently achieved by following a simple time and temperature schedule. It is important that the initial rise of temperature is slow enough to dry the ware thoroughly before the boiling point of water is reached at 100°C. An initial rate of 60°C per hour is about correct for average potting, but this should be reduced to something like

25°C per hour for very thick pieces. The rate of rise may be increased somewhat beyond 100°C but care must still be exercised until the second critical stage, in the region of 500°C, has been passed. A rate of 100°C per hour is now normally acceptable. The average biscuit temperature for most craft wares, especially *stoneware,* is in the region of 900°C–1,000°C. *Fine earthenware* is in excess of 1,100°C, and bone china 1,250°C, cf *water smoking.*

Bishop bowl   a mitre-shaped bowl originating in Scandinavia and used to serve a punch known as 'bishop'.

Bismuth sub nitrate   used in the preparation of a *lustre glaze* to obtain a 'mother of pearl' quality.

Bitstone   small pieces of *calcined flint*, about ⅛ inch across, used during the nineteenth century to prevent glazed *ware* sticking to *kiln furniture*, in the same manner in which *stilts* are used today. The bitstone was the coarser layer of *flint* obtained from the bottom of the *settling ark*, cf *parting sherd*; *stilts*; *kiln furniture.*

Bitting edge   otherwise known as a 'scrapping edge'; see *bittings* (ill 14).

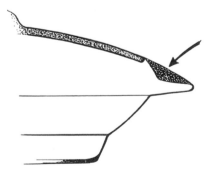

14   *Part section of a plate on a jigger mould, showing the bitting edge (arrowed)*

Bittings dried scraps of clay which remain at the edge of a piece still resting on the mould. If this scrap holds to the outside edge of a plate mould it can cause uneven contraction of the piece, especially as it usually holds on one side and not the other. To avoid this, the edges of plate moulds are sometimes made with what is called a 'bitting edge' (see ill 14) in which a more substantial amount of scrap clay resides causing the plate to break away more cleanly at the *welt*, cf *scrapping*.

Black ash crude *barium sulphide*; cf *barium carbonate*.

Black cores *biscuit-firing* fault; a dark discolouration at the centre of a piece caused by the outer surface of the ware becoming dense too early in the firing, thus preventing the interior from following the normal sequence of change and entrapping carbon.

Black-figure painting the name given to the first of the two great eras in Greek vase painting, the other being 'red-figure painting'. As the name implies the black-figure vases are decorated with figure subjects in black on a red ground. The secret of the Greek potters' technique remained one of the mysteries of ceramics for centuries. However, recent researchers point to the likelihood that a highly ferruginous *slip* was used to paint the pattern onto a *red clay* containing less iron. During the firing the wares were first subjected to a reducing atmosphere (cf *reduction*) which turned the entire piece black. As the kiln cooled an oxidising atmosphere (cf *oxidation*) caused the clay to return to its former red colour but the extra iron in the slip pigment was in excess of that which could be re-oxidised in the time, therefore it remained black, cf *Greek vases*; *amphora* (ill 3).

Black-figure vase Greek vase decorated with figure motifs in black on a red ground, cf *black-figure painting*; *red-figure vase*; *amphora* (ill 3).

Black iron oxide FeO, ferrous oxide. See *iron oxide*.

Black-pencilled decoration use of metallic pigments, prepared from oxides, to produce a fine black linear design, as though

33

executed with a pen. First introduced into Europe from China on the so-called *eggshell porcelain* of the Yung Cheng period of the Ch'ing dynasty (see appendix 1). Subsequently copied by the leading European factories of the time, notably Worcester, Chelsea and Longton Hall.

Black pottery culture ware   ware of a neolithic race originating in China to the north-east of the Yellow river; so called by virtue of the outstanding black pottery which they produced, cf *painted pottery culture ware.*

Black wad   variety of iron ore often found mixed with manganese (cf *manganese oxide*), mined in Derbyshire in the seventeenth and eighteenth centuries. It was probably from this material that many of the early potters made their brown glazes. Otherwise known to the potters as *magnus.*

Blanc de chine   name given in Europe to a white Chinese porcelain imported in the late seventeenth and early eighteenth centuries. The whiteness varies slightly from piece to piece, some being a sharp white, others ivory. This suggests a variation in kiln atmospheres (cf *reduction*; *oxidation*) rather than in the glazes themselves.

Blanc fixe   French term relating to much the same type of decoration as the Italian, *bianco-sopra-bianco.*

Blebbing   small raised blisters on the surface of fired *ware*, caused by pockets of entrapped gases in the *clay* which have expanded during the firing. The remedy lies in the careful preparation of the clay to the exclusion of all air. Overfiring may also be a cause of blebbing, cf *wedging.*

Bleeding bowl or barber's bowl   shallow dish about ten inches diameter with a broad rim, out of which was cut a moon-shaped section which permitted the barber to hold it close to his client's neck, in order to catch the lather during shaving. There is also to be found on most examples, a small modelled indentation to one side of the cutaway. This is to provide a firm thumb hold.

The fact that these bowls were also used for blood letting, and that such surgical practices were part of the barber's trade gives origin to both terms, and is illustrated by the combined decorative motifs of barber's and surgeon's instruments which frequently adorn such pieces (see ill 15).

15 *Tin-glazed earthenware barber's bowl or bleeding bowl in blue ; Bristol c 1760 (Victoria & Albert Museum)*

Blending preparation of *plaster of Paris* by mixing with a prescribed quantity of water and stirring to exclude air until it just begins to thicken. The proportion of water to plaster will vary according to the type of plaster, the quantity required and the use to which it is to be put (see appendix 4), cf *slake*; *plaster of Paris*; *gypsum*; *blowing*; *blibbing*.

Bleu céleste (sky blue); a delicate turquoise *enamel*, one of a series of *grounds* developed at Vincennes and Sèvres during the eighteenth century, cf *bleu de roi*; *gros bleu*; *rose Pompadour*; *vert pomme*; *jaune jonquille*; *oeil de perdrix*; *caillouté*; *vermiculé*; *jewelled decoration*.

Bleu de roi one of a series of *grounds* developed at Sèvres during the eighteenth century. Otherwise known as 'bleu royal' or 'royal blue', 'bleu lapis' or 'lapis lazuli', it is a rich *enamel* blue succeeding the earlier and less bright underglaze *gros bleu*; cf *gros bleu*; *bleu céleste*; *rose Pompadour, vert pomme*; *jaune jonquille*; *oeil de perdrix*; *caillouté*; *vermiculé*; *jewelled decoration*.

Bleu lapis see *bleu de roi*.

Bleu persan French tin-glazed *faience* (cf *tin glaze*) after the style of *bianco-sopra-bianco*; made at Nevers in the late eighteenth century. Decorated in white opaque-glaze pigments on a blue *ground* and occasionally gilded. At one time thought to have originated in Persia, in fact it is more likely to have been inspired by similar imported wares from China in the seventeenth century, cf *blanc fixe*; *bianco-sopra-bianco*; *berittino*.

Bleu royal see *bleu de roi*.

Blibbing fault in *mould making*; air pockets on the surface of the mould caused by pouring the plaster too quickly or too late after *blending*, cf *blowing*.

Blistering *glaze* fault in which broken bubbles or blisters appear on the surface. Usually caused by overfiring or glaze applied too thickly.

Bloating when *clay* is fired to the point of vitrification (cf *vitreous*), gas bubbles may form causing an expansion in volume. In most clays additional shrinkage takes place at this stage, but some do not and the expansion due to the gases remains permanent, which is termed bloating.

Blocking (1) making a *block mould*, cf *mould making* (see ill 86); (2) alternative term for *thwacking*, when used in relation to making curved roof tiles over a wooden former block.

Block handle type of cup handle in which the attachment to the cup is by one solid piece of clay as opposed to the usual two points of contact in the case of an *open handle*. Frequently used on *hotel ware* when strength and economy of manufacture are required (see ill 16).

16   Block handle

Block mould   sometimes referred to as a 'master mould'; it is the first impression taken from the original *model*. Always carefully preserved as the model may have become damaged in the process. The *case mould* is made from the block. *Working moulds* are made from the case, cf *mould making* (see ill 86).

Blood stone   burnishing stone for gold, cf *burnished gold*; obtained from *haematite,* otherwise known as 'kidney stone', a naturally occurring oxide of iron. The origin of the name stems from the fact that when this stone is ground and polished in water to the right shape and size to make a burnishing tool, the slurry so formed becomes stained to look like blood. It has no connection with the semi-precious stone, cf *agate* (2).

Blotching   see *blushing*.

Blow hole   hole or vent in the top of a kiln through which water vapour may be allowed to escape during the *biscuit firing* and so prevent *blowing* of ware, cf *water smoking*.

Blowing   (1) too rapid firing of biscuit (cf *biscuit firing*) causing the moisture in the *clay* to blow its way out and damage the ware, cf *bursting ;* (2) *mould making* fault manifested by pinholes on or

37

just below the surface of the mould; caused by faulty preparation of the *case*, cf *mould making*; *facing-up*; *blending*; *slake*.

Blown blue   see *powder blue*.

Blue and white transfer ware   otherwise known as 'Staffordshire blue'; see *printed decoration*.

Blue and white ware   *cobalt oxide* as a ceramic colourant was known in China as early as the T'ang dynasty (see appendix 1), but its successful use there as a painting pigment was not achieved until the Persian cobalt, Mohammedan blue (cf *asbolite*), already known in the Near East, was introduced during the Ming dynasty at Ching-te Chen (see appendix 1). Strained trading relationships limited the amount of Ming wares reaching Europe in the fifteenth and sixteenth centuries, but the appeal of such blue and white pieces as were imported was immediate and had a marked influence upon the style of contemporary European tin-glazed wares, cf *tin glaze*; *maiolica*. The constant counter influences of style between European, Near Eastern and Far Eastern wares are marked throughout the history of ceramics, but the eventual establishment of trade routes in the seventeenth century, by the English and Dutch East India Companies, had a far-reaching effect upon the European styles throughout the eighteenth and nineteenth centuries. Many of the imported wares were made to order for markets in Europe and the USA, with patterns according to specification, some copies of European originals, interpreted in the Chinese style. Early European *blue and white ware* in both *under-glaze decoration* and *enamel*, in turn copied and re-copied the Chinese, and so the counter influence continued into the mid-eighteenth century with the introduction in England of engraved transfer patterns. Such patterns, of which the 'willow' pattern is probably the best-known example, were the popular staple product of numerous potteries for something like a century. The number of engraved patterns is legion, whether *chinoiserie* or more indigenous in character, cf *engraved decoration*; *transfer decoration*; *Bristol blue*.

38

Blue-dash charger boldly decorated English *delftware* dish; made during the late seventeenth and early eighteenth centuries, so called because such pieces frequently bear a border of blue dashes. The subjects of decoration vary from boldly conceived floral designs to contemporary royal portraits, cf *delftware* (ill 33).

Blue lustre can be made by mixing one part by weight of *bright gold* with four parts by weight of bismuth lustre.

Blue scale pattern see *scale pattern*.

Blue vein see *stent*.

Blunge to mix raw materials in water as part of the preparation of a body, cf *blunger*; *flow chart*.

Blunger wet mixing tank used for the preparation of raw materials, *body* etc. In the past the normal structure has been a hexagonal tank in which paddles, mounted on a vertical shaft, rotate, thereby mixing the contents. More recent designs are cylindrical and the mixing takes a fraction of the time due to the vortex action caused by more efficient paddle design and very high speeds.

Blushing fault in glazes which shows as a faint pink discolouration. Occurs when *chrome oxide* and *tin oxide* are indiscriminately fired in the same *glost* kiln. Also known as 'blotching'.

Bocage decorative floral background frequently used in the modelling of *china* and *porcelain* figures. Technically it is a modeller's device to provide a means of support in the firing.

Boccaro or Buccaro name originally given by the Portuguese to a much-prized, perfumed, porous red *earthenware*, which they imported from Mexico in the seventeenth century. Subsequently the name has become used to denote several types of *redware* including *stoneware*. It is notably applied to such ware as the Chinese Yi-Hsing, imported into Europe in the seventeenth century. Being made of *red clay*, there is a variation in colour

39

from red, known as 'aka', if *oxidised*, to a metallic blue, called 'ao', if *reduced*.

Body (1) man-made mixture of clays and other ceramic materials, calculated to produce *ware* of desired characteristics, such as colour, texture, strength (dry and fired), translucency etc. In the case of *porcelain* the term 'paste' is often used to mean the same; (2) the main portion of a piece, ie as opposed to the neck, foot, handle, spout etc.

Body stain prepared metallic oxide colouring for introduction into a *body* to impart a desired colour (see appendix 5).

Boetja or Botijo spouted *apothecary jar* for containing and dispensing liquid drugs. A common shape in the Spanish and Italian maiolica wares of the sixteenth and seventeenth centuries, cf *apothecary jars* (ill 4); *biberon*; *cantaros*.

Bolting cloth fine bolting silk used in the preparation of silk screens for *screen-printed decoration*.

Bombentopf pear-shaped cooking pot dating back to the eighth century in Lower Saxony. A development of the fuller rounded *kugeltopf*, cf *grapen*.

Bonbonniere small box made of silver, enamel ware or *porcelain*. Often elaborate in shape and decoration. Used to contain sweetmeats.

Bone ash $Ca_3(PO_4)_2$, 'calcium phosphate'; calcined bone (cf *calcine*). Introduced as a *flux* in *bone china* bodies. In glazes it is sometimes used to give opacity and opalescence, cf *opalescent glaze*.

Bone china *vitreous*, translucent ware of high quality and strength. So named following the use of calcined bone (cf *bone ash*) as a *flux* to obtain a vitreous *body* originally made in emulation of the *porcelain* imported from China. Not a true *hard-paste* in the sense of felspathic porcelain, nor yet *soft-paste* as in *glassy porcelain*, bone china has become recognised as a class of hard porcelain in its own right. Biscuit fired in the region of 1,250°C–1,280°C, and glost at 1,060°C–1,080°C. The original use of *bone ash* can be traced back to a patent granted to Thomas Frye of Bow in 1794. These early experiments included fritted glass (cf *frit*) and therefore are more properly classified as soft-paste. Bone china as we now know it, containing *china clay*, *Cornish stone* and *bone ash* was first made by Josiah Spode in about the year 1800. In Britain the standard requirement for the definition of bone china is a translucent body with a content of 45–50 per cent of calcined animal bone. In the USA the requirement is a translucent *whiteware* with a minimum of 25 per cent of bone.

Bone edge   expression used in Stoke-on-Trent to describe a nicely rounded edge to a plate, cup or any other piece of clayware. It is most important that such a well-smoothed and rounded edge is achieved in order to ensure that the glaze does not run off any sharp edges, which in turn would provide problems for gilders and decorators.

Borax $Na_2B_4O_7$, sodium borate; owing to its slightly soluble nature, borax is normally used as a *frit*; it is a source of *boric oxide* and *sodium oxide*. Sometimes used in combination with salt for 'salt-glazing' (cf *salt-glaze*) when it contributes towards a smoother, richer quality glaze. At one time brought from Tibet, but in more recent times it has become available from the USA, especially California.

Boric oxide   a powerful *flux*, used mostly in lower-temperature glazes (cf *glaze*) but it can also be used in small quantities at high temperatures as an aid to colour brilliance. Its main qualities as a flux are to intensify colours and in some cases it is useful towards reducing the expansion of a glaze, thus lessening the likelihood of *crazing*. It is also useful to combine with or to replace *lead oxide*. A relatively non-soluble source of boric oxide is colemanite, but most other sources, such as *borax*, are soluble and require fritting (cf *frit*). The *tableware* industry frequently makes use of a fritted form of boric oxide in which it is combined with lead oxide and other essential glaze materials such as *silica*; such frits are known as *lead boro-silicates*.

Bosch   bath of cold water used for quenching *frit,* cf *frit kiln.*

Boss   (1) cushion-like pad for the support and easy manoeuvrability of a copper plate when being engraved; (2) transfer printer's pad, often faced with corduroy, used to clean the surplus colour from an engraving, after the *scraper* has removed the greater amount and before the transfer paper is applied, cf *engraved decoration.*

Botijo   see *boetja.*

Bottle oven   see *kilns.*

Boulder clay   *conglomerate clay* of glacial origin, found in the north of Britain, used for brick making. Also known locally as 'till'.

Boulder flint   originally *chalk flint,* but by reason of coastal erosion have become beach stones, such as are obtainable on the south-east coast of England, cf *flint; chalk flint.*

Bourdaloue   seventeenth-century ladies comfort pot, used in France during church sermons. Supposedly named after Louis Bourdaloue, a Jesuit priest renowned for his long sermons, cf *chamber pot; coach pot; skaphion.*

Bowing   warping of *flatware* during firing, the centre of the ware rises upwards; such pieces are known as 'humpers'. The opposite fault is known as *dishing,* and the pieces so formed as 'whirlers', cf *whirler.*

Bowl-pin   type of *pip* or *spur;* small conical, *refractory* pieces of *kiln furniture* placed in *saggars* to support bowls in an inverted position, cf *kiln furniture.*

Bowl-tile   see *cachala.*

Boxing   placing the tops of *hollow ware,* such as cups, together

42

in order that they occupy less space in the kiln and tend to keep each other from warping during the *biscuit firing*.

Brandenstein pattern   see *ozier pattern*.

Bread crock   item of *kitchenwear* for storing bread, popular in the days of large kitchens. It usually took the form of a large, 'thrown' (cf *throwing*) *earthenware crock* glazed internally, covered with a wooden lid.

Break-up   mottled glaze effect caused by the presence of *rutile*, popular for use on fireplace tiles since the 1930s. The term is sometimes used as a common name for the material of rutile itself.

Bright gold   otherwise known as 'liquid gold'; a less expensive quality of gold *lustre* than *burnished gold*, 'best gold' or *brown gold*. It emerges from the kiln bright and shiny, not requiring to be burnished (cf *burnishing*). Compared with the more expensive varieties it tends to have a somewhat brassy quality and is much less durable, cf *liquid lustre*; *screen gold*.

Brinjal   Chinese three-coloured *ware* of the K'ang Hsi period of the Ch'ing dynasty (see appendix 1), with floral sprays incised into a coloured *ground*, cf *sgraffito*.

Bristol blue   fine quality of *smalts*, made available to British potters by the Prussians after their war with Saxony (1756–63). Hitherto the export from Saxony of the best-quality smalts had been banned. The sole English importer of this special concession was an apothecary in Bristol.

Bristol glaze   so called because it is thought to have been used first in Bristol. It is a glaze for once-fired techniques (cf *once-fired ware*), can be transparent, opaque or coloured but the original as used at Bristol was probably opaque white, consisting of *zinc oxide, potash, lime, silica* and *alumina. Lead oxide* was never used. Bristol-type glazes are economical in use on account of the once-only firing, they are frequently to be found on *stoneware* storage jars and bottles, *sanitary* ware and *hotel ware*, cf *green-glaze*; *once-fired ware*; *slip-glaze*.

British gum   see *Anglo gum*.

Brocaded imari   see *Imari*.

Broderie ware or lace work decoration   decorative technique using lace or net patterns. Actual pieces of lace may be used, they are dipped in *slip,* dried and fired. During the firing the lace burns away leaving the clay replica in its place, cf *pierced decoration*.

Bromias   a type of tall *skyphos*, cf *Greek vases*.

Brookite TiO_2, a relatively rare form of titania, cf *titanium oxide*; *anatase*.

Brown gold   form of gold which is quite pure having been precipitated from gold chloride. Used by potters who prepare their own gold for decorating as opposed to purchasing ready prepared varieties, cf *bright gold*; *burnished gold*; *screen gold*.

Brushes   see *pencils*.

Brush jar   deep cylindrical Chinese pot for holding calligraphy brushes.

Buccaro ware   see *boccaro ware*.

Bulging   distortion during firing in which the sides of the *ware* swell outwards. Due to faulty *placing* in the kiln; faulty *casting* (too thin); faulty *body* mixture, either in calculation or poor materials; faulty design.

Bullers rings   flat rings of *ceramic* material so constituted as to shrink uniformly when fired. They are placed in the kiln in such a position that will enable the fireman to withdraw one at intervals throughout the firing. The greater the amount of *heat work* achieved, the greater the shrinkage of the ring, this is measurable on a Bullers ring gauge in units known as *pips*. Invented by Bullers Ltd of Stoke-on-Trent at the beginning of the twentieth century, cf *pyrometer*; *pyroscope*; *cones*; *Holdcroft bar*.

Bung (1) column of *saggars* in a kiln. Otherwise, similarly a stack of *flatware*, cf *bunging-up*; (2) *refractory* stopper placed in the spyhole of a kiln; also in a *frit kiln*, a stopper or plug used in to hold back the molten *frit* until the *charge* is ready to be drawn off; (3) a wooden stopper or plug used in wet grinding pans (cf *pan mill*) or *arks*.

Bunging-up *setting* of articles in *saggars* ready for *placing* in the kiln.

Burning a term sometimes used to mean *firing*. Particularly applicable in circumstances where solid fuels are, or were, at one time predominant.

Burnished gold the best quality gold is burnished gold, also known as 'best gold'; made from an amalgam of mercury and *brown gold* mixed with fluxes. It is fired at about 720°C–740°C when the mercury volatalises to leave a layer of almost pure gold. On withdrawal from the kiln this gold appears dull, being made up of malleable grains of gold which are burnished or sanded with a very fine sharp polishing sand, and in some cases with polishing stones such as *agate* or *blood stone*, cf *liquid gold*; *bright gold*; *screen gold*.

Burnishing polishing of *burnished gold*, cf *agate*; *blood stone*.

Burrow see *stent tip*.

Bursting term used in connection with *ware* which 'blows' (cf *blowing*) as a result of moisture or impurity in the clay. This fault sometimes occurs in craft pottery if plaster becomes mixed with the clay. In such cases it is not uncommon for bursting to take place some time after firing, especially in low-fired wares which will allow moisture to reach the plaster, cause it to swell and blow.

Buttonhole launder now obsolete, but at one time a wooden lining insert within the *washing shaft* of a *china clay* mine. So called on account of the holes made in one side of the *launder*, each of which was temporarily closed with a wooden cover known as the *button*. The top button, which was at the level of the clay being excavated, was removed to allow the clay in suspension to flow into the launder and thereby to be pumped to the surface for purification. As the level subsequently became lower so the next button would be removed and the surplus length of launder cut away.

Cabaret or **tête-à-tête set**   tea, coffee or chocolate service for two persons; comprising two cups and saucers, a milk jug, sugar bowl and an oval tray. Normally made in *porcelain* or *bone china* (including the tray), cf *solitaire*.

Cabbage-leaf jug   ornate style of *ware* peculiar to Caughley and Worcester during the eighteenth century. A shallow relief pattern, based upon the form of cabbage leaves and cast in the mould, was used as a background for hand-painted decoration (see ill 17).

17 Caughley porcelain jug. Painted decoration over a cast relief background of cabbage leaves c 1722-99 (Victoria & Albert Museum)

Cachala   an old German word meaning 'bowl'. It is thought that as bowls were used at one time in the manner of tiles (cf *bacino*), cachala may be the origin of *kachel*.

Cachemire   tall Delft vase (cf *delftware*), highly decorated with a floral design in polychrome with a predominance of a dull red. Made in the late seventeenth and eighteenth centuries.

Cachepot   French term for a plant pot holder.

Cadborough ware   type of red *earthenware*, sometimes decorated with *slip*, and glazed with a rich *lead glaze*. A ware with a distinctive style, made at Cadborough, Sussex, in the eighteenth and nineteenth centuries. The original *Sussex pigs* were made here.

Cadmium   used in combination with *selenium* to produce low-temperature red glazes and ceramic painting colours, the preparation of which is a fairly critical chemical process. For the best results it is advisable to seek the guidance of the materials supplier upon suitable glazes to use.

Cadogan tea-pot   late eighteenth-century novelty tea-pot having no immediately apparent means of filling. A spiral tube with an aperture at the base of the pot is so designed that once filled, through the tube, the pot may be turned the right way up without

18   Cadogan tea-pot

47

fear of spilling. Usually decorated with crude floral relief motifs and glazed in the characteristic *Rockingham glaze*. First made by Thomas Bingley at Swinton (later to become Brameld's Rockingham works) to the model of a peach-shaped wine pot of Indian origin, given to the Bramelds by the Hon Mrs Cadogan. Subsequently made in considerable numbers at the Rockingham pottery; also made by John Turner of Lane End, and by Spode.

Cadus   Roman equivalent of the Greek *amphora*.

Cage mill   see *bar-crusher*.

Cailloutages   French term for *creamware*; derivation from 'caillou', the French for flint, which was used in its manufacture.

Caillouté   one of a series of grounds (cf *ground*) developed at Sèvres during the eighteenth century; a tracery-like diaper pattern resembling pebbles outlined with gold. Often superimposed on one of the coloured grounds for which Sèvres is also famous, cf *gros bleu*; *bleu de roi*; *bleu céleste*; *rose Pompadour*; *vert pomme*; *jaune jonquille*; *oeil de perdrix*; *vermiculé*; *jewelled decoration*.

Calcareous glaze   a glaze in which calcium-bearing materials provide the main source of *flux*, cf *calcium oxide*.

Calcine   to make brittle by means of heating. Hard, raw materials such as flints or animal bone are heated to a red heat in order to drive off combined water and organic impurities, after which they emerge brittle in preparation for crushing and milling, cf *bone ash*; *flint*.

Calcite or calc-spa $CaCO_3$, calcium carbonate; sometimes known as 'Iceland spa'. A mineral constituent of *chalk*, limestone and marble which are ground to produce *whiting*, cf *calcium oxide*.

Calcium carbonate $CaCO_3$, see *calcite*; *whiting*; *calcium oxide*.

Calcium fluoride   see *fluorspar*.

Calcium metasilicate   see *wollastonite*.

48

Calcium oxide CaO, a most useful *glaze* ingredient as it contributes many desirable properties and is readily available as calcium carbonate in the form of *whiting*. Mainly used as a *flux* in high-temperature glazes, it has no marked effect upon colour though its presence does favour the development of 'reduced' iron colours (cf *reduction*), eg *celadon*. Although it is used as a flux it is very *refractory* on its own account, having a melting point in the region of 2,500°C. Therefore, if used in relatively large proportions it will cause mattness. In low-temperature glazes it is always used in combination with other more powerful fluxes such as *lead oxide, sodium oxide* or *boric oxide*. In such circumstances calcium oxide contributes towards hardness, durability and relative insolubility, cf *low solubility glaze*.

Calcium phosphate see *bone ash*.

Calc-spa see *calcite*.

Calix type of Roman drinking cup.

Callot figures otherwise known as 'Callot dwarfs' or 'Mansion House dwarfs'. Figures of dwarfs made in *soft-paste* porcelain, first made at Meissen in the eighteenth century, also at Vienna, Chelsea and Derby. So called from the book *Il Calotto Resuscitato*, the engravings in which were the origin of the first Meissen examples.

Callow term used in some localities to mean *overburden*, cf *plat*.

Cals noirs common French *earthenware*, made at Rouen, Paris and elsewhere in northern France. Brown in its lower half and blue above.

Calyx krater Greek shape, a bowl for mixing wine and water; this version of the krater is so called on account of its main body shape resembling the calyx of a flower, cf *Greek vases* (ill 47).

Camaieu French–'en camaieu'; painted decoration in tones of one colour. Also known as 'chiaro-oscuro', cf *grisaille*.

49

Cambrian argil type of cream-coloured *earthenware* made by Miles Mason in Staffordshire at the end of the eighteenth century. So called on account of the Welsh clay used in its manufacture. The style was distinguished by the use of relief decoration with superimposed *enamel*, cf *creamware*.

Cameo Parian *Parian* simulation of *jasper ware*. Though technically quite different, there is a superficial similarity between these two *pastes* and this was exploited during the mid-nineteenth century by T. J. & J. Meyer of Burslem. However, in the case of cameo Parian, the *body* of the piece and the relief decoration are both cast (cf *casting*) in one operation in the mould, no separate 'sprigging' (cf *sprigged decoration*) is involved. The coloured background to the relief decoration is applied by painting a thin film of stained *slip* (cf *body stain*) direct to the mould in the appropriate areas. The slip for the body of the piece is then poured in, whereupon the two become bonded without mingling. The normal colour schemes to be found have white slip for the body with tinted relief. Others use a pale tint for the decoration with a deeper tone for the background. Some pieces were unglazed externally, others are to be found with a *soft glaze* applied to the background only.

Cameo relief modelled relief decoration in which the motif is usually superimposed on a background of contrasting colour, cf *jasper ware*; *sprigged decoration*; *cameo Parian*.

Can cup of cylindrical shape.

Candeliere decoration of a somewhat flamboyant and grotesque style, in which animals and human figure motifs are arranged symmetrically about a central figure, creating a candelabra-like pattern. A popular style of the Italian *maiolica* painters at Castel Durante or Urbino.

Cane ware or bamboo ware buff-coloured *stoneware* introduced by Wedgwood in the eighteenth century as an improvement on the earlier *red stoneware*. Pieces were often moulded in the form of bamboo cane. It was soon superseded in the main by the more appealing white *earthenware*, but it continued in use right through the nineteenth century. Some of the less-refined wares of the nineteenth century are sometimes referred to in the USA as *yellow ware*. In later years some pieces were lined with white *slip*, cf *pie-crust ware*.

Canopic jar Egyptian burial jar in which the viscera of a dead person were placed. Such jars are often to be found at the foot of, or close to, the mummy.

Cantaros Near Eastern and Mediterranean drinking vessel, having a globular-shaped body enclosed at the top except for a filling spout offset to one side and a drinking spout to the other. By holding aloft at the correct angle a stream of water may be directed into the mouth without the lips touching the vessel, cf *gorgelet*; *biberon*; *boetja*.

19   Cantaros

Cantharides lustre yellow *lustre* with an iridescent quality similar to that of an insect's wing, particularly that of the cantharides fly. Made by mixing *bismuth sub nitrate* and silver nitrate with a *lead glaze* and fired in a moderate reducing atmosphere, cf *reduction*.

Canton blue violet-blue obtained by the combination of *barium carbonate* with *cobalt oxide*.

51

Carboy storage vessel for acids. Formerly made of *stoneware* but nowadays of glass.

Carpet bowls see *taws*.

Carquois eighteenth-century decorative theme using, bows, arrows, quivers, flowers etc, cf *décor à la corne*.

Carrageen or Irish moss seaweed boiled in water to extract *alginate,* a sticky syrup suitable for use as a *glaze hardener* and *suspender*. Equivalent of the Japanese *funori*. Favoured by some craft potters in the preparation of *green glazes* for *once-fired ware,* cf *gum Arabic*; *Anglo gum*; *gum tragacanth*.

Carrara ware Wedgwood equivalent of *Parian*. Named after a white marble of Tuscany.

Carrying-off transporting ware from the maker to the drier, kiln or whatever the next process may be. Formerly a manual task, the ware being carried on boards over the shoulder or on the head (see ill 139). The advent of mechanised conveyor systems has caused the term to become less used.

Cartouche scroll ornament, often gilded, used as a framework for a decorative panel. Applicable to all forms of decorative art.

Case mould mould taken from the *block mould*; that from which the *working moulds* are made, cf *mould making* (ill 87).

Cash pattern term sometimes applied to a Chinese pattern motif based upon the shape of a round coin with a square hole in the centre.

Casserole covered cooking dish, made of coarse *earthenware* or preferably ovenproof ware, cf *oven ware*; *kitchenware*.

Cassius purple see *purple of cassius*.

Casting casting appears to have been introduced into the pottery industry in Staffordshire in the eighteenth century. The technique makes use of *plaster of Paris* moulds and clay which has been rendered into *slip* by means of deflocculation. The mould is filled with slip and allowed to stand for a period of time which varies according to the type of ware—*bone china* casts at a much faster rate than *earthenware*. The porosity of the plaster absorbs some of the water out of the slip, there is also a slight flocculating action on the part of the calcium in the plaster on the surface of the mould. The longer the casting time, the thicker the cast. Once the required thickness has been built up, the surplus slip is poured off and the mould allowed to drain in an inverted position. This type of casting is sometimes referred to as 'thin-casting', the characteristic of which is that the inner shape of the article closely relates to the outer shape formed by the mould. For thicker pieces, or when the inner shape is different to the outer profile, a core or inner mould is used. This technique is known either as *double casting* or 'solid casting' (both terms are used in different factories to mean the same thing). Another meaning of double casting refers to the process of casting *ware* in two colours. This is achieved as follows: the first colour is allowed to cast for a short period only, this is then poured off, drained and the second coloured slip is cast inside the first until the total required thickness has been cast.

Casting spot   dark stain sometimes apparent on *whiteware* after biscuit firing. Occurs at the point of impact of the slip as it is poured into the mould. May be prevented by more gentle pouring and by using a piece of wood, zinc, plastic or other such non-ferrous material to serve as a shoot which will take the first impact of the slip.

Catinus   Roman dish for serving fish.

Caudle cup   seventeenth-century cup having two handles and a spout through which beverage may be supped; the same as a *posset pot, sallibube cup, wassell cup, skinker*. Caudle is a warm, sweet drink made from curdled milk, ale and spices.

Cauliflower ware   decorative *tableware* in the form of cauliflowers (see ill 20). The surface in low relief, being modelled to resemble fruit or vegetables, is *cast* in the mould and further depicted with colour glazes. First made as a cream-coloured

53

earthenware (cf *creamware*) by Josiah Wedgwood in the mid-eighteenth century during his partnership with Wheildon. Variations of this type of ware continued to be made by numerous small potteries up to the present day, such pieces are of doubtful aesthetic merit and in no way match the quality of those of the eighteenth century. The term also applies to similar imitations of other vegetables and fruit such as melons and pineapples.

20   *Wedgwood, lead-glazed cauliflower-ware tea-pot c 1760 (Victoria & Albert Museum)*

Caulk stone   an impure form of *barytes* found in Derbyshire.

Celadon   name of French origin given to imported Chinese *stoneware* and *porcelain* with delicate green to grey-blue glazes, much prized in the eighteenth century for their close resemblance to green jade. The colour is due to a small porportion of *iron oxide* in the *felspathic glaze* fired in a reducing atmosphere, cf *reduction*. Celadon glazes are still much favoured by craft potters, The quality and depth of colour can vary greatly according to the amount of iron present in the glaze (up to 2 per cent) and the influence of the iron content in the clay of which a piece is made. The type of fuel will also have a marked influence, wood fuels giving the most exquisite results. In this respect it is interesting to note that the northern Chinese celadons, fired with coal fuels, tend to be darker than those of the south fired with wood. A similar comparison can be observed between the use of town gas or wood fuels in craft kilns. The term celadon is sometimes erroneously used to describe other wares, including *tablewares*, of a remotely similar green but of copper origin, cf *copper celadon*.

Celebe   Greek vase similar to a krater but shallower, cf *Greek vases*.

Celeste blue   see *bleu céleste*.

Centre   term used to describe the first stage of *throwing*; to cause the initial, solid mass of clay on the potter's *wheel* to run in a true concentric manner prior to hollowing out.

Ceramic   from the Greek, 'keramos', meaning pottery. In recent times it has been adopted in Britain as a generic term to include not only products made of fired clay but also those of allied materials made by similar processes of manufacture and firing, eg electrical, nuclear and scientific equipment etc. In the USA the term is officially recognised as embodying all silicate industries, thus including glass, metal enamels etc.

Cerquate   decorative idea used on sixteenth-century Italian *maiolica,* using wreaths of oak leaves and acorns. Usually in yellow on a blue *berittino* ground.

Chaire   also known as 'chaki'; tea-caddy used in the Japanese tea ceremony; sometimes made in *raku* ware and having an ivory lid, also made in laquer ware, cf *chatsubo*; *furidashi*; *chawan*; *kensui*; *mizusachi*; *mukozuki*; *futaoki*.

Chaki   see *chaire*.

Chalk   soft rock consisting of *calcium carbonate,* cf *whiting*; *calcite*; *calcium oxide*.

Chalk body type of white *earthenware* in which *chalk*, *(calcium carbonate)* is added to an otherwise cream or buff firing clay.

Chalk flint flint pebbles obtained from chalk outcrops in southern England, cf *flint*; *boulder flint*.

Chamber pot item of *sanitary ware*, so named on account of its provision as a night convenience in the bedchamber in the days before modern indoor sanitary systems were in common use. P. Amis, 'Some Domestic Vessels of Southern Britain', in *Journal of Ceramic History* no 2 (1968), points to the existence of such wares in ancient Greece, cf *bourdaloue*; *coach pot*; *skaphion*.

Chambrelan the French equivalent of the German *hausemaler*; outside decorators.

Chamois lustre yellowish-red *lustre* made by mixing yellow and red lustres.

Chamotte alternative term for *grog*. Chamotte ware is made from coarse clays using grog, and/or sand, to give a textured quality.

Champlevé *sgraffito* technique in which large areas of the *slip* coating are cut away to produce a broad pattern as opposed to a linear design. Originated in the Near East in the tenth century, and was probably influenced by earlier metalwork techniques. The term is derived from the same term in enamelled metalware, used to indicate a method of keeping broad areas of enamel colours apart by shallow raised ridges. A nearer parallel in ceramics would be the techniques of de *cuenca*, de *arista*, *tube lining*.

Chantilly sprig blue and white pattern of delicately painted sprays of flowers, openly spaced out but centred on a cornflower or pink, as a focal point. Of Chinese origin, popular in the late 1780s when it was made at Caughley, Worcester, Spode, Derby and Bristol. Later, blue and white transfers of the pattern were made to succeed the hand-painted versions, cf *blue and white ware*.

Charge complete *batch* of materials weighed and measured out for a specific purpose, such as may be loaded into a mill for grinding, a *blunger* for blunging, a *frit kiln* for fritting etc.

Charger large serving dish for roast meat, game etc; English medieval origin, cf *blue-dash charger*.

Chaser mill an *edge-runner mill* with a fixed pan in which the *runners* revolve and rotate in a stationary pan, the manner of which appears as if they are chasing each other, cf *edge-runner mill*; *pan mill*.

Chatironné or fleurs chatironnées late eighteenth-century French style of flower painting, a characteristic of which was the flat tonal quality surrounded by a firm outline.

Chatsubo bowl used in the Japanese tea ceremony for containing leaf tea, cf *furidashi*; *chaire*; *chawan*; *kensui*; *mizusachi*; *mukozuki*; *futaoki*.

Chattering fault caused by the vibration of a *turning tool,* either because the tool is not sharp or because it is not held correctly.

Chawan Japanese *tea bowl* used in the tea ceremony, cf *chaire*; *chatsubo*; *furidashi*; *futaoki*; *kensui*; *mizusachi*; *mukozuki*.

Chemical ware articles made of *vitreous* acid-resisting *stoneware* or *porcelain*. Designed for scientific use, eg acid containers, carboys, mortars and pestles, crucibles etc.

Chert stone or cherts type of stone of high *silica* content, formerly used in the milling of *flint*. At one time the bases of the mill pans were lined with chert *pavers* from North Wales or Yorkshire. The *runners* were also cherts but of a softer variety, from Derbyshire.

Chiang t'ai Chinese term—a near equivalent to *soft-paste*.

Chiaro-oscuro see *camaieu*.

Chicken-brick unglazed porous *earthenware* cooking pot, in which a chicken is virtually sealed to bake in its own fat; popular in Scandinavian countries. The traditional method of making is to 'throw' (cf *throwing*) an enclosed vase shape, turn it on its side and slice it lengthwise with a wire, so forming the base and lid in one operation, cf *ovenware*.

21   Chicken-brick

Chi hung Chinese—'massed red', 'sacrificial red' or 'sky-clearing red', interpretation according to the Chinese character used to represent 'chi'. Descriptive term for a particular quality of *copper-red glaze* or under-glaze colour, cf *under-glaze decoration*; *copper-red glaze*; *sang de boeuf*; *hsien hung*; *pao shi hung*; *lang yeo*.

China short for *bone china*. Commonly misused term outside the *Potteries* as a generic term for a wide range of *tableware* products, in the sense of crockery, and irrespective of composition. This is quite mistaken, it should only be used as an abbreviation for bone china.

In the USA the term appears to have been used during the eighteenth century, before bone china. In different localities it had different meanings, varying from a general term for porcelains to that of a particular style or type.

China clay Al_2O_3 $2SiO_2$ $2H_2O$, *kaolin*; a highly *refractory* white burning *primary clay* with a melting temperature in the region of 1,800°C. An essential constituent of *hard-paste* porcelain and most *soft-pastes*. In glazes it is a rich source of *alumina* and *silica*, unlike most other clays it is free from unwanted colouring impurities such as *iron oxide*. It is also useful in helping to maintain the suspension of other materials in the glaze mix.

22   Cornish china-clay pit

China stone   see *pegmatite*.

China trade porcelain   see *Chinese export ware*.

Chinese blue   see *asbolite*.

Chinese export ware   also called 'Chinese export porcelain', or 'China trade porcelain'. *Hard-paste* porcelain made in China to European and American requirements. During the nineteenth century such pieces were attributed to Lowestoft and the name of this factory continued to be used in error for some time—such ware was referred to as 'Oriental Lowestoft'. However, this fact is now recognised in Europe and the name of Lowestoft is not now normally used in this connection. In the USA the term 'Oriental Lowestoft' is still used sometimes.

Chinese shapes   some of the more usual of the traditional Chinese shapes are gourd vase; double gourd-vase; square vase; square club-shaped vase; club-shaped vase; *potiche*; *coup*; *ginger jar*; *gallipot*; *cup-stand*; *hill-jar*; *granary urn*; *stem bowl* (see ill 23).

23 (facing page) Chinese shapes: 1 double gourd-shaped vase; 2 potiche; 3 gallipot; 4 club-shaped vase; 5 square club-shaped vase; 6 granary urn; 7 stem bowl; 8 square vase; 9 hill jar; 10 coup; 11 ginger jar; 12 cup stand

Chinoiserie   pieces of European manufacture made or decorated after the Chinese style. Applicable in fields other than pottery or porcelain.

Chittering   fault usually attributed to poor *fettling* which shows as a series of split-like cracks around the rims of ware.

Chock   spherical or domed-shaped object used to true the rims of *leather-hard* cups and similar hollow ware which may have become mis-shapen during manufacture. Usually made of glazed pottery.

Chrome oxide Cr_2O_3, a highly *refractory* colouring oxide which is not easily absorbed into glazes. Under most conditions it will give a dull-green colour sometimes know as 'Victoria green', but in other circumstances it can contribute towards yellow, orange, red, pink and brown:

Low-fired *lead glazes*, low in *alumina*   orange and red.
Low-fired *lead glazes*, including *sodium oxide* yellow.
Glazes containing *zinc oxide*   brown.
Glazes containing *tin oxide*   pink or dull brown-pink.

In high-temperature glazes chromic oxide may be used to good effect to modify other colours such as blue from *cobalt oxide*. For the full effect of its more colourful properties it is necessary to prepare chrome oxide chemically with other materials, such as tin oxide. Glaze stains and painting pigments prepared in this way are readily available from pottery materials suppliers, cf *Paris green*; appendix 5.

Chuck   support made of clay, wood or other suitable material to hold pots firm in the *turning* process. The term is generally used for both the conical and hollow varieties (see ill 24) though the conical type is sometimes called a *chum*.

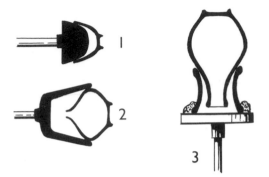

24   *1 Chum set on lathe; 2 chuck set on lathe; 3 chuck set on throwing wheel*

Chucker or pitcher   flat iron disc, used in conjunction with a *knocker* or 'punch', to release tight moulds. The derivation of the term is thought to stem from the fact that at one time this tool was also used as a component of a spare-time game of pitching, indulged in by mould makers during meal breaks.

Ch'ui ch'ing   see *powder blue*.

Chum   an interesting term in that some of the older potters believe that it may be so called by being a craftsman's friend, his 'chum'. Certainly a chum is an aid to his work in whatever sense it is used. (1) a type of *chuck* (see ill 24); (2) a type of *hump mould* used as a former to pre-shape a *bat* of clay prior to pressing into a hollow mould. In this way the likelihood of clay cracking on the outer radii of acute curves is minimised.

Chun glaze   name given to delicate opaque *celadons* of a pale duck-egg to lavender blue. Glazes of this type, with occasional reduced (cf *reduction*) copper-red blushes were typical of the Chun wares of the Sung dynasty (see appendix 1). The blue is due to a small proportion of *iron oxide* in the glaze or clay; the opacity may be caused by opalesence due to phosphorous present in wood *ash* used as a *flux* (cf *ash glaze*), this can be reproduced by the introduction of a small quantity of *bone ash* in the order of 5 per cent. Alternatively, Bernard Leach—*A Potter's Book* (1940) —points out that the Chinese used rice-straw as the source of ash for this type of glaze, and that, as this particular ash is rich in *silica*, it is likely that the opacity is due to fine particles of silica suspended in the glaze. It is probable that both factors have a bearing on the true secret of the original Chun glazes, as undoubtedly does the method of *firing*, ie the natural sequence of alternative *oxidation* and *reduction* caused by wood firing. The red blushes are decorative applications of *copper oxide*, and are not due to the partial reduction of an otherwise copper-blue glaze, as was thought at one time.

Cistercian ware English, black glazed, *redware* of the sixteenth and seventeenth centuries, so called on account of the fact that much of this type of ware has been found on abbey sites. The glaze is rich, smooth and glossy, almost mirror black, and probably the first use in Britain of a water-suspended glaze and dipped application. Typical shapes are tall, elegant beakers and mugs with two handles, known as *tygs* (see ill 132).

Clair-de-lune pale lavender-blue Chinese glaze of the Ch'ing dynasty (see appendix 1), obtained from *cobalt oxide*. One of a number of self-coloured glazes developed, or revived from earlier dynasties, under the influence of the court of K'ang Hsi, cf *peach bloom*; *mirror black*; *kingfisher blue*; *peacock blue*; *Nankin yellow*; *imperial yellow*; *coral red* and *apple green* enamels, cf *enamel*; *sang-de-boeuf*; 'sang-de-pigeon', and *celadon* revivals of the Sung dynasty (see appendix 1).

Clamin or clamming clay sealing of the bricked door of a kiln; otherwise known as a *wicket*.

Clamp primitive type of kiln in which a structure is built over the pots, partly of combustible material and partly of unfired clay.

At one time used extensively for firing common clay bricks, cf *kilns*.

Clapmutsen or klapmutsen   Dutch name for shallow bowls imported from China.

Clay   is formed as a result of the decomposition of *felspar*, a mineral found in crystalline rocks such as granite. Hence the name, *mother rock of clay*, which is sometimes given to granite. Decomposition takes place as a result of the chemical and physical action of the elements, water and ice in particular, over a period of millions of years. Some clays are to be found in their place of origin, ie on the site of the former granite deposit, such clays are known as *primary clays*. Others, by reason of various geological phenomena, notably river and glacial action, have been moved some considerable distances—these clays are known as *secondary clays*. The prime property of all clays is plasticity, this is due to the flat, laminar shape of the clay particles, which when lubricated with water, slide upon each other, cf *ball clay*; *primary clay*; *secondary clay*; *china clay*; *body*; *paste*; *clay substance*.

Clay bed   bank or mound of *weathering* clay, cf *banking of clay*; *beater*; *packer*.

Clay substance   theoretically pure *clay* has the formula, Al_2O_3 $2SiO_2$ $2H_2O$ and is called clay substance. Such clays do not occur naturally for all clays, including the relatively pure *kaolin*, contain some impurities.

Clean ark   see *ark*.

Climbing kiln   see *kilns*.

Cloam   ancient Cornish word for an *earthenware* clay.

Clobbered ware or clobbered china   imported wares, usually of Chinese origin, which have been decorated after importation. Not to be confused with *clobbering*.

Clobbering   method of decoration in which an under-glaze (cf *under-glaze decoration*) transfer outline is first applied and subsequently used as a guide for coloured *enamel* decoration. Not to be confused with *clobbered ware* or *clobbered china*.

Cloisonné   in ceramics, a decorative technique in which a design is outlined with a raised clay line, sometimes formed in the mould, to act as a barrier between different coloured glazes (see ill 25). *Cuenca* is the alternative and more usual term for this process; cloisonné being derived from, and more appropriate to, a similar metal enamelling technique, cf *tube lining*; *cuerda seca*; *san ts'ai*.

25   Doulton vase cast with raised cloisons and decorated in three shades of blue with amber at the rim and foot c 1910

Clot   see *bat*.

Clothing   (pronounced cloth-ing), final finishing of dry surfaces of new, dry moulds before being used for production. Carried out with the use of a piece of soft felt or baize.

Clouder or dabber   small stick with a number of sponges attached, used for *clouding*.

Clouding   method of decoration in which a variegated or mottled effect (resembling clouds) is achieved by dipping a sponge into a coloured glaze and dabbing the ware prior to glazing all over with a transparent glaze, cf *sponged ornament*.

Coach pot   an oval-shaped variation of a *chamber pot*; used in the eighteenth century as a means of convenience when travelling, cf *bourdaloue*; *skaphion*.

Coalad flint   type of *flint* found near Cork in Eire, it is easily ground without the need for *calcination*.

Cobalt oxide   CoO, a blue colouring oxide, the strongest of all the ceramic stains, and should be used sparingly—$\frac{1}{2}$ per cent in a glaze will give quite a strong blue. In *alkaline glazes* it will give a more vivid blue than in *lead glazes*. As a painting pigment the best results are obtained if it is combined with other oxides such as *manganese oxide, iron oxide, copper oxide* (see appendix 5). A violet blue, known as *Canton blue* is made by combining cobalt oxide with *barium carbonate*. On its own, cobalt oxide tends to produce a harsh and relatively uninteresting blue, cf *zaffre*; *smalts*.

Cobbler   the last piece made in a day's work, cf *running*.

Cockspur   piece of *kiln furniture* for *setting* glazed ware. Formerly used for plates but in this particular use it has now been replaced by *thimbles* and *cranks*, cf *kiln furniture* (see ill 62).

Cod placer   Staffordshire name for an operative in charge of a gang of *placers*.

Coiling   hand method of building pots without the aid of a *wheel*. Ropes of clay are rolled out and coiled upon each other to form the walls, being finally joined together by smoothing the inside, the outer surface may also be smoothed or partially left as a decorative feature.

Colcothar   form of red iron peroxide, cf *iron oxide*.

66

Cold-colours unfired oil colours; sometimes referred to as 'lacquers' or 'Japanned-colours', occasionally used for pottery decoration up until about the mid-nineteenth century. The wear resistance of such colours was very poor and they soon became replaced with fired *enamel*.

Colmanite source of *boric oxide*.

Colluvial clay classification given to clays which have been deposited as a result of violent water action. Such clays are seldom of much value since they are usually 'conglomerates', cf *conglomerate clay*.

Cologne ware variety of *Rhenish stoneware* (see ills 12, 115); Cologne being an important centre of stoneware manufacture from the fifteenth to early seventeenth centuries, cf *salt glaze*; *red stoneware*.

Columbine glaze late eighteenth-century red and blue mingled glaze, used on Konigsberge cream-coloured *ware*.

Column krater or kelebe Greek shape used for mixing wine and water; a type of 'krater' distinguished by having two column-like handles attached to a broad rim, cf *Greek vases*.

26   Column krater with red-figure decoration

Combing decorative technique using *slip,* a coating of which has been partially allowed to dry, just until the shine has disappeared. It is then combed with a broad comb of stiff leather, rubber, wood or even cardboard. The pattern so formed may be varied according to the width and spacing of the teeth, together with the manner in which the comb is drawn through the slip.

Comport dessert or fruit dish, usually raised on a stem foot though some examples are unfooted. The latter often take the form of a shell dish.

Cone three-sided, conical, or more accurately, pyramidal-shaped piece of unfired *ceramic* mix, so composed to fuse and melt at a predetermined temperature. Each cone is marked on one face with a reference number indicating the temperature at which it is designed to melt (see ill 27). Like other *pyroscopes* a cone is a measure of *heat-work* rather than actual temperature. It is placed in the kiln opposite a spy hole so that it may be seen to bend. Short for pyrometric cone, otherwise known as a 'Staffordshire cone' in Britain; 'Seger cone' (after the inventor) in Germany; 'Orton cone' in the USA (see appendix 2), cf *Bullers ring*; *Holdcroft bar*; *pyrometer*.

27   *Pyrometric cones as they appear after firing*

Conglomerate clay an impure *clay* containing a high proportion of rounded stones. Usually of little commercial value, cf *agglomerate clay*; *colluvial clay*.

68

Coperta glaze a second, transparent glaze, sometimes applied over Italian *maiolica* glazes after decorating, to ensure a glassy finish and full development of the colours in the painting. The Dutch equivalent is called 'kwaart'.

Coppa d'amore Italian *maiolica* bowl made for presentation to a lover or betrothed; usually painted with a portrait or alternative amatory emblems, cf *bacile amatori*.

Copper carbonate $CuCO_3$. $Cu(HO)_2$, favoured as a source of *copper oxide* in 'reduced' glazes (cf *reduction*); in 'oxidised' glazes (cf *oxidation*) it gives green. Converts to copper oxide in the process of firing, cf *copper oxide*.

Copper celadon a misnomer, see *lang yao*; *celadon*.

Copper oxide CuO, cupric oxide or black copper oxide; Cu_2O, cuprous oxide or red copper oxide. A colouring oxide which gives greens in oxidising atmospheres (cf *oxidation*) and red under *reduction,* as in *sang-de-boeuf* and *rouge flambé* glazes. A rich turquoise is obtainable in highly *alkaline glazes*, especially at low temperatures, as exemplified by the early Egyptian and Persian wares. *Copper carbonate* may be used as a source, in fact, as it is usually ground finer than the oxide it is often preferred, especially when reducing atmospheres are being used.

Copper-red glaze glaze containing *copper oxide* and which is fired in a reducing atmosphere (cf *reduction*) to obtain red. Clear, bright ruby-reds are among the most difficult glazes to achieve and are highly prized (not to be confused with other low-temperature *oxidised* reds from *selenium* and *cadmium*). The best results are obtained on relatively iron-free bodies (cf *body*), and in highly *alkaline glazes* containing *boric oxide* and *tin oxide*. Variously known on Chinese *porcelain* according to its quality as, *chi hung*, *hsien hung*, *pao shih hung*, cf *sang-de-boeuf*; *sang-de-pigeon*; *flambé glaze*; *peach bloom*.

Coraffine type of fused *alumina* used in the manufacture of refractories, cf *refractory*.

Coral red an iron-red *enamel*, one of a number of K'ang Hsi self colours of the Ch'ing dynasty (see appendix 1), cf *clair-de-lune*; *peach bloom*; *mirror black*; *kingfisher blue*; *Nankin yellow*; *Imperial yellow*; *apple green*; *sang-de-pigeon*, *sang-de-boeuf* and *celadon* revivals of the Sung dynasty.

Corded ware primitive wares decorated by means of impressing rope or cordage, cf *cording*.

Cording or cord-mark decoration form of impressed decoration to be found on early culture wares, and sometimes still used by craft potters. Flowing or geometric textured patterns may be built up by pressing rope or cordage into the soft clay.

Cord throwing method of hand building in which the shape is first made by winding a rope or cord round a core, usually a wooden dowel. The clay is then built up around the cord shape and allowed to stiffen a little. The core is then removed and the cord unwound from the centre.

Corne 'à la corne'; a style of decoration used on eighteenth-century French *porcelain*, in which cornucopias, flowers, bees and butterflies predominate.

Cornish stone or cornwall stone see *pegmatite*.

Costrel a *pilgrim bottle*.

Cottle wall of stiff roofing felt, linoleum or other suitable material used to retain wet *plaster of Paris* until it sets to make a mould, cf *mould making*.

Coup Chinese ink-pot, cf *Chinese shapes* (see ill 23).

Coupe plate or shallow dish without a rim.

Cover-coat protective coating applied over ceramic transfers, cf *transfer decoration* (3).

Cow creamer late eighteenth and nineteenth-century Staffordshire *earthenware* cream or milk jug in the form of a cow. It is filled through a hole in the animal's back, and the contents are poured through the mouth; the tail serves as a handle, cf *fairings*.

28   Cow creamer; early 19th-century Staffordshire earthenware with pink lustre decoration

Cow's lip or ox's lip   leather smoothing tool used by a *presser* in the eighteenth century; actually made from a piece of a cow's or ox's lip because of its suitability for constant use in water. Eventually superseded by rubber, cf *presser's rubber*; *kidney palette*; *diddler*; *pressing*; *potter's horn*; *pitcher*.

Coyotlatelco ware   Ancient American, Toltec pottery of the Post-Classical period (AD 980 – 1521); similar in characteristics to *Matlatzinca ware*, cf *Matlatzinca ware*; *Mazapan ware*; *fine orange ware*; *plumbate ware*.

Crab's-foot crackle   see *crackle*.

Crabstock handle   an eighteenth-century Staffordshire design for handles, also spouts, which resemble gnarled and knotted tree branches (see ill 29).

29   Crabstock handle

Crackle or craquele   Chinese – 'sui yu'; deliberate *crazing* of a *glaze* to produce a decorative effect, caused by the unequal contraction of the glaze and *body* or *paste*. Probably accidental at first, the Chinese learnt to control the degree of crackle by adjusting the composition of their glazes. In Europe the larger scale of crackle became known as 'crab's foot', the finer (and sometimes almost round crackle) as 'fish roe'. Coloured stains are frequently rubbed into the cracks to enhance the effect.

Crank   composite piece of *kiln furniture* for firing tiles or *flatware*. The 'tile crank' is a thin refractory *bat* raised on three legs or *dots*. The type used by the *tableware* industry for the *glost* firing of flatware is made up of three column supports, into which *thimbles* or *pins* are inserted. A third variety is a three-legged bridge-like support, used for the same purpose, cf *kiln furniture* (ill 62). The term also applies to a low *saggar* for holding a single plate, as used at one time in the manufacture of *porcelain*, cf *refractory*.

Crate-man   in the seventeenth century, the Staffordshire potters sold their ware direct from the kiln to crate-men, who proceeded to peddle them throughout the country.

Crater   see *krater*.

Crawling   otherwise termed 'ruckling'; if a *glaze* recedes during *firing*, leaving unglazed areas, it is said to have crawled. This is a fault more likely to occur in *matt glazes* rather than glossy ones. The reasons for crawling may be glaze application over dusty, greasy, or otherwise dirty *biscuit* ware, or merely as a result of over-handling prior to glazing. Some matt glazes, rich in *clay* content, may show cracks before firing, these should be gently smoothed over before *placing* in the kiln.

Crazing   the development of slight cracks in the fired *glaze*. These may be apparent immediately upon taking from the kiln or may develop progressively afterwards. It is a particularly undesirable fault in *earthenware* as it is likely to cause the ware to be porous; for obvious reasons of hygiene it is equally undesirable in other *tableware, sanitary ware etc.* Crazing occurs whenever a glaze is in tension. This usually happens on cooling if a glaze has a tendency to contract more than the body. It can also occur some time after firing if the *body* is too *soft* and able to absorb water, causing it to expand. The causes of crazing may be incorrect formulation of a glaze relative to the clay; incorrect firing of the biscuit, especially in the case of earthenware; expansion of the body after firing due to moisture intake; heat shock; incorrect application of glaze—glaze uneven or too thick. The remedies may be to increase the *silica* or *alumina* in the body, particularly in the case of earthenware; to increase the firing time and maximum temperature of the biscuit, especially in the 1,100°C range (earthenware); to avoid uneven or too thick application of glaze, cf *cristobalite.*

Creamware and Queen's ware   the introduction of cream-firing *ball clays* from Devon and Dorset in the early eighteenth century heralded a turning point in the development of English pottery, which was consolidated by the subsequent discovery that the addition of calcined *flint* gave added whiteness and strength. The early experiments were largely concerned with the manufacture of white salt-glazed *stoneware* (cf *salt-glaze*), but the development of cream-coloured earthenware soon followed. Such were the beginnings of creamware, later to be improved by Josiah Wedgwood in the 1750s, which, following the patronage by Queen Charlotte, became known as 'Queen's ware', the forerunner of modern white earthenware. The early creamware resembled in shape and decoration the preceding sprig decorated (cf *sprigged decoration*), salt-glazed stonewares, but the advantages of the applied liquid glaze soon brought about *under-glaze decoration* in *cobalt oxide* and *manganese oxide* (see appendix 5), then in *enamel* 'on-glaze'. *Transfer decoration,* both in under-glaze and enamel followed. The new fine body also made possible *pierced decoration* exemplified by Leeds ware, cf *steingut; faience fine; terraglia; terra de pipa; Cambrian argil.*

73

30   Wedgwood Queen's ware bowl with cover, 1780. Decorated by handpainting in red enamel

Crime cottages novelty-ware models of cottages cited in the notorious nineteenth-century murders, eg Potash Farm and Polstead.

Cristobalite crystal formation of *silica* which increases the thermal expansion of bodies (cf *body*) and therby contributes towards the prevention of *crazing*. At temperatures above 1,100°C a proportion of the silica in bodies combines with *alumina* to form *mullite*. The remaining silica, having already converted to beta quartz between 500°C and 600°C (cf *biscuit firing*), converts again into another form of silica—beta cristobalite, with an accompanying increase in volume. On cooling below 200°C, at which temperature the glaze will have hardened, beta cristobalite converts to alpha cristobalite with a decrease in volume. This is known as the cristobalite squeeze and is an important factor in subjecting a glaze to the correct amount of compression to prevent *crazing*.

Crock piece of pottery, particularly a basin, jug, bowl or large piece of *kitchenware*, eg a bread crock.

Crockery common generic term for domestic wares.

Crock-pie see *pie-crust ware*.

Crocodile's teeth see *dog's teeth*.

Crocus martis Fe_2O_3, purple iron oxide; see *iron oxide*.

Crouch ware a buff to off-white salt-glazed (cf *salt-glaze*), *stoneware* made from a Derbyshire clay. It is suggested that the name is derived from the Derbyshire village of Crich. First made at Nottingham and then in Staffordshire in the early eighteenth century, until it was replaced by the whiter-burning *ball clay* of Devon and Dorset.

Crowsfoot descriptive term for a type of crack sometimes found on pottery. It takes the form of several small cracks emanating from a centre. Usually caused as a result of a sharp knock.

Cryolite Na_3AlF_6, sodium aluminium fluoride; a natural source of *sodium oxide* in a form not requiring to be fritted (cf *frit*). Useful in *alkaline glazes* to develop colour, but should not be used in excess as the volatilisation of the fluorine may cause *pitting*.

31 Doulton bottle with crystalline glaze c 1900

Crystalline glaze   beautiful starred effects (see ill 31), due to the formation of crystals, may be achieved by the slow cooling of a *glaze* low in *alumina* content. Additions of *zinc, rutile* or *titanium oxides*, in proportions of up to 20 per cent, will encourage crystallisation. Other oxides may be added to give varying colours (see appendix 5); *iron oxide* is favoured in this respect and the glazes so formed are termed *aventurine*, cf *devitrification*.

Cuenca   otherwise 'de cuenca' or 'de arista'; decorative technique used for tiles in Spain since the sixteenth century. Ridges of clay are formed to enclose the main areas of the design, the reservoirs so formed are then filled with coloured glazes. The art nouveaux wares of the early twentieth century employed a similar technique, the ridges in this case being formed in a mould (see ill 25) and not always strictly used as a division between colours. The so called *tube-lined decoration* is a modern equivalent (see ill 130), cf *cloisonné*; *cuerda seca*; *tube-lined decoration*; *san ts'ai*.

Cuerda seca   Spanish—'dry cord'; decorative technique used on tiles; the outline of the design is incised into the soft clay, these lines are subsequently filled with a greasy medium which serves as a resist to prevent different-coloured glazes running together during application. Likewise, the incised line prevents them merging during the firing, cf *cuenca*; *cloisonné*; *tube-lined decoration*; *san ts'ai*.

Culinary ware   generic term for all kitchenwares including *pipkins, casseroles, bread crocks, beakers, jugs* etc.

Cullet   pieces of broken or crushed glass, as may be used in *mosaic*, otherwise in a finely ground form which may be used as a *frit* in a *glaze, body* or *paste*.

Cup   average capacities for modern cups are breakfast 9oz; tea 7oz; coffee 4oz.

Cupboard set   see *kast-stel*.

Cupric oxide   see *copper oxide*.

Cuprous oxide   see *copper oxide.*

Cup-stand   Chinese shape in which a *tea-bowl* may be stood, cf *Chinese shapes* (ill 23).

Curtain glaze   that which has run down in a wave-like formation on the vertical surfaces of an article; caused by overfiring, use of too *soft* a *glaze* or too thick a glaze application.

Cut-glass decoration   faceted style of decoration after the manner of cut glass in which the fired ware is cut and polished on a glass-cutter's wheel. To be found on European red stoneware of the eighteenth century, especially Meissen, cf *red stoneware.*

Cut glaze decoration   *sgraffito*-like technique in which the design is scratched through the glaze to reveal the clay beneath. This may be carried out on the *biscuit* ware or by using a *once-fired* glaze on the dry, unfired clay. Glazes for this type of decoration must be stiff enough at their maturing temperature to retain the detail of the incised pattern. Once-fired glazes are particularly suited to this technique as they normally contain a fairly high proportion of *clay*. It is a method best suited to *stoneware.*

32   18th-century Meissen tea-pot in red stoneware with cut-glass decoration

Cut liner   pottery-decorator's brush, or otherwise known as a 'slant liner' or 'liner', cf *pencil* (ill 94).

Cutter hoe-like cutting tool, at one time used in the *china-clay* industry to cut *clay* into squares as it dried in the *pan hearth*, thereby facilitating easier removal from the pan to the *linhay*.

Cutting a plate to make the model for a piece of *flatware* by rotating a mix of plaster on a *whirler* and cutting it with a template and turning tools to form the required shape, cf *running*.

Cutting spade Dorset *ball-clay* digger's tool; formerly used to make the vertical cut when excavating clay. The horizontal cut was made with the *tubal* (see ill 129), cf *skivet*; *biddy shovel*.

Cutting-up term sometimes used by decorators and gilders for the process of putting the final touches to a *raised-paste* decoration by carving the finer details with a sharp scalpel-like knife.

Cutty clay term used for the type of *clay* once used for the manufacture of clay pipes of the churchwarden type, cf *pipe clay*; *ball clay*.

Cylix see *kylix*.

Dabber (1) see *clouder*; (2) wooden tool used by engraved-transfer printers for forcing colour into the engraved image on the plate, cf *engraved decoration*.

D'alva bottle seventeenth-century term for a *bellarmine* or 'greybeard'.

Damascus ware a misnomer for a group of sixteenth-century Turkish wares, pottery and tiles, made at Isnik but at one time erroneously thought to have been made at Damascus, probably on account of the many buildings there which are clad with such tiles. Decorated with designs of conventional plant forms, in blue and greens with a black outline, under a clear glaze, cf *Rhodian ware*; *Miletus ware*.

De-air removal of air from plastic *clay*, *slip*, *plaster of Paris* etc prior to use. De-airing of plastic clay increases its plasticity and reduces the danger of *bursting* during the *biscuit firing*. The traditional hand method of removing air from clay is by *wedging*. The mechanised method used by industry is achieved by placing a vacuum chamber in line with the barrel of a *pug mill*. In the case of plaster, air is removed by careful *blending*. If plaster is allowed to set with air bubbles still entrapped, the *face* of the mould is liable to appear pitted, cf *blibbing*.

Decal   term used in the USA for a lithographic transfer. From the Greek—'decal'—'off paper', cf *lithography*; *transfer decoration*.

Decalcomania   term used in the USA for the process known in Britain as *lithography*.

Décor à la corne   style of decoration used on French *faience*, especially that made at Rouen in the eighteenth century, in which the subject matter of the pattern is based upon bows, arrows, quivers etc, together with birds and foliage, cf *carquois*.

Décor à pochoir   see *pochoir*.

Décor aux cinq bouquets   decoration on French *faience* comprising five sprays of blossom; on *flatware*, one as a central motif the others spaced around the rim.

Deflocculant   electrolyte used in the preparation of casting *slip*. When added to a stiff mixture of *clay* and water it charges the clay particles and creates forces of repulsion causing dispersion, thereby reducing the viscosity without adding water, cf *sodium silicate*; *casting*.

Dégourdi   from the French—'to warm'. A term used to indicate a low-temperature *biscuit firing*, in the range of 900°C, as used for *stoneware* and *porcelain*.

Delft doré   variety of eighteenth-century *delftware*, in a *chinoiserie* style, in blue, red, green and gold, cf *delft noire*.

Delft noire   variety of eighteenth-century *delftware* having decoration painted in blue, green, red and yellow on a black glaze, cf *delft doré*.

33   English delftware blue-dash charger

Delftware   otherwise known as 'tin-enamelled ware', cf *tin enamel*; tin-glazed earthenware, cf *tin glaze*; the English and north European version of *maiolica*. So called as it was first made in England in the mid-sixteenth century by Flemish potters invited to England by Henry VIII, who was much taken with this type of ware being produced on the continent. Whilst the technique undoubtedly came to England from Holland, the term—delftware—is thought to be a misnomer, in that it presupposes that the tradition came from the Dutch town of Delft. In fact, the wares of Delft are of a later date. The name was probably adopted in subsequent years on account of the fame that this pottery centre eventually gained in Europe. In England, tin-enamelled wares were formerly known as *gallyware*. It is now customary to differentiate between the wares of Delft and those of other centres by using a small letter 'd' for the latter, eg English delftware. In England, the main centres of manufacture were first at Norwich, from whence in the seventeenth century the Dutch potters moved to London at several places along the Thames, in particular Lambeth and Southwark. By the middle of the seventeenth century some of the potters had moved westwards and set up workshops at Brislington, Bristol, Wincanton and Liverpool. There were also delftware potteries in Dublin and Glasgow for a short time. Meanwhile, some of the London potters had set up a workshop in the USA, at Burlington, New Jersey. It is curious to note that tin-glazed ware does not seem to have been made in Stoke-on-Trent.

Perhaps one of the greatest misconceptions of delftware is that it is often thought of as blue and white ware of Dutch influence. In fact, the earliest examples in England are the colourful *Malling jugs* which would seem to indicate a greater influence from the *Rhenish stoneware*. In later times the imported blue and white Chinese Ming *porcelain* did influence the style towards blue and white and the Dutch followed with their own brand of *chinoiserie*. The Chinese influence continued, particularly in terms of painted decoration, throughout the seventeenth and eighteenth centuries until the decline of delftware in the face of *creamware* and *porcelain*. Nevertheless the story of English and Dutch tin enamels embodies much in the way of important developments in terms of national styles. The most outstanding examples of English delftware are the seventeenth-century *blue-dash chargers*, wine bottles, mugs and *posset-pots*. Later the *bleu Persan* and *bianco-sopra-bianco* techniques were developed at Lambeth and Bristol respectively. Liverpool used a particularly individual style of polychrome

34   English delftware bottle

decoration known as *Fazackerley colours*. There were also a few examples of *enamels* on tin glaze. In Holland, tin enamelling is probably most outstanding for its contribution to decorative tiles. The tradition of tin enamelling is continued to the present day by craft potters and in some of the decorative wares of factories such as De Porcelayne Fles at Delft and Poole Pottery in England.

Demi-grand feu the middle range of *firing* temperatures, eg for *earthenware* glazes; as used in France for *faience* and glazes on *soft-paste* porcelain.

Dentil see *dontil*.

Derby blue *enamel* blue introduced by Duesbury at the Derby factory during the eighteenth century. Somewhat akin to the Sèvres *bleu de roi*, being brighter than the mazarine blue previously used.

Deutsche blumen 'German flowers', flower painting on German *porcelain* in a naturalistic European style. On French porcelain a comparable term is *fleurs fines*.

Devil's work see *kuei kung*.

Devitrification the formation of crystals in a *glaze*. This may be carried out intentionally as in *aventurine* and other *crystalline glazes* or *matt glazes*; otherwise if it occurs as a fault the cause may be a deficiency of *alumina*, too slow cooling or a combination of both.

Diddler piece of flannel or chamois-leather used by pressers for smoothing and finishing plastic clayware, cf *cow's lip*; *presser's rubber*; *tommy stick*; *kidney palette*; *pitcher*; *potter's horn*.

Dieper decorator's brush of the type used by Dutch tile painters. It is a full, broad brush used for shading or filling in larger areas. Used in conjunction with the *trekker* which is a fine-pointed brush used for outlining, cf *pencil*.

Dimples glaze fault; see *pinholing*.

Dinner ware   *tableware* specifically made for use at dinner or luncheon, cf *tea ware*.

Dinos   Greek shape; a *krater* set on a tall base, cf *Greek vases*.

Dipping   method of *glaze* application in which the *biscuit* ware is immersed in a tub of glaze; also termed 'giving'. Sometimes a dipper may use three wire claws attached to his thumb, first and little fingers, to facilitate a firm hold and at the same time exposing the maximum area to attain full coverage of glaze. This form of aid is particularly useful when dipping *flatware*, cf *pouring*; *spraying*.

Dipylon   term which has become applicable to the *Greek vases* of the middle and late geometric attic-type. So called because a great many of such pieces have been found in a cemetery near the Dipylon gate of Athens.

Dirty ark   see *ark*.

Dishing   warping of *flatware* in the kiln, the centre of the piece sinks so that it will not stand firm; such pieces are known as *whirlers*. The opposite fault is known as *bowing*.

Dobbin   drier for *tableware*. The *ware*, having been cast (cf *casting*) or jolleyed (cf *jigger and jolley*) is placed (still in the mould) into a rotary cabinate drier, the shelves of which rotate taking the ware through a warm zone. After a single revolution the ware is dry enough to remove from the mould and the mould is ready for re-use, cf *mangle*.

Dod   die aperture placed in a *dod box*.

Dod box   hand-screw press device for extruding strips of clay to a section determined by the *dod*, a shaped orifice. Used for preparing clay to make *interlaced* and *dod handles*, *basket ware* etc. Also termed a 'wad box' on account of its use in the preparation of *wads*, or strips of clay used as a seal between *saggars* in a *bung*.

35   Simple dod handle   36   Double-interlaced handle

Dod handle   ribbon-like handle, made from extruded strips of
clay from a *dod box*. Sometimes two strips are used in an inter-
twined fashion, called an 'interlaced' or 'double-interlaced handle',
according to the number of plaits (see ills 35, 36). Used extensively
on seventeenth- and eighteenth-century salt-glazed wares (cf
salt glaze) and *creamware*.

Dog's teeth   otherwise termed 'dragon's teeth', 'alligator's
teeth' or 'crocodile's teeth'. Fault occurring at the edges of clay
extrusions such as *dod handles*, appearing as a serrated or ragged
edge. Caused by the tearing of the clay due to friction as the result
of *short clay* or it may be because the shape of the *dod* presents too
sharp an edge section compared to the centre mass.

Dolomite $CaCO_3$ $MgCO_3$, natural rock containing approximately equal parts of calcium carbonate and magnesium carbonate. Used in high-temperature glazes as a *flux*, cf *calcium oxide*;
magnesium oxide.

Dontil, dontil edge or dentil   type of decorative gilding on the
edges of articles (see ill 37).

Dot   small *refractory* piece of *kiln furniture* used as a spacer
between *tile cranks,* cf *kiln furniture.*

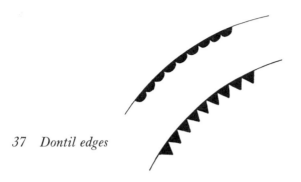

37   Dontil edges

Dotted green   enamel ground colour used at Worcester during the eighteenth century, cf *enamel*; *ground*.

Dottling   *placing* of glazed *flatware* horizontally into *cranks* ready for firing, cf *rearing*.

Double casting   (1) also referred to as 'solid casting'; a method of *casting* in which the inside as well as the outside of the piece is formed by the mould. Especially for some types of *flatware* which are required to show a smooth surface inside when the outer surface may be embossed, cf *embossing*; (2) the term is also used for the process of casting ware in two different colours, cf *casting*.

Double glaze   use of two glazes to achieve a decorative effect. The manner in which it is possible for glazes to react upon each other and to influence the final result will vary according to their composition, cf *glaze*. Probably the most outstanding examples are those of *rutile* or titanium. One of the properties of rutile, commonly called *break-up*, is to cause mottling, especially when used as the underneath glaze of a double dip.

Double-gourd vase   see *Chinese shapes* (ill 23).

Double-interlaced handle   see *dod handle*.

85

Drag (1) fault in cast ware (cf *casting*), appearing as a fracture caused by an error in *mould making* when an undercut or acute curve in a profile may be too great to cope with the clay shrinkage; (2) cracking in fired ware due to sticking to the kiln *bats* or *cranks*, cf *stuck ware*; *bat-wash*; (3) see *micas*.

Dragon lustre   see *fairyland lustre*.

Dragonskin glaze   see *ja katsu*.

Dragon's teeth   see *dog's teeth*.

Draw (1) to remove a piece of clayware from a mould; (2) to remove the contents of a kiln after *firing*; (3) to remove one plaster-cast from another, ie the *block mould* from the *model*; the *case mould* from the block etc.

Dressing any means of smoothing or imparting a finish to ware, cf *fettling*; *towing*; *facing-up*.

Drift horizontal shaft at one time used at the bottom of a *china-clay* mine to connect the *buttonhole launder* to the pump shaft; now obsolete.

Drillingsbecher German equivalent to the English *fuddling cup*.

Droppers drops of *glaze* which have become adhered to *ware* during the *glost* firing, having dropped from above. Possibly caused by too thick or too *soft* a glaze on a piece set above, or as the result of overfiring. In salt-glazed wares, (cf *salt-glaze*) after a time the kiln arch may become overcoated with a glaze deposit which will then have a tendency to drip at peak temperatures. A protective kiln *bat* should be placed over the ware.

Drug jar see *apothecary jars*.

Dry in a *china-clay* mine, the storage area for excavated and purified clay, consisting of two main portions: (1) the 'pan hearth' or 'trough' (now obsolete), a large, heated area for drying the china clay *slurry* from the *micas*. Now replaced with *filter presses* and rotary driers; (2) the *linhay*, a term still in use for the storage area for the dried clay awaiting dispatch.

Dry blue   vivid-blue *enamel* used at Worcester in the eighteenth century.

Dry body   term sometimes used to indicate a *vitreous* unglazed body, cf *jasper*; *basalt*; *rosso antico*; *parian*; *cameo parian*; *red stoneware*; *biscuit figure*.

Dry edge   fault; an area on the edge of a *glost* article from which the glaze has been rubbed before *firing* so leaving a rough *starved glaze* surface.

Dry-edge figure   descriptive term for some early glazed figures, particularly Derby, in which the *glaze* was left off the base, and occasionally for some distance up the side of the piece, in order to prevent sticking to the kiln during *glost* firing. Later pieces were set on *bitstones* and subsequently *stilts*.

Dry foot   an unglazed foot.

Dry-pan   type of *edge-runner* mill for grinding raw materials. The term is also sometimes used to mean the same as a 'slip-pan', *sun-pan* or 'sun-kiln', though in these circumstances 'drying pan' would be a more appropriate term.

Dubber   single-headed tool (something like a ball-clay worker's *pug*) used at one time in the *china-clay* mines to remove obstructions likely to impair the flow of water over the *strakes*.

Dry pressing   see *dust pressing*.

Duck-egg porcelain   porcelain with a pale duck-egg colour discernible through its translucency. Characteristic of ware made at Swansea for a short time early in the nineteenth century.

Dulling   *glaze* fault in which the surface appears less glossy than it should. Normally caused by a slight degree of *devitrification* or by *sulphuring*.

Dumont's blue   see *smalts*.

Dump   early name for a *stilt*.

Dunting   cracking of ware caused by too-rapid cooling of the kiln, cf *fled*.

Duster   type of pottery painter's brush, cf *pencil* (ill 94).

Dust pressing   method of making tiles using almost dry clay dust in place of plastic clay, so reducing the problems of drying and warping. The body is first prepared in the normal wet mix process, filter pressed (cf *filter press*) and kiln dried, after which it is milled and a small percentage of water added, sufficient only to achieve the binding of the clay dust under pressure. The dust is then fed into a powerful screw press, or its modern hydraulic equivalent. The moisture content varies on an average from 5–15 per cent, according to the pressure used and the section of the piece; high pressures require less moisture, low pressures and complicated sections require more to achieve a satisfactory flow in the die. The technique is also used in the manufacture of scientific components requiring a high degree of dimensional accuracy.

Dutch   otherwise known as 'gawdy Dutch' or 'gawdy Welsh'; see *gawdy ware*.

Earthenware   opaque, non-*vitreous*, *soft*-fired ware. The normal firing temperature of the *biscuit firing* is 1,100°C–1,150°C; the *glost* is in the region of 1,080°C. However, some *red-clay* craft wares may be found to benefit from a lower biscuit temperature, in the region of 1,000°C, and glost at 1,080°C–1,100°C. *Fine* white earthenware is composed of *china clay*, *ball clay*, *Cornish stone* and *flint*, cf *slipware*; *maiolica*; *delftware*; *creamware*; *faience*; *faience fine*; *steingut*; *terraglia*; *loza-fina*; *terra de pipa*.

Easy fire   relatively low-temperature *firing*; also referred to as *soft* fire.

Edge-runner mill   there are two basic types of edge-runner mill; (1) *chaser mills*, in which the pan remains stationary and the *runners* (two heavy, horizontally mounted rollers) are made to rotate about horizontal and vertical axes; (2) *pan-mills*, which have the opposite action, the pan is made to rotate and the runners revolve freely about their horizontal axis only.

Efflorescence sometimes referred to as 'kiln white', 'scum', 'scumming' or *soluble salts*. This fault appears as a white scum on unglazed *redware* and bricks. It may be obviated by the addition of a small quantity of *barytes* to the clay during preparation, cf *barium carbonate*.

Egg and spinach glaze see *tiger glaze*.

Eggshell porcelain an exceptionally thin *hard-paste* porcelain made in China for export to Europe. Imitations in *soft-paste* were made in Staffordshire during the nineteenth century, cf *t'o t'ai*; *black-pencilled decoration*.

Egyptian black black unglazed *vitreous* ware made by the addition of *manganese oxide* or *cobalt oxide* to *red clay*. This type of ware was already in use in Staffordshire in the mid-eighteenth century, when Wedgwood, realising that such a body would be ideal for his neo-classical designs, developed and improved it to produce the *ware* known as *basalt*.

Egyptian blue (glaze) a rich turquoise blue formed by using copper compounds (cf *copper oxide*), in an *alkaline glaze* (see appendix 5). The early Egyptian and Persian blues were basically of a similar nature. *Natron*, a source of *sodium oxide*, likely to produce such colours, was readily available in the Near East and is most likely to have been a significant factor in the development of glazes by the Egyptians several millennium BC, cf *Egyptian paste*.

Egyptian paste otherwise known as 'fritware' or glazed 'quartz fritware'. A non-plastic mixture of *silica*, an alkaline *flux* and *copper oxide*. The original Egyptian paste was most probably made of *quartz*, *natron*, *copper oxide* and a small amount of *clay* to give a modicum of plasticity. Simple shapes were made by pressing the paste into clay or carved stone moulds. The glazed surface is due to soluble sodium salts in the paste which, as the pieces dry, become deposited on the surface forming a coating of alkaline flux. At low temperatures, in the region of 950°C, this flux combines with the other materials near the surface to form a *glaze*, cf *ushabti figure*.

Elutriation   method of grading a material by means of suspension in a gentle stream of water. The heavy particles settle out first, the finer ones continue in suspension. This process is sometimes combined with *magnetic purification* to extract free iron impurities.

Émaillé sur bisque   French term for a Chinese technique of decorating in *enamel* colour on unglazed *porcelain*.

Émaux ombrants   mid nineteenth-century French decorative technique, using a delicate low-relief (cf *bas relief*) design impressed into the *leather-hard* clay and ultimately glazed with a coloured transparent glaze, usually green. The highest points of the relief tend to shed the glaze whilst it flows deeper in the low-lying areas, giving light and dark tones respectively. Similar wares using the same technique were made by Wedgwood in the 1860s.

Embossing   the use of relief stamps or rollers to impress decorative motifs into the soft clay. A wide variety of effects may be achieved according to the condition of the clay, ie wet or *leather-hard*; whether the stamp is used with freedom or precision; the ultimate treatment, ie glazed or unglazed. The stamps may be made by carving sticks of wood, *plaster of Paris* or even clay which is subsequently fired. Alternatively, ready-made objects and natural forms often provide interesting sources of pattern, eg *corded decoration*. Repetitive patterns can be obtained by using an *embossing wheel*. Industrially embossed relief, known in this case as 'embossment', is usually cast in the mould, not to be confused with *sprigged decoration*.

Embossing wheel   wheel or roller with a pattern carved around the rim. Used to decorate in the *leather-hard* state, cf *embossing*.

Embossment   see *embossing*.

Enamel   extensively used in China on K'ang Hsi wares (see appendix 1) since the seventeenth century. Sometimes referred to as 'on-glaze' or 'over-glaze' decoration; prepared from the same metallic sources as other *ceramic* pigments, but blended with fluxes so that it may be fused onto the surface of the fired glaze at low temperatures. The normal enamel kiln temperature is in the region of 750°C to 800°C, but for some colours may reach 900°C. Such relatively low temperatures make possible the use of many materials which would burn away at the higher *glost* temperatures needed for *under-glaze decoration* or *maiolica*. Therefore the colour range is comparatively extensive and unlike most other instances of colour in ceramics, enamel colours before *firing* often closely resemble their fired qualities. This property, together with its ease of application, makes enamel ideal for the intricate hand-painted decoration so popular since the eighteenth century. Subsequent developments have evolved numerous mechanical methods of application which remain a prominent feature of the *tableware* industry today, cf *enamel painting*; *groundlay*; *aerography*; *engraved decoration*; *lithography*; *screen-printed decoration*.

Enamel glaze   term sometimes used erroneously to refer to a *tin glaze*, the expression 'tin enamels' is similarly used.

Enamel painting   the medium used for painted *enamel* is pure turpentine and *fat oil*. The colour is first ground in turpentine and the fat oil added as required to give flow to the pigment. Sometimes the oils of *aniseed*, *fennel* or *lavender* are added to keep the colour open and workable for a longer period. Camel-hair brushes, known as *pencils*, are made in a variety of sizes and shapes each devised for a specific purpose (see ill 94).

Encaustic decoration   meaning 'burned in' decoration; the term is used to define two types of *ware* similar only in that both use clay as a medium and therefore require *firing* or 'burning in' (cf *burning*) to complete. (1) using coloured *slip* to paint a design on the fired ware, after the manner of Wedgwood's red-painted *basalt* made in imitation of Greek *red-figure vase* painting, such pieces are normally made of *vitreous* ware and left unglazed, cf *Etruscan ware*; (2) the term is also used in relation to 'inlaid' tiles; plastic clay, or sometimes *slip*, is laid into channels incised into clay of a different colour, as exemplified by European medieval floor tiles. In this sense the term encaustic does not seem entirely appropriate but it has been accepted as such since the nineteenth century, cf *Henri deux ware*.

End set   see *sets*.

Energy regulator   controlling device for electric kilns, comprising an automatic mercury switch which varies the intervals of off and on from 0–100 per cent, according to a selected setting.

Enghalskrug   seventeenth-century German *faience* jug, having a globular body and a long neck. These shapes also usually had a spreading foot, thick lip and a plaited handle. They are occasionally further adorned with pewter lids, cf *Rhenish stoneware*.

Engine turning   mechanical method of decoration in the *leather-hard* state. The *ware* is set in a lathe equipped with an eccentric motion. The lathe may be set to obtain geometric, diced and fluted patterns. It can also be used for normal turning. The first lathe of this type was built for Josiah Wedgwood by Matthew Boulton in 1763 (see ill 38).

English pink   the name given to chrome-tin pink when it was first produced in England in the eighteenth century, cf *chrome* oxide (appendix 5).

Engobe   Coating of *slip*, white or coloured, applied to wares as decoration or to present a finer surface by concealing an inferior clay beneath.

Engraved decoration   method of producing '*on-glaze*' and '*under-glaze*' *transfer decoration*, first introduced in the eighteenth century, supposedly at Battersea, and subsequently used profusely in the production of *blue and white ware,* of which the *Willow pattern* (see ill 39) is probably the most well known.

*38 Engine-turning
at the Wedgwood
factory, Barlaston*

Spode's *Blue Italian Pattern* (see ill 40) introduced in 1816, is
also worthy of particular mention on account of the distinct
advance in engraving technique which it represents. The improved use of half-tone in this and later patterns succeeded in
producing a noteworthy quality of depth, hitherto not achieved.
The design is engraved on copper plates or rollers in the normal
way. The printing process itself is also similar to the conventional
methods of engraving except that the image is filled with *ceramic*
pigment suspended in printer's oil.

For *under-glaze decoration* the print is taken on tissue paper
(see ill 127) which has previously been prepared with a soapy
solution in order to facilitate its eventual removal from the ware
without damage to the image. The transfer is applied immediately
to the clean *biscuit* ware when the sticky image adheres to the dry
and slightly porous surface (see ill 128). After a firm rubbing down,

39   Spode, printed 'Willow Pattern' plate

the tissue may be removed by soaking in water; it is now that the soapy solution assists in its release from the ware. A 'hardening-on' firing (cf *harden-on*) is required in order to fuse the image to the ware and to burn off the printing oils, which would otherwise prevent the adherence of the glaze (cf *crawling*).

For 'on-glaze' engraved transfers, *enamel* colour is used in place of 'under-glaze' pigments. The method of printing is virtually the same but there are two methods of application—one is the same as the under-glaze method already described, except that when printing on-glaze it is sometimes necessary to apply a *size* to the ware in order to achieve a satisfactory adherence of the printed image.

The second method is known as *pull and dust*. The print is applied but the particular colour being used may not be strong enough if left to itself. Therefore, after removal of the tissue (which in this case is pulled off as opposed to being soaked), an extra quantity of the appropriate colour, in powder form, is dusted on to the print while it is still tacky, thus reinforcing its quality, cf *printed decoration*; *clobbering*; *Pratt ware*.

40 *Spode, selection of pieces decorated with the engraved 'Blue Italian Pattern'. Introduced about 1816 and in continuous production ever since*

Epergne   composite centre piece for a table; made to contain sweetmeats, fruit etc. Usually made in *porcelain* or silver.

Escudelles ab orelles   Spanish *lustre*-ware bowl with ear-shaped handles. Dating from the fifteenth and sixteenth centuries.

Essex jug   large jugs, sometimes up to three feet high were made at Hedingham in Essex in the nineteenth century.

Etruscan ware   black *basalt* ware with red figure *encaustic* decoration produced by Wedgwood in the eighteenth century after the style of the Greek *red figure vases.*

Etui   lady's vanity box made of *porcelain,* silver, pinchbeck etc.

Eulenkrug   see *Rhenish stoneware* (ill 115).

Ewer large jug or water container. Generally associated with nineteenth-century toilet sets, consisting of an ewer and a wash basin.

Extrusion the forcing of clay through a shaped orifice or die. As used in the manufacture of drainpipes, bricks and some types of tiles, cf *dod box*.

Face the surface of a mould or article which is deemed to be the most important. In a mould, the surface from which the piece is made. On an article, the upper surface as opposed to the back of a piece of *flatware*, or the outside as opposed to the inside of a piece of *hollow ware*, cf *mould making*.

Facing up coating a *plaster of Paris* surface with soap *size* which serves as a release agent between it and the subsequent pouring of fresh plaster. Inadequate facing-up of the *case mould* or *sets* can contribute to sticking and *blowing*.

Faience originally French tin-glazed ware (cf *tin glaze*) after the *maiolica* tradition, and this is the most accurate use of the term, but it has become loosely used in connection with any glazed *earthenware*.

Faience d'oiron see *Henri Deux ware*.

Faience fine French term relating to *fine* white or cream-coloured earthenware, cf *creamware*.

Faience Japonnée name given to a high-quality French *faience* made by the Sceaux factory in Paris during the mid-eighteenth century. The style closely followed that of Sèvres.

Faience parlantes (story-telling *faience*); pictorial dishes with satirical inscriptions, made at Nevers in the eighteenth century.

Faience patronymiques pictorial commemorative wares depicting family occasions, patron saints etc. Made at Nevers during the eighteenth century.

Fairings originally inexpensive wares of various kinds made at one time especially for sale at country fairs. Many of the now much-treasured eighteenth-century pieces, such as *cow creamers,* were first produced as fairings.

Fairyland lustre and dragon lustre highly decorative style of *lustre* ware made by Miss Daisy Mackaig-Jones for Wedgwood between 1914 and 1931. The technique, which makes some use of earlier researches by William Burton into lustres, involves a fairly complex combination of printed outlines on the *biscuit,* followed by hand painting, glazing, application of lustre and finally an 'on-glaze' printed outline in gold. Patterns are based upon folklore ('fairyland lustre'), many in the contemporary art nouveau style, others are *chinoiserie* in character ('dragon lustre') after the K'ang Hsi porcelains (see appendix 1).

Famille jaune (yellow family); French name for a style of imported K'ang Hsi (see appendix 1) *porcelain* profusely decorated in *enamels* of which the predominant colour of the design or *ground* colour is yellow. Famille jaune is often found to be painted in enamel on *biscuit,* cf *famille verte; famille noire; famille rose.*

Famille noire (black family); French name for a style of imported K'ang Hsi (see appendix 1) *porcelain* profusely decorated in *enamels* of which the predominant colour of the design or *ground* colour is black. The famille noire is often to be found painted in enamel on *biscuit,* cf *famille verte, famille jaune; famille rose.*

Famille rose (pink family); French term for a style of imported Chinese *porcelain* which features a pink *enamel* obtained from gold, *purple of cassius.* This pink enamel first appears as a dull reddish-brown in the late K'ang Hsi period (see appendix 1) but was subsequently developed into a ruby-pink during the Yung Cheng period (see appendix 1). In the nineteenth century the term was used in relation to a similar range of *rose colours,* also developed from purple of cassius, used at Worcester, Chelsea,

Bow and Staffordshire, cf *famille jaune*; *famille noir*; *famille verte*.

Famille verte (green family); French name given to a style of imported K'ang Hsi and early Yung Cheng (see appendix 1) *porcelains*, often profusely decorated in *enamels* of which the predominant colour is green. The term has also become accepted as a collective name for the whole range of K'ang Hsi enamelled wares in yellow, green, blue, black, purple and pink, cf *famille jaune*; *famille noire*; *famille rose*.

Fancies trade term for non-utilitarian decorative wares often of a novelty nature.

Fan Hung Chinese red *enamel* derived from *iron oxide*.

Fantasievogel (exotic birds); the term originates from a style of decoration using imaginative bird motifs at Meissen in the latter half of the eighteenth century. The style itself is undoubtedly influenced by imported oriental *porcelain,* and in turn was taken up at Sèvres and Worcester, cf *Indianische blumen*; *streu blumen*; *Meissner blumen*.

Fat clay plastic clay of an easily workable consistency, cf *lean clay*; *short clay*.

Fat oil (fat oil of turpentine); obtained as a result of the evaporation of pure turpentine; used with turpentine as a medium for *enamel painting*.

Fayence the German for *faience*.

Fazackerley colours eighteenth-century style of brightly coloured *delftware* attributed to Liverpool. The name is derived from one Thomas Fazackerley, whose name appears on some mugs of this style.

Feathering *slipware* technique in which a background coating of *slip* is applied to the *ware* and then followed immediately by a second slip of a contrasting colour which is 'trailed' (cf *trailing*) into the first before it dries. The whole is then given a slight bump in order to sink the trailed slip into the background. A sharpened feather quill, stiff bristle or other suitable instrument with a long, flexible, fine point is drawn across the trailing causing the latter to break into fine hair-lines.

Felspar mineral found in *igneous rocks* such as granite and *pegmatite*, felspar is one of the most important raw materials used by potters. It contains all the essential ingredients for a *glaze*, ie *silica, alumina* and *flux*, the latter usually in the form of *potassium oxide, sodium oxide* or *calcium oxide*. Less-common varieties contain other fluxes, lithium (cf *lithium carbonate*) for example. Felspars vary in composition and are broadly classified under names appropriate to their respective dominant flux. The three most common in use being 'orthoclase'—potash felspar, $K_2O\ Al_2O_3\ 6SiO_2$; 'albite'—soda felspar, $Na_2O\ Al_2O_3\ 6SiO_2$; 'anorthite'—calcium felspar, $CaO\ Al_2O_3\ 2SiO_2$. The most useful variety used in potting is orthoclase, it is this type which is normally inferred when just the name felspar is quoted. Orthoclase felspar melts in the region of 1,200°C and will form a milky glaze on its own account, in fact felspars may be regarded as natural *frits* forming a useful basis for high-temperature glazes, requiring only slight additions of other materials to achieve a satisfactory glaze. Felspar may be introduced in the form of 'Cornish stone', cf *pegmatite; glaze*.

Felspar china see *felspar porcelain*.

Felspar porcelain modified *bone-china* introduced by Spode in 1821; so called because felspar was used to replace *Cornish stone* (used in the earlier recipes), being added to *ball clay, bone ash* and a sand *frit*. A point of interest is that the felspar originally used was mined at Middleton Hill on the North Wales border, having been identified by a Thomas Ryan who discovered it amidst waste overburden in a disused lead mine. More aptly called 'felspar china' it is *biscuit* fired at a higher temperature than most *soft-pastes*. A similar paste was made at Coalport,

Worcester and Derby. For a fuller account of the background to the introduction of felspar as a raw material in English ceramics, the reader is referred to Leonard Whiter. *Spode: 1733-1833* (1963).

Felspathic glaze high-temperature *glaze* for *stoneware* and *porcelain* in which *felspar* constitutes the principal *flux*, either in the form of pure felspar or included in other materials such as 'Cornish stone', cf *pegmatite*.

Fennel (oil of fennel); alternative to the oils of aniseed or lavender, used in *enamel painting* to keep the colour open for a longer period to allow for fine painting, cf *enamel painting*.

Fen ting Chinese—'flour ting'; one of the varieties of white Ting wares of the Sung dynasty (see appendix 1), the others being 'pai ting' (white ting) and 't'u ting' (earthy ting).

Ferric oxide Fe_2O_3, red iron oxide; see *iron oxide*.

Ferronerie French term for patterns similar in character to, or derived from, wrought-iron work.

Ferrous oxide FeO, black iron oxide; see *iron oxide*.

Fettling removal of surplus clay, rough edges and seam marks from clayware before *firing*. Usually carried out in the *leather-hard* to dry state using a sharp blade and followed with a damp sponge, cf *scrapping*; *towing*; *pencilling* (2). Similarly used in connection with the cleaning up of moulds. It is suggested that the term may originate from the expression to be in fine 'fettle'.

Figuline relief-modelled decoration using natural form as subject matter. A term introduced by Bernard Palissy to describe the characteristic style of his full relief decoration consisting of casts taken from snakes, beetles, ferns and other plant forms.

Figure making see *sprigged decoration*.

Filter cake a slab of plastic clay as produced by a *filter press*.

Filter cloth formerly made of cotton twill, with a jute backing cloth, but now replaced by stronger man-made fabrics such as nylon or terylene. Filter cloths form the actual filters through which *slip* is strained in order to remove excess water, to produce plastic clay, cf *filter press*; *filter cake*.

Filter press (1) equipment for straining *slip* under pressure through cloths to extract water in order to obtain plastic clay; (2) to produce plastic clay by forcing *slip* through *filter cloths*.

Fine pottery made of relatively pure, white-burning materials.

Fine earthenware see under *fine* and *earthenware*.

Fine orange ware Ancient American, Toltec ware of the Post Classic Period (AD 980–1521). So called on account of the pinkish-orange colour of the fired clay; it is finer in texture than other ancient Central American wares which normally contain a proportion of *grog* or other similar materials. Decorative style seems to vary, including some *slip* painted ware and some *incised decoration*, cf *Matlatzinca ware*; *Mazapan ware*; *plumbate ware*; *Coyotlatelco ware*.

Finger vase see *quintal flower horn*.

Fireclay *refractory* clay capable of withstanding high temperatures. Often associated with coal seams being *seat earths* found immediately below the coal. Normally sedimentary, containing fine-grained *kaolin* and *silica* (in the form of *quartz*) together with impurities in common with other *secondary clays*.

Firing heating of a *kiln*; derived from the time when combustible fuels were the only source of heat, but now applicable also to electric kilns, cf *burning*.

Firsts perfect ware of first quality without blemish, as opposed to *seconds*, *lump* or *wasters*.

Fish-roe crackle see *crackle*.

101

Fit *transfer decoration* purposely shaped so as to fit the curve of a particular piece, eg most shapes are resolved as parts of a cone rather than discs (flatware), or cylinders (hollow ware), and the transfers are shaped accordingly, cf *sheet pattern*.

Flambé glaze or rouge flambé reduced (cf *reduction*) *copper-red glaze* with a streaky appearance somewhat reminiscent of flames. Essentially similar to *sang de boeuf* and other glazes with such descriptive names. First made in China during the Ming dynasty (see appendix 1) and at recurring intervals since. During the early twentieth century, flambé glazes became a vogue in western countries and the term became more loosely used to cover all reduced copper glazes. Such wares were produced by a number of individual potters, notably Bernard Moor of Longton, and some larger companies—The German Porcelain Company; Doultons and Moorcrofts of Stoke-on-Trent; Pilkingtons of Manchester; Carter Stabler and Adams of Poole; Ruskin Pottery of Birmingham; in the USA, Rookwood Pottery of Cincinnati.

Flashing occurs when the flames in a *kiln* are allowed to lick across the ware causing variegated *glaze* effects. Sometimes considered a fault, but it is also carried out intentionally particularly in *studio pottery* and in brick manufacture, cf *reduction*; *oxidation*; *bag-wall*.

Flash lustre see under *lustre glazes*.

Flash wall term used in the USA for a *bag-wall*.

Flatware shallow articles such as plates, saucers, disches etc, as opposed to *hollow ware*.

Fled alternative term for *dunting*, particularly applicable to cracking which occurs in the *enamel* kiln. Normally caused by the internal strains of a piece being exposed to sudden differences of temperature or a sudden cold draught.

Fleurs chatironnées see *chatironné*.

Fleurs fines flower painting in *enamel,* following a naturalistic style usually depicting actual species, cf *deutsche blumen.*

Fleurs Indes flower painting in a pseudo-oriental style after the manner of *kakiemon* patterns and often outlined as in *chatironné.*

Flint SiO_2, source of pure *silica*; a hard siliceous material generally thought to have originated from plants and animals such as sponges and diatoms, which made their skeletons and shells from silica, and which became deposited as a gelatinous substance on the floor of the Upper Cretaceous Sea, forming as nodules or tabular masses in chalk. Now still found in chalk (cf *chalk flints*) or as beach pebbles. The latter, known as *boulder flints,* are used in Britain as the main source of calcined flint in *ceramics.* The pebbles are calcined (cf *calcine*) and ground to a fine powder for use in the preparation of bodies and glazes, cf *coalad flint*; *body*; *glaze.*

Flint-enamelled ware mid nineteenth-century development of Rockingham ware (cf *Rockingham glaze*) having a deliberately mottled or streaky glaze applied over a relatively hard, buff-coloured *body.* Patented in the USA by the Fenton factory at Bennington, Vermont.

Flintporslin Swedish term for *creamware.*

Flow blue *cobalt oxide* pigment for under-glaze printing, (cf *printed decoration*) fired in a chlorinated atmosphere to induce the colour to blend or 'flow' into the glaze. The intention was to create smooth even tones as a means of increasing the sense of depth in a pattern, particularly in the case of the landscape patterns with which it is usually associated. Sometimes the flow would be overdone and a blurred image would result. In such cases the term *flown,* indicating a fault, is strictly more appropriate, cf *flow powder.*

Flow chart diagrammatic representation of a process sequence.

103

TYPICAL FLOW CHART FOR BODY PREPARATION

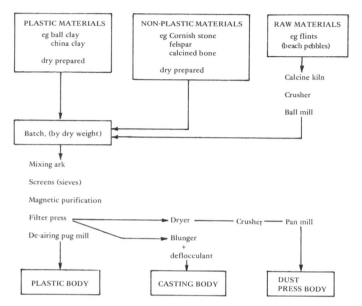

Flower-brick   rectangular container with holes in the top as a basis for floral arrangement (see ill 41). First made in England during the eighteenth century in tin-glazed *earthenware*, cf *tin glaze*. Possibly in imitation of imported Chinese wares. Some varieties have large and small holes, these occasionally double as ink stands, the large holes for containing an ink well and the smaller ones for pens.

Flown   colour which has run in a glaze, becomes blurred or transferred from one article to another placed too close in the *glost* kiln. *Cobalt oxide* and *copper oxide* are particularly susceptible, especially in chlorinated atmospheres, cf *flow blue; flow powder; striking.*

Flow powder   preparation to induce the flowing of colour by means of creating a chlorinated atmosphere. It is placed in the *glost* kiln close to wares decorated with *flow blue*. May be made

*41 Bristol tin-glazed earthenware flower-brick c 1750
(Victoria & Albert Museum)*

with two parts of *whiting* to one part of calcium chloride, or lead chloride can be used on its own, cf *flow blue*; *flown*.

Fluorspar CaF_2, calcium fluoride; may be used in glazes as a source of *calcium oxide*, though its use in *soft* glazes is limited due to a tendency for the volatilised fluorine to cause bubbling.

Fluting *incised* form of decoration by cutting flutes in the *leather-hard* clay. In the case of moulded or cast ware the flutes are cast in the mould, having been originally cut on the model, cf *moulding*; *casting*; *mould making*.

Flux constituent of glazes (cf *glaze*), some bodies (cf *body*) and *enamel* colours; added to glazes to reduce the melting point of the other materials, ie *silica* and *alumina*, to within a workable temperature relative to the body to which it is applied. Used in the preparation of bodies to encourage the fusion of other materials, imparting strength and reducing porosity. In enamels to facilitate fusion to glazes.

Foglie manner of decoration in which the pattern is made up totally of leaves.

105

Foliated scroll-handle decorative handle modelled with scroll-work. Made by *casting*, cf *crabstock handle, interlaced handle, dod handle, open handle, block handle, pulled handle*.

42   Foliated scroll-handle

Fond écaille tortoiseshell glaze produced at Sèvres in the eighteenth century.

Foot or foot-ring raised, integral support at the base of a pot; made by *turning* when the piece has become *leather-hard*, or initially by *jigger and jolley* or by *casting* in the mould, cf *stem*; *footer*.

Footer *foot* mould used by pressers to form the foot on a pressed dish (cf *press moulding*). After the main shape of the piece has been pressed, the footer is located on the dish and held firm while a roll of clay is pressed against it to form the foot-ring (see ills 43, 107-9).

43   Footer mould

Former (1) simple *hump mould* or *chum* over which a *bat* of clay is pre-shaped prior to pressing into a hollow mould. Useful when the hollow shape involves complex or acute curves, when pre-shaping on a former helps to prevent *retching* on the outer surface—a fault which if it should occur in a hollow mould is not easy to rectify; (2) hand-held template as used for early hand jolleying, cf *jigger and jolley* (ill 60).

French chalk   see *steatite*.

Frit   all or part of the constituents of a *glaze*, pre-melted in a *frit kiln*, cooled and ground to a fine powder. The purpose being to render water-soluble materials insoluble (water being the medium of glaze application); to render lead compounds non-toxic; to achieve a greater degree of homogeneity, thus producing a higher glaze quality, cf *lead glaze*; *leadless glass*; *low-solubility glaze*.

Frit kiln   crucible-like furnace designed to accept dry, raw materials for *glaze* making, so that they may be melted into a molten glass or *frit*. The molten *charge* is poured off and quenched in a bath of cold water, known as a *bosch*, causing it to shatter into granular fragments suitable for milling. There are a number of types of frit kiln, either reverberatory or rotary.

Fritted porcelain   see *glassy porcelain*.

Fritware   see *Egyptian paste*.

Frizzling   fault in enamel-decorated ware, particularly transfer decorated, cf *transfer decoration*. Due to too rapid firing in the early stages of the *enamel* kiln, causing the media of application, eg *fat oil*, printing oils, *size*, *cover-coat* etc to boil or burn before they can evaporate, causing the colour to curl.

Frog mugs   novelty ale mugs, in the bottom of which life-sized replicas of frogs have been modelled as a prank to the drinker. Eighteenth-century Staffordshire examples are usually in *slipware* or *creamware*. Also made well on into the nineteenth century at Leeds, Nottingham and Sunderland.

Fruti manner of decoration in which the pattern is made up of fruit and leaves.

Fuddling cup composite cup made up of three or more cups joined together and linked internally so that to empty one, all must be drained.

44   Fuddling cup

Funori Japanese term for a sticky syrup or gum obtained from seaweed; used as a glaze hardener and binder for decorating pigments, cf *carrageen moss*; *alginate*; *gum Arabic*; *gum tragacanth*; *Anglo gum*.

Furidashi bowl used in the Japanese tea ceremony for containing powdered tea, cf *chatsubo*; *chaire*; *chawan*; *futaoki*; *kensui*; *mizusachi*; *mukozuki*.

Futaoki Japanese ladle rest used in the tea ceremony, made of pottery, bamboo or metal, cf *chaire*; *chatsubo*; *chawan*; *furidashi*; *kensui*; *mizusachi*; *mukozuki*.

Gabri ware alternative name sometimes given to the *champlevé*-decorated *slipwares* of the Near East. So called because some authorities held the view that these wares may have been made by the fire-worshipping Gabri inhabitants of Persia.

Galena PbS, *lead sulphide*; an ore of lead, a low-temperature *flux* and the basis of medieval glazes. In the very early days, galena, being a friable mineral, was crushed into a powder, known as *smithum*, and dusted onto the ware before firing. It was sometimes mixed with *iron oxide* and *manganese oxide* to give dark-brown or black glazes. It contains impurities, notably sulphur which can be a source of trouble in glazes (cf *sulphuring*), therefore its use is not recommended. Furthermore, its use on domestic items is not permitted by law owing to solubility, cf *low-solubility glaze*. Neither is it permitted to be used in factories nor schools.

Gallipot   name given in Europe to a Chinese shape; a tall jar with full shoulders and a short, narrow neck, cf *Chinese shapes* (ill 23).

Gallonier   seventeenth- and eighteenth-century measure; a pot containing one gallon, cf *pottle pot*; *pot*; *little pot*.

Gallyware   early name for *delftware*; derivation obscure but thought on one hand perhaps to be from an old word meaning clayware, or alternatively because such wares were transported in galleys from Italy or Spain (both views are expressed by differing authorities).

Ganister   siliceous rock or earth deposit found immediately below a coal seam, cf *seat earth*.

Gardenware   flower pots, containers, planters, edging tiles etc. Usually made in *soft*-fired *redware*.

Garnitures de cheminée   as the name implies, decoration for the mantelpiece. Matching sets of five vases, normally comprising

45   *Garnitures de cheminée*

109

three baluster shapes (cf *baluster vase* or *jug*), sometimes with lids, and two open vases or beakers with flared rims. Originally produced in China, of K'ang Hsi (see appendix 1) *porcelain*, to meet western tastes and subsequently copied in most European factories, cf *kast-stel.*

Gaulus   a Roman drinking cup.

Gawdy ware   otherwise known as 'Gawdy Dutch' or 'Gawdy Welsh'; early nineteenth-century Staffordshire *earthenware* made as a cheap imitation of the colourful *porcelain* with *Imari* decoration. It was decorated with gay floral patterns in red, yellow and blue; sometimes the blue was applied first as an under-glaze print (cf *engraved decoration*). A great deal of this *ware* seems to have been exported to the USA, as much has been found in Pennsylvania. This gave rise to an earlier, but erroneous, belief, that it was made there, cf *Pennsylvania Dutch.*

Getting   see *winning.*

Gilding   application of gold decoration. The early techniques of the eighteenth century made use of gold leaf and various fixitive *sizes*, fired to a very low heat. Subsequent developments during the nineteenth century up to the present day, using various forms of gold in solution, have produced a range of qualities of high durability together with adaptability to the modern hand and mechanical methods of application, cf *acid gold*; *bright gold*; *burnished gold*; *screen gold*; *raised gold*; *brown gold.*

Ginnetting   see *sorting.*

Ginnetting wheel   see *sorting lathe.*

Ginger jar   Chinese shape in which ginger and other spices were exported to Europe, cf *Chinese shapes* (see ill 23).

Giving   alternative term for 'glazing' (not commonly used).

Glassy porcelain   otherwise known as 'fritted porcelain'; *soft-paste* porcelain containing powdered glass or *frit* as a *flux.*

Originating in Europe as an attempt to reproduce wares similar to the imported Chinese porcelains. The first known experiments were carried out in Florence at the end of the sixteenth century. Whilst the characteristics of glassy porcelain are quite different to true *hard-paste* they soon became established as a class in their own right, reaching a peak at Vincennes and Sèvres during the eighteenth century. The technique was brought to England from France but gained little favour owing to its high rate of loss. Instead English potters turned to alternative materials in search of a more commercially viable *body*, cf *bone china*; *felspar porcelain*; *ironstone china*; *stone china*; *Turner's patent*.

Glaze glassy coating applied to pottery as a combined practical and aesthetic measure; as a practical measure to render porous bodies (cf *body*) non-porous—essential in the case of *earthenware*— and to provide a smooth easily cleaned surface; as an aesthetic measure by providing surface colour and texture of an infinite variety.

The exact date and origin of the first uses of glaze are not known, but it is certain that the technique was known in Egypt between 2000 and 1500 BC at least. The natural resources in the Near East of glass-forming materials, such as *sand* (silica) and *natron* (sodium carbonate), tend to support the theory that the first, perhaps accidental, discoveries were indeed made in this part of the world.

Glass and the glaze coating on pottery are essentially similar in composition, both being formed by the melting of *silica*, which on cooling does not return to its former crystalline state but remains rather as a super-cooled liquid or glass. The melting point of silica is in excess of $1,700°C$ so that a *flux* is added to reduce this to within workable limits. The type and quantity of flux used is selected according to the temperature at which the glaze is required to melt, eg for earthenware ($1,000°C$–$1,100°C$), two parts of silica to one of all other materials; for stoneware ($1,250°C$–$1,300°C$), four parts of silica to one of all other materials (see appendix 3). Examples of fluxes in common use are *lead*

111

oxide, lead carbonate, borax, sodium oxide, potassium oxide. Alumina is the third main constituent of a glaze, introduced to control the viscosity in the molten state. Colour is introduced by using metal oxides (see appendix 5). Other qualities and textures are achieved by variations on the basic composition, cf *matt glaze*; *opaque glaze*; *opalescent glaze*; *crystalline* and *aventurine glazes*; *tin glaze*; *raw glaze*; *Bristol glaze*; *slip glaze*; *lustre glaze*; *salt glaze*; *ash glaze*; *frit*.

Glaze-fit   the relationship between the rates of expansion and contraction of the glaze and that of the *body*. The perfect glaze-fit is that when the glaze is under slight compression to prevent *crazing*.

Glaze hardener or binder   additives, such as alginates, gum, starch or cellulose substances, which facilitate ease of handling and decorating on the unfired glaze. Used by some manufacturers to reduce loss by *starved glaze*, *cut glaze* or *dry edge*, cf *gum Arabic*; *sodium carboxymethylcellulose*.

Glaze suspender   additive, usually a fine plastic material such as *ball clay* or *bentonite*, included in small amounts in glazes to hold the other constituents in suspension.

Glost   glazed state; a glost kiln is that in which the glaze is being fired.

Goat and bee jugs   ornate jugs with relief-modelled goats, plants and a bee. The handle is in the form of a branch or twig. Made at Chelsea in the eighteenth century.

Godet   late medieval drinking vessel; sometimes refers to a shallow cup, or, in the seventeenth century, a beaker without a handle.

Goglet   see *gurglet*.

Gold   see *bright gold*; *burnished gold*; *brown gold*; *screen gold*; *gilding*.

Gold rubber extremely fine abrasive stick for burnishing gold, cf *burnishing*; *agate*; *blood stone*.

Gombroon ware sixteenth- and seventeenth-century Persian wares, ordered by Dutch merchants for export to Europe and made in the style of contemporary Chinese wares which at the time had become difficult to obtain. Hard, white and thinly potted, decorated with *incised* and *pierced* designs, the glaze often running into the holes as in the so-called *rice pattern* (see ill 46). Term derived from the port of Bender Abbas, formerly Gombroon, on the Persian Gulf from where the wares were exported, cf *transparencies*.

Gorgelet oriental drinking vessel with a full, rounded body and a spout through which the liquid was poured into the mouth rather than supped, cf *cantaros*.

46 *Persian Gombroon ware, porcelain bowl decorated with transparencies, 17th or 18th century (Victoria & Albert Museum)*

Gosu cobalt blue used on Chinese *porcelain*, cf *asbolite*; *cobalt oxide*; *smalts*.

Graft gouge-shaped spade, formerly used in the Dorset *ball-clay* mines for digging clay from the *clay beds* after *weathering*. It is straight from the blade to handle, and the metal strapping extends from the blade to the handle, cf *biddy shovel*; *cutting spade*; *beater*; *spudgel*; *packer*; *pug*; *treader*; *tubal* (see ill 129).

Granary urn large Chinese pot of the Han dynasty (see appendix 1). The shape tapers inwards towards the base and stands on modelled feet. The top resembles a tiled roof with a hole, cf *Chinese shapes* (ill 23).

Grand feu French term for a high-temperature glost *firing*, cf *demi grand feu*; *petite feu*.

Granite ware *creamware* with a mottled grey glaze imitating granite, made in the eighteenth century at Leeds, and in Staffordshire by Wedgwood, Ralph Wood and others.

Grapen eighth-century *skillet* or cooking pot with three legs; a development of the *bombentopf* and the *kugeltopf* from Lower Saxony.

Grease-spot pattern textured *ground* made up of large and small ovals of gold on a coloured background, after the effect formed by grease floating on a hot liquid such as broth. A variant of *caillouté*.

Greek vases collective term in common usage to cover the unparalleled range of wares made in Greece between the fourteenth and second centuries BC, and reaching a climax with the Attic black-figure and red-figure vases of the sixth to fourth centuries BC. The Greeks' mastery of technique shows a virtuosity of manufacture unique in the history of ceramics. The shiny but unglazed decoration remained a mystery for centuries, until recent researches revealed that the use of fine, siliceous, colloidal and highly ferruginous *slips* together with an alternate *oxidation* and *reduction* firing cycle will reproduce ware of similar identity, cf *black-figure vases*; *red-figure vases*. The shapes of the Greek vases are purposive and may be classified into the following categories (for a fuller description of each shape, see under the appropriate heading and ill 47).

Storage jars: amphora, stamnos, kados, sitella, pithos, pelike, panethenaic amphora.

Water jars: hydria, kalpis, loutrophorous.

Jugs: oenochoa, olpe.

Mixing bowls: kraters—volute krater, column krater, calyx krater, bell krater or oxybaphon.

Oil containers: lekythos, aryballos, askos.

Perfume containers: alabastron, plemochoe.

Trinket boxes: pyxis.

Cups: kylix, skyphos or kotyle, kantharos, kyathos or kathos, rhyton, head cup.

Plates and dishes: phaile, pinax, lekanis.

Other shapes: psykter (a wine cooler), lebes and lebes gamikos lebes (ceremonial pedestal bowls).

Green glaze   glaze of the *Bristol* type, applied to *greenware*. This type of glaze is sometimes erroneously referred to as a *raw glaze*, cf *once-fired ware*.

Green-hard   clayware in the *leather-hard* state; also used to refer to ware in the plastic state, particularly stiff plastic state, ie when it is not dry enough to be termed leather-hard but too stiff to be considered as plastic, cf *white hard*.

Greenhouse   heated warehouse in which clayware is stored and dried prior to *biscuit* firing.

Greenware   unfired clayware; particularly that in the *leather-hard* or *green-hard* state, but in general used to include *white-hard* ware also.

Grès   French term meaning *stoneware*.

Greybeards   see *bellarmine*.

115

Grisaille painting in tones of grey to give the effect of relief decoration. Particularly appropriate to the pictorial motifs to be found on some Sèvres *porcelain*. A term not restricted to ceramics, eg also applicable to similar painted panels on furniture, cf *camaieu*.

Grog grit made from fired and ground *pitcher*. Blended with clays to give texture, to reduce shrinkage, to minimise warping and cracking in *heavy clayware* due to improved drying properties, cf *chamotte*.

Gros bleu one of a series of *grounds* developed at Sèvres during the eighteenth century. Gros bleu is an 'under-glaze' blue (cf *underglaze decoration*) which preceded the brighter *bleu de roi*, cf *bleu céleste*; *rose Pompadour*; *vert pomme*; *jaune jonquille*; *oeil de perdrix*; *caillouté*; *vermiculé*; *jewelled decoration*.

Ground background colour or texture over which the main pattern is superimposed, or into which it is let.

Ground-hog kiln in the USA, a craft potter's kiln which is partly let into an earth bank.

Groundlay application of a *ground* colour. A special *size* is painted onto the area to be groundlayed, using a soft, flat brush. Once the size has become tacky it is dabbed vigorously with a padded silk boss in order to achieve an even coating. The whole is then liberally coated with powdered *ceramic* colour which adheres only to the sized area. If further colours are to be painted or transferred over the ground, the latter must be fired first. In such cases care must be taken to ensure that the nature of the ground colour is not such as requires a softer firing than subsequent

47 (facing page) Greek vases: 1 pithos; 2 stamnos; 3 amphora; 4 pelike; 5 panathenaic amphora; 6, 7 oinochoae; 8 olpe; 9 loutrophorous; 10 kalpis; 11 hydria; 12 bell krater; 13 volute krater; 14 cylix krater; 15 column krater; 16 skyphos; 17 kyathus; 18 kylix; 19 kantharos; 20 kothon; 21 guttis; 22 askos; 23 pyxis; 24 lekanis; 25 plemochoe; 26 lekythos; 27 aryballesque lekythos; 28, 30 aryballos; 29 alabastron

colours. Hard-firing enamels are to be preferred for groundlay, cf *wool-drag*.

Grout   cement, mortar or other proprietary filling for the spaces between *tiles* and *tesserae*.

Growan stone   local Cornish name for *Cornish stone*, cf *pegmatite*.

Guelder rose vase   eighteenth-century German *porcelain* vase with naturalistic modelled flowers, either attached or made separately and arranged within it. In the case of the latter the porcelain blooms are usually attached to gilded-bronze wire stems.

Gum arabic   vegetable exudation obtained from some species of acaciae. It is occasionally used by craft potters as a *glaze hardener*, giving a tough, dry surface prior to *firing* as an aid to handling and decorating, eg *maiolica* (decoration on the unfired glaze). As a binder for under-glaze painting (cf *under-glaze decoration*) it should be used in moderation to avoid the possible side effect of glaze *crawling*, cf *Anglo gum*; *gum tragacanth*; *carrageen*; *funori*; *alginates*.

Gum tragacanth   vegetable exudation obtained from a species of shrub—'astragalus'. Occasionally used by craft potters as an alternative to *gum Arabic*, cf *Anglo gum*; *carrageen*; *funori*; *alginates*.

Gurglet or Goglet   long-necked water cooler made of porous *earthenware*.

Gurtfurchen   in German—'girth grooves'. Ribbed impressions made by the thrower's fingers as a deliberate form of decoration, cf *throwing*.

Gutbrennblau   late eighteenth-century Meissen copy of the Sèvres *bleu de roi*.

Guttus   Roman shape comparable with the Greek *askos*.

Gypsum   natural hydrated calcium sulphate used in the manufacture of *plaster of Paris*, cf *alabaster*.

Habaner ware   from the Hebrew 'ha-banim'—true children of God.   The Habaner were a Slovakian religious sect whose pottery decoration was restricted to floral patterns, the portrayal of human form being forbidden to their creed.

Haematite   see *iron oxide*.   A naturally occurring iron oxide, sometimes called 'kidney ore'; it is from this material that the *blood stone*, used for burnishing gold, is obtained, cf *burnished gold*.

Hafner ware   *earthenware* tiles made in Germany in particular but also in Switzerland and France during the fifteenth and sixteenth centuries, for the purpose of cladding the great decorative stoves of the period, cf *kachel*; *kachelnoven*.

Hakeme   Korean term for a free style of brushwork decoration using coarse brush marks, often with *slip* as a medium. Exemplified by the wares of Karatsu, on the island of Kinshiu, from about the seventh or eighth centuries AD.

Hammer mill   see *bar crusher*.

Hand-and-cup vase   small vase of *parian ware*; the form being that of a human hand holding aloft a narrow cup.

Handling   fixing handles to ware. Formerly an entirely hand process but in recent years it has become mechanised for smaller items, such as cups, on long production runs.

Hanging arms   vertical hardwood slats attached to the *sweep arms* of the old type of *pan mill*. Their function being to act as a non-ferrous buffer between the 'sweep arms' and the *chert runners*.

Hard   high fired.

Hardener   see *glaze hardener*.

Harden-on   to fix under-glaze colour (cf *under-glaze decoration*) by means of an additional low-temperature firing, after the *biscuit firing* and before the *glost*. The function of this extra firing is

119

twofold; first, to burn away any printing oils and other media used in application, so that they do not impair the application of the glaze; secondly, to fuse the colour to the *biscuit* slightly, thus preventing damage to the pattern during the glazing process.

Hard-paste high-fired porcelains, especially the original true felspathic pastes, as opposed to the *soft-paste*, *glassy* or *fritted* porcelains. *Bone china* is also considered to be a class of hard-paste in its own right, cf *ironstone china*; *stone china*.

Hare's-fur glaze iron glaze (containing *iron oxide*) of the *tenmoku* type having yellowish fur-like streaks following the flow of the glaze, cf *oil spot*.

Hatchel simple *presser's* tool made of metal or wood, of any convenient shape to scrape away the excess clay from a *press-mould*. The clay being pressed against the rim which forms the edge of the mould causing the surplus material to be discarded, cf *press moulding*.

Hausemaler outside decorator of German *faience* and *porcelain*. Each worked individually and in his own style, cf *chambrelan*.

Head cup Greek drinking vessel in the form of a human head, cf *Greek vases*.

48   Greek head cup

Head pins old form of *kiln furniture*. Pin-like pieces of *refractory* which may be inverted into holes in *saggars* to support *glost* ware.

Heat fuse   an emergency safety measure for electric kilns; if the safe working temperature is exceeded the fuse will melt breaking the circuit and switching off the electricity.

Heat work   actual effect upon clay being fired of the combined factors of temperature and time. During the firing process, *ceramic* materials are subjected to a number of chemical changes (cf *biscuit firing*), such changes take time to become fully effective. Therefore, temperature alone may not be a complete indication of the true state of the ware being fired. Heat work may be measured by the use of *pyroscopes* such as *Segar*, *Orton* or *Staffordshire cones*, *Holdcroft bars* and *pyrometers* such as *Bullers rings*.

Heavy clayware   *sanitary ware*; drainpipes, bricks etc.

Heavy spar   alternative name for *barytes*.

Henri deux ware   otherwise known as 'Saint Porchaire' ware or 'Faience d'oiron'; ornate sixteenth-century French *earthenware* made at or in the region of Saint Porchaire, decorated with a very thin black and red clay inlay. Copies were made in the late-nineteenth century by Minton, Wedgwood and Worcester, using impressed rouletted patterns inlaid with coloured slips. Both the French originals and the English reproductions use a *fine* white-burning earthenware and a slightly ivory-tinted transparent glaze.

Hill jar   Chinese shape of the Han dynasty (see appendix 1); cylindrical but distinguished by a lid modelled in the form of a hill surrounded by waves; cf *Chinese shapes* (ill 23).

Hino-oka   rock used by the Japanese *raku* potters to make iron-red glazes, cf *to-no-tsuchi*.

Hispano-Moresque ware   Spanish tin-glazed *earthenware* of the fourteenth and fifteenth centuries, decorated with boldly painted lustres (see ill 49). A technique introduced by the Moors but which originated in Persia, cf *maiolica*; *faience*; *delftware*; *tin glaze*.

121

49   *Reverse of a large tin-glazed earthenware dish, painted in gold and purple lustre, with the arms of Morelli of Florence. Hispano-Moresque ware, made at Valencia, 15th century. Diameter 18in (Victoria & Albert Museum)*

Historical blue   term used in the USA for a nineteenth-century Staffordshire *blue and white ware* with patterns depicting historical events in the USA. Later replaced by pink, sepia or black prints.

Holdcroft bar   *pyroscope*; similar to a *cone* in that it is composed of *ceramic* materials in carefully calculated proportions to fuse and melt at predetermined temperatures. Unlike a cone, which is set in a near-vertical position, a Holdcroft bar is set horizontally and allowed to sag (see ill 50), cf *Bullers ring*; *pyrometer*.

50   *Set of Holdcroft bars as they appear after firing*

Hollow casting *casting* of *hollow ware*, sometimes termed *thin casting*, cf *casting*.

Hollow ware hollow articles such as vases, cups, jugs and teapots, as opposed to *flatware*.

Horizontal kiln see *kilns*.

Horn see *potter's horn*.

Horse ('oss) special type of wooden steps with a platform at the top, used in Staffordshire for carrying *saggars* to the top of the *bungs* in *bottle ovens* (see ill 100).

Hotel ware *tableware* of practical design and strength, usually cast thicker than domestic tableware, cf *block handle*; *once-fired ware*.

Hoval bottle-shaped outer protective brickwork shell of a Staffordshire *bottle oven* (see ill 51).

51 *Hoval kilns at the Gladstone Pottery, Stoke-on-Trent*

Hsien hung   Chinese—'fresh or vivid red'; descriptive term for a particular quality of Chinese *copper-red glaze* and under-glaze colour, cf *under-glaze decoration*; *chi hung*; *pao shih hung*; *sang-de-boeuf*; *flambé*.

Hua Shih   constituent of some Chinese *porcelains*; identified by Père d'Entrecolles as being *steatite*, but there is some scientific evidence to suggest that in fact it is a form of *pegmatite*.

Hump   large piece of clay 'centred' (cf *centre*) on the *wheel*, from which the *thrower* makes several small pots.

Humpen   German cylindrical tankard often with a pewter lid, cf *Rhenish stoneware* (see ill 115).

Humper   see *bowing*.

Hump mould   simple convex press mould over which a *bat* of clay may be pressed to form a dish or bowl, cf *pressing*.

Hydria   Greek water container (see ill 52), cf *Greek vases*.

52   Hydria with black-figure decoration

Hydrofluoric acid   acid used for *acid-etch decoration*.

Hygroscopic water   *water of plasticity*; present in *clay* until fired to 500°C, cf *biscuit firing*; *interlayer water*.

124

Iceland spa   see *calcite.*

Ichotero   red *earthenware* bowls with tall stems, made by the Twa pygmies and used to burn twigs to produce an aromatic smoke to cure animal skins for clothing, cf *redware.*

Igneous rocks   rocks formed as the result of cooling magmas. Those which have cooled below the surface are called intrusive, they include granite, *pegmatite* and syenite which provide most of the minerals used in pottery manufacture, eg *felspar, quartz* and, by decomposition, *clay* itself. Those which erupt and cool on the surface are called extrusive and include lava, basalt, obsidian, pumice etc. Metal ores, the source of colour in *ceramics*, are associated with igneous rocks, sometimes having penetrated the more porous forms, or occur as concentrated veins.

Illite   generic term for clays associated with mica-bearing sediments. First discovered in clays from Illinois, USA, from which the name is derived, cf *mica clay.*

Ilmenite $FeO.TiO_2$, ferrous titanate. An ore containing *iron oxide* and *titanium oxide*, similar to *rutile*, but coarser and containing more iron. Used in *glazes* to give speckled effects or in conjunction with rutile or titanium to induce *break-up* or mottled glazes.

Imari   originally a style of Japanese *porcelain* made at Arita in the eighteenth century and exported via the port of Imari. Heavily decorated in polychrome *enamels* after the style of contemporary brocade (see ill 53), these wares were made specifically for export to Europe by the Dutch East India Company. Also copied by the Chinese potters at Ching-te-chen, probably under instructions from the Dutch traders. European copies were introduced in the late eighteenth century at Worcester and Chelsea. These patterns proved so popular that they accounted for a major proportion of the output of many factories, including Spode and Derby, during the early nineteenth century. Sometimes referred to as *Japans.*

*53 Japanese porcelain vase and cover. Painted in colours
and gold in the Imari style, made at Arita, 17th or
18th century. Height 2ft 9½in (Victoria & Albert
Museum)*

Impasto ware   method of decorating *earthenware* by applying a thick coating of *slip* to the extent that a very low relief is built up. Similar in technique to *pâte-sur-pâte*, but not to be confused with this finer type of ware, cf *barbotine decoration*.

Imperial yellow   Chinese *glaze* of the K'ang Hsi period (see appendix 1); a medium-temperature *lead glaze*, which is said to have been coloured by the use of *iron oxide* alone. Opinion is divided, it is thought that as *antimony* was already in use for other glazes and painting pigments, it may also have been added to the iron. The wares themselves are often thinly potted and decorated with incised (cf *incised decoration*) patterns, which, if intended for imperial use include dragon motifs, cf *Nankin yellow*; *clair-de-lune*; *peach bloom*; *mirror black*; *kingfisher blue*; *peacock blue*; *coral red* and *apple green* enamels; *sang-de-boeuf, sang-de-pigeon* and *celadon* revivals of the Sung dynasty.

Impressed decoration   see *embossing, embossing wheel.*

Incised decoration   cutting a decoration into dry or *leather-hard* clay, rather after the manner of engraving (see ill 83), cf *sgraffito*; *scrat*; *scratch blue.*

Indian flowers   see *Indianisch blumen.*

Indianische blumen   stylised patterns of oriental flowers. First adopted at Meissen in the mid-eighteenth century, and soon after in England where such patterns became known as 'Indian flowers' or 'Indian plants', cf *streu blumen*; *Meissner blumen*; *fantasievogel.*

In-glaze decoration   decoration on the unfired glazed surface, so that the oxides sink into the *glaze* during the *glost* firing. The normal craft method of decorating stoneware; it is also the principle of *maiolica* and *delftware.* Sometimes a thin coating of transparent glaze is applied over the whole to ensure full-colour development and avoiding dryness, cf *coperta glaze.* In-glaze decoration is used by some manufacturers to decorate *tableware*, in which case it is usual to use a *glaze hardener to provide* a firm

127

surface for painting or screen printing (cf *screen-printed decoration*). A variation sometimes used is to decorate on the fired glaze with oxides or under-glaze colours (cf *under-glaze decoration*), this is followed by re-firing to a temperature just below that of the glaze.

Inlay   see *encaustic*.

Intaglio printing   obtaining an image from an engraved line, ie from below the surface of the plate, as opposed to letterpress (raised) or *lithography* (on the same plane). Used in pottery decoration as a method of obtaining transfers for *under-glaze* and *on-glaze* decoration (see ill 54). Exemplified by the blue and white transfer-printed wares of the late eighteenth and nineteenth centuries (see ills 39, 40), and still in use today, cf *engraved decoration*; *transfer decoration*.

Interlaced handle   (see ill 54). See also *dod handle* (ill 36).

54   Adams ware, earthenware   Mariner's mug with interlaced handle.   Decorated with   black under-glaze engraved transfer c 1896-1900

Interlayer water term used in the USA for *water of plasticity*, ie that added to dry clay sufficient to render it plastic, cf *hygroscopic water*; *plasticity in clay*.

Iridium oxide can be used as a black pigment for *under-glaze decoration*.

Irish moss see *carrageen*.

Ironing over-concentration of decorating pigment in any one spot causing a burnt metallic effect. Paradoxically the term is normally used in relation to cobalt-blue decoration, cf *cobalt oxide*.

Iron oxide one of the most useful colouring oxides available to the craft potter, but to the *tableware* industry it may be considered to be an impurity to be avoided at all costs. The latter situation arises where high-quality *whiteware* 'bodies' are essential. In such circumstances all traces of iron are eliminated by the use of extraction equipment such as electro-magnetic filters. Craft potters on the other hand, utilise the iron content of clays to gain aesthetic advantage. The colour range available from this oxide is extensive, varying according to the type and quantity of iron present, the type of *glaze* used and the kiln atmospheres in which they are fired, cf *oxidation*; *reduction*.

In a *body* the colour may vary between cream, buff, tan and dark brown according to the amount of oxide present, eg natural *red clay* contains about 8 per cent of finely divided *red iron oxide*. Low-temperature *lead glazes* over iron-bearing bodies will give rich ambers and browns. Under clear *stoneware* glazes, buff clay and other similar bodies will give fawns to grey under *oxidation*, but under *reduction* the iron in the clay is frequently sufficient to combine with the glaze to produce green or blue-grey *celadons* without further additions of iron into the glaze itself.

In a *glaze* the range of colour is similar, ie cream, yellow, tan, browns to black in an oxidising atmosphere; under reduction, pale green-grey or blue-grey celadons through darker celadons to the rich broken blacks traditionally known as *tenmoku* and *aventurine* glazes.

As a painting pigment, iron oxide gives mainly straw yellows and browns of varying depth, but quite diverse qualities can be achieved according to which form of the oxide is used, eg *red iron* and *crocus martis* are similar when applied thinly, but a heavy application of crocus martis produces a characteristic *lustre* quality especially when reduced.

The usual forms of iron oxide used by potters are:

Red iron oxide; haematite, ferric oxide, Fe_2O_3. (readily available and inexpensive, disperses easily in glazes).

Purple iron oxide; *crocus martis*, ferric oxide, Fe_2O_3. (favoured as a painting pigment on stoneware).

Black iron oxide; ferrous oxide, FeO (slightly stronger than red iron, containing more iron in proportion to oxygen, not so fine as red iron).

Iron spangles or magnetic iron; magnetite, ferroso-ferric oxide, Fe_3O_4. (used as a painting pigment to give broken lustrous textures, difficult to mix and apply).

Yellow ochre; ferric hydroxide, $Fe(OH)_3$.

Iron chromate; ferrous chromate, $FeCrO_4$. (used in glazes to obtain grey).

Ironstone cane ware   see *pre-crust ware*.

Ironstone china   fine felspathic ware (cf *felspar*) made by C. J. Mason in the early nineteenth century, sometimes referred to as 'Mason's ironstone', (patent 3724, taken out in 1813). Not a *china* in the sense of a *bone china*, but more accurately described as a white *stoneware*. Early indications that the body contained 'prepared iron stone' are now considered to be fallacious. Even the possibility that the so-called 'prepared iron stone' may have been *Taberner's mine rock*, a mineral found in association with ironstone, is also thought to be unlikely. It is generally supposed that the name was adopted merely as a highly successful commercial trade name to introduce this very strong *tableware* body.

Istoriato from the Italian—'to tell a story'. Many of the six-teenth-century Italian *maiolica* painters, notably Nicola Pellipario, decorated plates and dishes with landscapes and figures depicting a story.

Itokiri Japanese term relating to the twisted wire-cut marks found on the bases of some unturned wares, formed as the piece is cut from the *wheel*.

Jackfield ware otherwise known as 'shining black'; generic term for a type of red *earthenware* with a brilliant black *glaze*, first made at Jackfield in Shropshire and some Staffordshire potteries in the late-eighteenth century. Sometimes decorated with floral and scrollwork relief, or at other times with *cold colours* and *gold*.

Jacobite ware salt-glazed *stoneware* (cf *salt glaze*) decorated with Jacobite motifs and emblems, eg portraits of Bonnie Prince Charlie, an oak or a butterfly, sometimes in a disguised form as part of a less-significant pattern.

Jacqueline north-European jugs modelled in the form of a seated figure.

Jagd service *tableware*, usually a dinner service, used by hunt-ing parties. Decorated in an appropriate style with hunting motifs, cf *stirrup cup*.

Ja katsu Japanese 'dragon-skin' glaze; the term usually applied to the thick, coarse and shrivelled glazes produced by the Chosa potters of the Satsuma princedom in the seventeenth century. Other Chosa glazes are *namako*; *tessha*; *bekko* and an inlaid decora-tion called *mishima*.

Jakobakanne tall *baluster jug*, made of unglazed buff *stoneware* at Seigburg during the fifteenth century, probably used as a wine jug, cf *Rhenish stoneware* (ill 115).

Japanned colour see *cold colours*.

Japans term loosely used to describe the popular eighteenth- and nineteenth-century English patterns after the style of the imported brocaded oriental wares, whether of Japanese or Chinese origin, but mainly applicable to the *Imari* or *Kakiemon* styles.

Jardinière French—a 'garden pot' or 'planter'; the term also applies to containers for cut flowers, especially to a distinctive shape made at Sèvres (see ill 55) and later by Mintons of Stoke-on-Trent.

55 Sèvres porcelain jardinière, painted in enamels on reserved panels in a green ground c 1780 (Victoria & Albert Museum)

Jar mill small *ball mill* for laboratory use, consisting of a *porcelain* jar, set horizontally on two revolving rollers. The grinding balls are also of porcelain.

Jasper dip see *Jasper ware*.

Jasper ware probably the most well-known of all Wedgwood wares; a coloured, vitreous *stoneware* with white *sprigged decoration* in the classical style (see ill 56). Introduced by Josiah Wedg-

56 *Wedgwood jasper ware, selection of shapes in current production*

wood in 1774 in succession to his already established *basalt ware*, and still in production by the Wedgwood factory today. The characteristic qualities of the jasper *body* were not only perfectly suited to Wedgwood's own interest in classical art, but also to the popular vogue and architectural style of the time, for which he produced plaques, panels and other similar component inserts for furniture and fittings. Likewise, small personal items of jewellery, cameos, trinkets, buttons etc were produced, and on a grander

133

57 Wedgwood jasper-ware copy of the Portland vase

scale, portrait busts in relief, of famous contemporaries. At first the production of *hollow ware* was restricted to decorative pieces, mostly after the style of classical vases (cf *Greek vases*), culminating in 1790 with the copy of the famous Roman glass vase known as the Portland vase. In the period following the death of his partner (Thomas Bentley) in 1780, and prior to his own death in 1795, Wedgwood expanded the production of jasper ware to *tableware* and countless other utilitarian items—ink wells, candelabra, trinket boxes, even parts for opera glasses.

The composition of the body is noteworthy for its high content of *barium carbonate* in addition to *flint*, *china clay* and *ball clay*. Colour is obtained by staining with oxides, light and dark blues, lilac, lavender, sage green, olive green, black and more rarely, yellow. The sprigged decoration is made from the same body before staining. At first pieces were made solid with the stained body, ie the body of the piece was stained right through, but the expense of *cobalt oxide* brought about the introduction of a *slip*-coated technique, known as 'jasper dip' (see ill 58). Much of the finest early jasper ware was of this type, though there was a return to solid jasper in later years, cf *sprigged decoration* (ills 123, 124).

58 Jasper-dip trinket box, Wedgwood c 1785

Jaune jonquille (pale yellow), one of a series of coloured *grounds* developed at Vincennes and Sèvres during the eighteenth century, cf *bleu de roi*; *bleu céleste*; *gros bleu*; *rose Pompadour*; *vert pomme*; *oeil de perdrix*; *caillouté*; *vermiculé*; *jewelled decoration*.

Jaw crusher crushing machine with two inclined jaws, one or both of which are activated in a manner similar to a nutcracker. Used for preliminary crushing of raw materials prior to milling, eg for breaking down calcined flints or hard rocks into pieces small enough to be ground in a *ball mill,* cf *calcine*; *flint*.

Jesuit china Chinese imported *porcelain* of the eighteenth century, with Christian subjects used in the decoration. Thought to have been painted by two Jesuit priests, known to be working at the Imperial Palace at the time.

Jet ware *redware* used in the main for making *earthenware* teapots. Glazed with a *lead glaze* stained black with *cobalt oxide* and/or *manganese oxide*.

Jewelled decoration or jewelling also known as 'raised enamel'; enamel colours, notably white, coral and turquoise, applied thickly, usually in dots, giving a raised jewel-like quality.

Introduced at Sèvres in the late-eighteenth century and soon copied in England at Worcester, Derby, Spode (see ill 59), Coalport and later at most other major factories, especially by Copeland in the 1860s.

59 Copeland covered vase c 1870. Footed oval shape with pierced domed lid, decorated with jewelled panels on a celadon green ground and areas of jewelled pink ground. Signed— W. Ball

Jigger and jolley mechanical methods of making both *flatware* and *hollow ware* from plastic clay, using revolving *plaster of Paris* moulds and a template fixed to a lever arm or 'monkey'. In the case of hollow ware ('jolleying') the mould forms the outer face of the piece and the template the inner; for flatware ('jiggering') the process is vice versa. The original derivation of the terms is obscure and some contrary opinion exists as to their correct usage. In addition to the interpretations of the terms already described, jigger is sometimes used to refer to the revolving cuphead which holds the mould, the jolley being the combined lever and template assembly. The term jolley is more correctly applied to what is also called a *vertical* or 'upright' *jolley* (see ill 60). It was

136

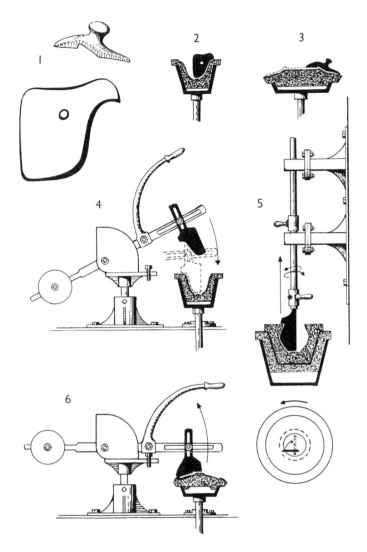

60 *Jigger and jolley : 1 hand-held formers used in the early'
method of jiggering ; 2 hand-held former used with a cup
mould ; 3 hand-held former used with a plate mould ;
4 cup jolley ; 5 vertical jolley ; 6 flatware jigger*

originally a cup-making machine, but since cups are also made by mounting the template on a lever arm, the original distinction has been lost. Modern jigger and jolley machines have become automated or semi-automated to a large extent, often being used in conjunction with a *batting machine* for the production of flatware. For long runs and high production speeds the automated *roller, making machine* has now replaced the jigger and jolley.

Joggle   little used but alternative term for a *natch*.

Jolley   see *jigger and jolley*.

Joseph jug   German salt-glazed jug, decorated in relief with motifs depicting Joseph and his brothers, cf *salt glaze*; *Rhenish stoneware*.

Juan ts'ai   Chinese—'soft colours'; descriptive term used for a particular quality of enamel *rose colour* used during the Yung Cheng period of the Ch'ing dynasty (see appendix 1), cf *yang ts'ai*; *enamel*.

Juraku-zuchi   Japanese *red clay* as used for making *raku* wares, cf *raku*; *akaraku*; *kuroraku*; *hino-oka*.

Kachel   German—'tile'; derived from *cachala*, meaning bowl. Tiles made from bowls or dishes were the original form of tiles used to clad the bulky stoves of the Middle Ages in Europe, cf *bacino*; *hafner ware*; *kachelnoven*.

Kachelnoven   German—'tiled stove'; cf *kachel*; *cachala*; *bacino*; *hafner ware*.

Kados or Kadiscos   type of Greek *stamnos*, cf *Greek vases*.

Kakiemon   a line of Japanese potters, one of whom, working at Arita in the seventeenth century, was so noted for his simple, elegant style of decoration that the name has since been adopted for this type of pattern (see ill 61). The original Japanese Kakiemon patterns used simple motifs of blossom, twigs with birds, children at play etc, painted with much delicacy in a finely balanced composition.

61 Japanese double-gourd vase, porcelain, painted in enamels in the Kakie-mon style. Made at Arita in the late 17th or early 18th century (Victoria & Albert Museum)

Kalpis Greek water pot; a type of *hydria* with the third handle attached to the neck rather than the lip, cf *Greek vases*.

Kameoka early Japanese primitive pottery, so called after the region in which the remains of such wares have been found.

Kantharos Greek drinking cup, deep in shape with two handles. Sometimes with a low *foot*, otherwise set on a pedestal or *stem*, cf *Greek vases*.

Kaolin Al_2O_3 $2SiO_2$ $2H_2O$, *china clay*; derived from the Chinese Kao-lin ('high ridge'), a descriptive name for the geographical location in China where this material was first thought to have been discovered. However, some authorities now believe that Père d'Entrecolles (a French missionary writing from China in 1712) was mistaken in this and that only *petuntse* was mined in the Kaoling mountains.

Kap when a large mural design is transferred from the original drawing onto actual tiles, it is usual to divide the design into easily handled units. The Dutch term for such a unit is a *kap*, conventionally a board of twenty-five tiles.

Kast-stel *cupboard set*; a group of five Delft vases (cf *delftware*), normally three pots with lids and two tall flared beaker-shaped vases. Made in tin-glazed *earthenware* (cf *tin glaze*) and intended to decorate the large cupboards popular in the late-seventeenth and early nineteenth centuries. The shapes and decoration show a distinct resemblance to the imported Ming *porcelain* sets known as *garnitures de cheminée* (see ill 45).

Kathos or Kyathos Greek ladle or deep, shaped cup with a single, long, looped handle. A shape probably derived from contemporary metalware, cf *Greek vases*.

Kelebe see *column krater*, cf *Greek vases*.

Kensui also known as a 'kobishi'; Japanese bowl used in the tea ceremony as a receptacle for waste water, a kind of parallel to the western 'slop basin', cf *chawan*; *chaire*; *chatsubo*; *furidashi*; *futaoki*; *mukozuki*; *mizusachi*.

Keros beaker of the Tiahuanaco culture of South America.

Ki Japanese—'yellow' glaze, produced at Seto in the thirteenth century; reputed to have been introduced by Toshiro II, the second of the Toshiro family of potters.

Kidney ore see *haematite*.

Kidney palette an oval or kidney-shaped piece of rubber, leather or spring steel, used for *press moulding* and of general use to craft potters as a shaping or finishing tool, cf *cow's lip*; *pitcher*; *diddler*; *tommy stick*; *presser's rubber*; *potter's horn*.

Kidney stone see *blood stone*.

Kiln furniture items of *refractory* material to support *ware* in the kiln during *firing* (see ill 62), eg *bats*, *props*, *cranks*, *stilts*, *spurs*, *pins*, *saddles*, *thimbles*, cf *bitstone*, *parting sherd*.

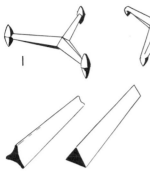

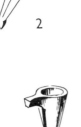

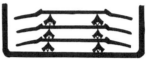

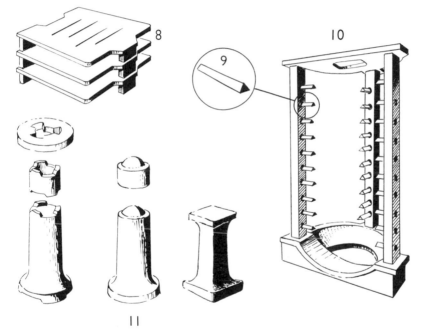

62 Selection of kiln furniture: 1 six-point stilt; 2 old
bowl-stilt; 3 spur or cockspur; 4 pip; 5 saddles; 6
thimble (for use with plate crank); 7 former method
of placing flatware using spurs; 8 tile cranks; 9 pin;
10 pillar plate crank; 11 props

141

Kilns there are many types of kiln, from the early *clamp* type (still in use by some primitive peoples) to the modern, highly controlled, intermittent and continuous-firing designs. The following illustrate some of the principal types and stages of development.

Clamp or open brushwood fire; a simple up-draught principle controlled by damping with green vegetation, used by early man and some present-day primitive peoples (see ill 63).

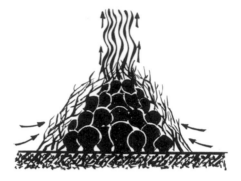

63   Primitive clamp or open brushwood firing

Simple up-draught kiln; improvement on the *clamp* by walling in the fire to conserve heat. Loaded from the top and sealed with

64   Simple up-draught kiln

142

brushwood as a damper for greater kiln control; Egypt 2000 BC
(see ill 64).

Horizontal through-draught kiln; built of clay and brick;
usually wood fired; Far East, first century AD (see ill 65).

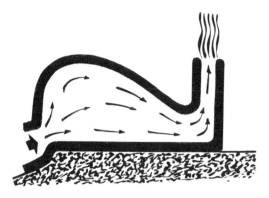

65   Horizontal through-draught kiln

Climbing kiln (Far East); the down-draught principle increases
efficiency by re-circulating heat. This is true even of single-
chamber kilns but the more so of multi-chamber designs in which
the excess heat from one chamber contributes to the next. Heat is
supplied initially by the main firemouth at the first chamber and
supplemented by others at intervals (see ill 66).

66   Climbing kiln

Roman wood-fired up-draught kiln; constructed from two shallow pits below ground level, one was a stoke-hole and connected to the second, a horseshoe-shaped pit which supported the hearth. The wares were stacked over the hearth and subsequently enclosed with a dome of clay and straw. This outer wall would be broken down after each firing (see ill 67).

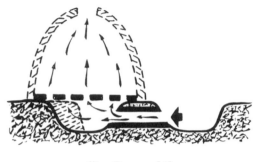

67   Roman kiln

Round up-draught kiln; built above ground level and heated by several firemouths situated around the circumference. Probably

68   Round up-draught kiln

originally fired by wood but later by coal, the availability of which in Staffordshire contributed to the rise of Stoke-on-Trent as the main centre of the industry in Britain (see ill 68).

Bottle oven, or 'hoval kiln'; a familiar sight in Stoke-on-Trent until the mid-1960s (see ill 51). Either up-draught or down-draught in design, the most efficient being the latter. Wares are placed in *saggars* to provide protection from the direct effect of the flames. Coal was the most common fuel until recent times when gas and oil fuels become more readily available (see ill 69), cf *water-smoking*.

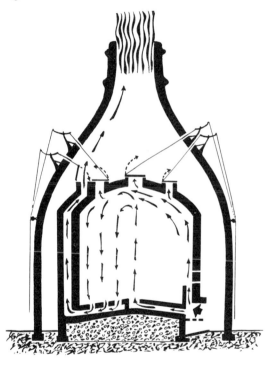

69   Up-and down-draught bottle oven

The introduction of oil and gas fuels enabled great advances to be made in kiln design, one of the most outstanding being the principle of the continuous-firing kiln as opposed to the hitherto intermittent method. Increased efficiency is gained by avoiding heat loss due to repeated heating and cooling. The ware is loaded onto specially designed trucks which pass through the tunnel which is cool at each end but has a heat zone at the centre (see ill 70). More recent developments of the continuous-firing principle are represented by such innovations as the gas-fired 'Trent' kiln in which a ram slides *refractory bats* along a track of similar refractory material. Other variations use a conveyor roller system, or for low temperatures, heat-resisting conveyor belts.

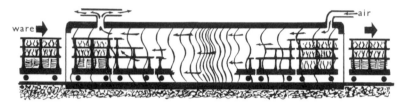

70   Tunnel kiln

Electricity opened up still further possibilities in the development of kiln design, eliminating the need for muffles or *bag walls*. Installation problems are simplified as no flues are required. This greater versatility is exemplified by the design known as the 'top hat' kiln in which one unit comprises two bases and a cover. The ware is placed on one of the bases and the cover lowered over the whole to be fired. During the firing the second base is loaded with ware in readiness (see ill 71).

The development of the small studio-type kiln owes much to the research into the use of electricity as a fuel, together with advances in the field of refractories and insulation materials; ease of installation being a particularly favourable factor for electricity as a fuel for craft kilns. On the other hand, combustible fuels such as gas, oil or wood have the advantage of cheap and easily achieved atmosphere control (cf *reduction*; *oxidation*), which since reducing atmospheres in particular play a significant part in studio potting, is also an important factor. Electric kilns can be fitted with silicon

146

carbide elements which will stand up to the strain of reduction, but these are expensive by comparison with the normal Kanthal-wire type

Kiln wash   see *bat wash*.

Kiln white   see *efflorescence*.

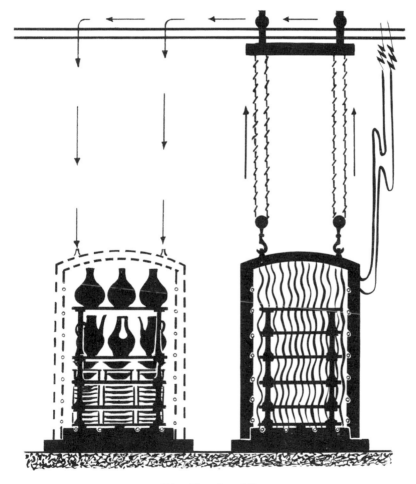

71   Top-hat kiln

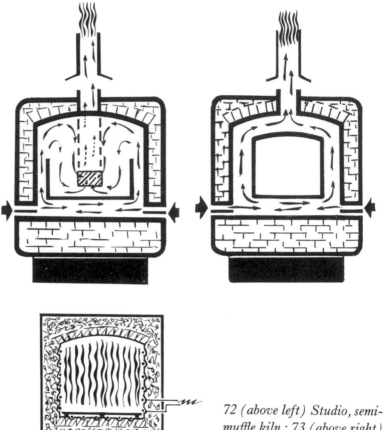

72 (above left) Studio, semi-muffle kiln; 73 (above right) Studio, muffle kiln; 74 (below) Studio, electric kiln

Kingfisher-blue glaze low-temperature turquoise *glaze* on *porcelain* of the K'ang Hsi period of the Ch'ing dynasty (see appendix 1), cf *clair-de-lune*; *peacock blue*; *Nankin yellow*; *mirror black*; *coral red* and *apple green* enamels; *sang-de-boeuf*; *sang-de-pigeon* and *celadon* revivals of the Sung dynasty.

Kinran-de Japanese term for the gold brocaded designs copied from the Chinese, cf *Imari*.

Kitchenware see *culinary ware.*

Kitu Fijian water vessel; usually unglazed but sometimes varnished. Elongated in shape, rather like that of an English rugger ball.

Klapmutsen see *clapmutsen.*

Kneading hand preparation of plastic clay, used in addition to *wedging* to obtain a more homogeneous texture and to improve plasticity.

Knocked glaze fault in *glost* ware; small unglazed areas appear as the result of physical damage to the *glaze* in the unfired state, cf *glaze hardener; dry edge.*

Knocker, knocker-out or punch short iron bar, about six inches long by one inch in diameter, used by mould makers to strike the *chucker* when releasing a tight mould, cf *mould making.*

Knocking-on to *centre* an article for *banding* or *lining* on a decorator's *banding wheel*; the technique involves a deft side-tapping or knocking action with the fingertips.

Knockings see *knottings.*

Knottings or knockings the scrap residue left in a screen after sieving *slip.*

Kobishi see *kensui.*

Kochi Japanese *ware* similar in technique to *raku*, except that the biscuit is *hard* fired to *stoneware* temperature before the *soft* glaze is applied.

Kothon Greek drinking vessel, probably similar to a *kotyle* and thought to have been a soldier's cup.

Kotyle see *skyphos.*

Krater Greek shape, a deep bowl used for mixing wine and water. There are various alternative shapes, eg *column krater, volute krater, cylix krater*, cf *Greek vases.*

Krause   see *pilgrim bottle*.

Kuei kung   Chinese—meaning 'devil's work', indicating a delicacy of craftsmanship in *pierced decoration* seemingly beyond human achievement.

Kugeltopf   eighth-century round-bottomed cooking pot from Lower Saxony, cf *bombentopf*; *grapen*.

Kuro   Japanese—'black glaze', produced by the Chosa potters of the Satsuma princedom in the seventeenth century.

Kuroraku   Japanese—'black raku'; black *raku* ware made of a coarse *red clay* and fired higher than most other varieties of raku, cf *akaraku*; *juraku-zuchi*.

Kwaart   see *coperta glaze*.

Kylix or Cylix   shallow, flat Greek cup with two horizontal loop handles, often having a tall *stem* foot, cf *Greek vases*.

75   *Kylix*

Labradorite   variety of *felspar* containing *calcium carbonate* and *sodium carbonate* as the principal *fluxes*.

Lace-work   see *broderie ware*.

Lacquers   see *cold-colours*.

Lajvardina   thirteenth-century Persian *on-glaze decoration* in gold leaf, white, red and black on blue or turquoise glazed ware, including bowls, dishes, ewers and tiles. A similar technique was also used in Turkey in the fifteenth century.

Lakabi ware   also known by the alternative spelling of 'laqabi ware'. Sometimes referred to as 'lakabi carved wares', which tends to be misleading since lakabi or laqabi means 'painted'. This is explained by the fact that the technique is one of carving a design into the surface of a white *body* and supplemented by painting on coloured glazes of blue, yellow, green and a reddish purple. In some ways the method somewhat resembles *cloisonné*, though there is a tendency for the colours to merge, especially on the more upright surfaces of *hollow ware* pieces. Made in Persia during the twelfth and thirteenth centuries.

Lambrequin   border pattern formed by two interlinking themes which are repeated alternatively.

76   *Lambrequin border*

Lange liszen   Dutch—'slender maidens'; descriptive term for the Delft copies of tall Chinese ladies painted on Dutch *chinoiserie* patterns. In England, where the term became corrupted to 'long Elizas', most factories making *blue and white wares* included a version of the theme in their pattern books, either as a painted design or as an engraved transfer, eg Spode's 'Lanje Lijsen' pattern.

Lang yao   Chinese copper glaze of the K'ang Hsi period of the Ch'ing dynasty (see appendix 1). Primarily a high-temperature *copper-red glaze* named after a family of potters noted for their success in producing these difficult glazes. It also appears as a delicate green glaze, not unlike *celadon*, and for that reason sometimes erroneously referred to as *copper-celadon*. It is thought by some authorities that such pieces may have occurred accidentally, having been fired in an oxidising part of the kiln, cf *oxidation*. This may indeed be so, especially at first and with those pieces which are partly red and partly green. However, the evenness of the green on some pieces suggests that the colour may have become recognised for its own sake and that the glaze was at times intentionally fired in an oxidising atmosphere to obtain green. Lang Yao green glaze is not to be confused with the K'ang Hsi *apple-green*, which is an *enamel* colour.

Lapis-lazuli   eighteenth-century *Derby blue* ground introduced in imitation of the Sèvres *bleu de roi*.

Laqabi ware   see *lakabi ware*.

Laubengrupen   German equivalent of *bocage* figures.

Launder   a water-course constructed and used in the *china-clay* industry as a means of carrying water to loosen the clay prior to hosing, or for conveying water-borne clay to the pumps or settling beds, cf *micas*.

Lava ware   see *agate*.

Lavender   (oil of lavender); alternative to *aniseed* for use in *enamel painting*.

Lawn   see *sieve*.

Lead antimonate   see *antimonate of lead*.

Lead bisilicate $PbO\ 2SiO_2$, *lead oxide* fused with *silica* to form a *frit*, and thereby overcoming the toxic nature of the lead, is called a 'lead silicate'. The usual proportion used in glazes is one of lead to two of silica, and is therefore known as a lead bisilicate.

Lead boro-silicate glaze   low-temperature glaze containing both *lead oxide* and *boric oxide* as *fluxes*. Used in the *tableware* industry, such glazes being favoured for their smoothness and good *firing* characteristics.

Lead carbonate $2PbCO_3\ Pb(OH)_2$, 'white lead'; preferred in the preparation of raw lead glazes (cf *raw glaze*) because of its fine particle size which facilitates an acceptable degree of suspension in the *slop* state. It is also a relatively pure form of lead, cf *to-no-tsuchi*.

Lead chromate   PbO PbCrO$_4$; may be used in low-temperature glazes to give coral reds.

Lead glaze   glaze in which *lead oxide* is used as the principal *flux*; normally a low-temperature glaze, cf *leadless glaze*; *lead carbonate*; *galena*; *lead bisilicate*; *lead boro-silicate glaze*; *lead sesquisilicate*; *lead monoxide*.

Leadless glaze   in Great Britain, a glaze which contains not more than 1 per cent by dry weight of PbO, see *Pottery (Health and Welfare) Special Regulations* (1950).

Lead mono-silicate   a lead silicate with the formula PbO 0·7SiO$_2$, cf *lead bisilicate*.

Lead monoxide   PbO, *litharge*, sometimes known as 'massicot'; similar properties to red lead (cf *lead oxide*). Often preferred by *slipware* potters as a *flux*, either in its raw state (cf *raw glaze*) or as a *frit* known as *lead sesquisilicate*, cf *lead carbonate*; *lead boro-silicate glaze*.

Lead oxide   the most powerful of *fluxes* used in glazing (cf *glaze*), therefore used in low-temperature glazes. It is valued for the ease with which a clear, brilliant glaze may be obtained and the wide range of colour available, afforded by the low temperature. The most common forms of lead oxide are *red lead* or *litharge*. Because of the toxic nature of these oxides it is necessary to use them in a fritted form, cf *frit*; *lead sesquisilicate*; *lead bisilicate*; *galena*; *lead monoxide*; *low-solubility glaze*.

Lead sesquisilicate   *lead silicate frit* using *litharge* as the source of *lead oxide*, cf *lead monoxide*.

Lead sulphide   PbS; see *galena*.

Leafer   see *pencil* (ill 94).

Lean clay   otherwise known as *short* clay; a *clay* or *body* of low plasticity; can be remedied, if need be, by the addition of *ball clay*, *bentonite* or other similar plastic materials, cf *fat clay*.

Leather-hard   partially dried clay; of a texture not unlike cheddar cheese. Articles to be *turned* are done so at this stage, cf *green-hard*; *white-hard*.

Lebes and Lebes gamikos   deep round-bottomed Greek bowls set on tall pedestals. Ceremonial pieces, the lebes gamikos as a trophy, the lebes for use at a wedding ceremony, cf *Greek vases*.

Lekanis   Greek shape, a flat, covered dish, cf *Greek vases*.

Lekythos   Greek oil container (see ill 77), cf *Greek vases*.

77   Lekythos

Lepidolite   lithium-based mineral; source of lithia in glazes; sometimes used as a secondary *flux* in high-temperature *alkaline glazes*. If used in excess it can produce *pinholing*, cf *lithium carbonate*; *petalite*.

Lime and limestone   see *calcite* and *whiting*.

Limoges enamels   white *enamel* painting, traditionally on a deep-blue *ground*. The original Limoges enamels being metal enamels on copper, these gave rise to a similar style of decoration for use on *porcelain*, which was developed to a notable degree by Thomas Bott for Worcester and E. H. Tryggelin for the Swedish Rorstrand factory.

Liner   sometimes referred to as a *cut liner*, or *slant liner*, cf *pencil* (ill 94).

Ling lung   Chinese term for the delicate *pierced decoration* of the Ming dynasty (see appendix 1), cf *kuei kung*.

Linhay   in the *china-clay* industry, storage area, silos etc, for dry processed clay awaiting dispatch, cf *dry*.

Lining   (1) coating of *slip* inside a *slipware* piece, or a similar slip coating on slipware as a *ground* for *sgraffito*, *trailing*, *feathering* etc; (2) a small thrown cylinder in *bone china* or *porcelain*, made as a basis for jolleying a cup (cf *jigger and jolley*) necessary on account of the low plasticity of this type of *body*; (3) painting of thin lines on *ware*, as opposed to *banding*, which generally refers to somewhat broader bands, cf *pencil*.

Liquid gold   see *bright gold*.

Liquid lustre   in contrast to the early reduced lustres (cf *reduction*; *lustre*) eg *Hispano-Moresque ware,* a more recent form of lustre made from precious metals such as *gold* or platinum (cf *platinum lustre*) may be applied on the fired glaze and fused to the *ware* under oxidising conditions (cf *oxidation*), at low temperatures, 750°C–900°C. Nitrates or chlorides are ground in media such as resin and spike oil of lavender. Ready prepared lustres are available from potters' materials suppliers.

Litharge   PbO; see *lead monoxide*.

Lithium carbonate Li_2CO_3; may be substituted for *sodium oxide* or *potassium oxide* in *alkaline glazes*. Its thermal expansion is less, therefore the likelihood of *crazing* is reduced. It tends to encourage brilliance and colour response.

Lithography   sometimes referred to as 'litho'; known in the USA as 'decalcomania'. A planographic process of printing, ie the printing surface is entirely flat. The image is obtained from a greasy ink, whilst the area to remain unprinted is protected with a film of water to repel the ink during rolling up. Lithography was invented in 1798 by Senefelder, an Austrian. The name is derived from the Greek 'lithos', a stone; 'graphio', to draw.

Originally large, flat, polished blocks of limestone were used as a printing surface, the porous nature of the stone was sensitive to grease and at the same time retained moisture when required. Stones have long since been replaced by zinc plates which are lighter to handle and are easily accommodated on modern printing machinery. The porous nature of the stone is simulated on the plate by graining, a slightly textured surface made up of minute recessions capable of retaining moisture and grease as required. The process is used extensively by the *ceramic* industry for the production of transfers (see ill 78). The process for ceramics is essentially similar to other aspects of the litho printing industry except that the image is usually printed in a sticky varnish on a transfer paper and dusted with powdered ceramic colour.

Lithophane   sometimes referred to as 'Berlin transparency'; nineteenth-century decorative technique on *porcelain*, making full use of its translucent qualities. The pattern motif, which sometimes takes the form of a portrait, is carried out in such low relief as to be imperceptible until held to the light, when it is revealed by the translucent qualities of the *paste*. Used to advantage on decorative ware, such as lanterns and nightlights, but also on *tableware* in the bases of cups so that the decoration was revealed when the cup was drained.

78   Wedgwood, Edward VIII coronation mug. Designed by Eric Ravilious and decorated by lithographic transfer

Little mine rock   see *Tabberner's mine rock.*

Little pot   seventeenth- and eighteenth-century measure; a pot containing one pint, cf *gallonier*; *pot*; *pottle pot.*

Littler's blue   a brilliant royal blue, obtained by staining *slip* with *cobalt oxide* and applying to the *ware* as a *ground*. Introduced in the mid-eighteenth century by William Littler, originally as a coloured ground for salt-glazed ware, (cf *salt glaze*), but later used on the *soft-paste* of Longton Hall.

Livering   a breakdown in the deflocculation (cf *deflocculant*), of casting *slip,* resulting in a lumpiness. Usually caused by allowing slip to stand for too long a period without agitation.

Lode   see *stent.*

Longbeard   curious form of jug, usually *stoneware*, on which the handle is modelled in the form of a man with a long beard.

Long Elizas   see *lange liszen.*

Loseta   Spanish *tile* about 10cm square; sometimes used together with a hexagonal tile called an *alfardone*, to form an octagonal unit, cf *alfardone* (ill 2).

Loutrophorous   Greek ceremonial water vase, used to carry water for the bridal bath. They are also found buried in the tombs of unmarried youths and maidens, in which case the vessels have no bases, signifying that a marriage has taken place with Hades. The shape is more that of a tall *amphora* than a *hydria,* having two long handles (sometimes partially filled in), a broad rim and the whole highly decorated, cf *Greek vases* (ill 47).

Loving cup   two-handled beaker, cf *tyg.*

Low-solubility glaze   in Britain, in accordance with the *Pottery (Health and Welfare) Special Regulations* (1950), a glaze which yields not more than 5 per cent of *lead oxide* (PbO) to dilute hydrochloric acid in a lead-solubility test, cf *frit; lead bisilicate.*

Loza fina   Spanish—high-quality *earthenware*, cf *faience*.

Lug handle   flat ear-shaped handle normally employed on shallow bowls used for soup, cereal etc; normally applied in pairs.

Lump   saleable but defective *ware,* not up to the standard of *firsts* or *seconds,* but not *wasters.*

Lustre   decoration whereby a film of metal is deposited on the surface of the *ware.* In its original form, sometimes known as 'Arabian lustre' but first developed in Persia in the tenth century and later by the Moors in Spain (see ill 49). Metallic salts, mixed with an ochreous earth, are painted on the unfired *glaze.* The ware is then fired in a reducing atmosphere (cf *reduction*). On removal from the kiln the ochre deposit is burnished away to reveal the lustre beneath (cf *burnishing*). If applied thinly the result is iridescent, if painted thickly a more metallic finish is achieved. The usual metallic salts used to produce lustres are copper sulphate—red to gold; gold chloride—rich purple-red; silver nitrate—yellow; bismuth sub nitrate—gives an iridescent effect.

The use of reduced lustres was revived to some extent in the early twentieth century being ideally suited to the art nouveau style of decorative art. Examples are to be found in the work of such artist/designers as Gordon Forsyth, Gwladys Rodgers and W. S. Mycock for Pilkingtons of Manchester (see ill 79); Carter Stabler and Adams of Poole and Maw & Co of Jackfield (see ill 80). In more recent years, some craft potters, notably Alan Caiger-Smith in Great Britain, have been responsible for a reintroduction of the technique.

Another form of lustre decoration made in Staffordshire, Leeds, Sunderland, Bristol and Swansea during the nineteenth century makes use of platinum (to give silver) and gold in the form of *liquid lustres,* fired at low temperatures in an oxidising atmosphere (cf *oxidation*). Some pieces being coated all over in simulation of contemporary silverware, others incorporating a resist medium to create a stopped out white decoration on a silver or gold back-

79 (left) Pilkington vase, painted in lustre c 1900; 80 (right) Earthenware bottle, painted in copper lustre. Maw & Co, Jackfield c 1890

ground (cf *resist*). *Pink lustre,* derived from gold, also enjoyed a popular vogue at this time, being used in a variety of ways including painting, banding, *oil-spot lustre* etc, cf *pink lustre*; *resist*; *liquid lustre*; *fairyland and dragon lustre*; *lustre glaze*.

Lustre glaze sometimes referred to as 'flash lustre'; obtained by adding metallic salts or carbonates to a *glaze*. The technique is usually confined to low-temperature glazes and subjected to a strong reducing atmosphere (cf *reduction*) during cooling. Like other forms of lustre decoration, lustre glazes were popular during the early twentieth century as part of the art nouveau style in pottery at that time, cf *lustre*.

Luting   joining together the component parts of a piece, eg fitting handles and spouts on *tableware*, or arms, legs etc on figures. A thin *slip* is applied to the surfaces to be joined, this acts as a bond in the *green* or *leather-hard* state, the whole becoming united in the *biscuit* firing, cf *sticking-up*; *pegging*.

Madreperla   *lustre* with a 'mother of pearl' quality.

Magnesia   MgO, magnesium oxide; a weak *flux* used in high-temperature glazes to which it imparts a soft, smooth texture. It is a refractory and therefore excessive quantities will produce dryness in glazes. Most glazes which contain this oxide are opaque. Usually introduced as *dolomite*, a rock containing equal proportions of magnesium carbonate and lime, or as *steatite*, otherwise known as *talc* or *French chalk*.

Magnesite $MgCO_3$, *magnesium carbonate*, cf *magnesia*.

Magnesium oxide   see *magnesia*.

Magnetic iron Fe_3O_4, ferroso-ferric oxide; see *iron oxide*.

Magnetic purification   removal of iron particles from *clay* and other *ceramic* materials by passing them in *slop* form over electromagnets. Essential in the production of *fine* white *tablewares*, cf *elutriation*.

Magnetite   *magnetic iron*; see *iron oxide*.

Magnus   term by which seventeenth- and eighteenth-century potters knew a variety of Derbyshire iron ore; otherwise known as *black wad*, it contained some manganese (cf *manganese oxide*) impurity and may have been the source of colour in many of the early brown glazes.

Maiolica   alternative spelling—'majolica'; term originating in Italy in the fourteenth century and referring to the Italian tin-enamelled *earthenware* (cf *tin enamel*) made in like manner to the

Valencian *lustre* wares imported from Spain by way of the island of Majorca from whence the name is derived. Eventually the name came into wider use throughout Europe, becoming applicable to most forms of tin-enamelled earthenware. This great tradition of tin-glazed wares began with the Persian lustres of the tenth century, and progressed through varying styles via the Moors to Spain (*Hispano-Moresque ware*), via Majorca to Italy (maiolica, see ill 81). One of the main centres of manufacture in

81 Italian maiolica plate, decorated by Nicola Pellipario at Urbino and lustred at Gubbio c 1530. Diameter 10½in (Victoria & Albert Museum)

Italy was Faenza from which the term *faience* is derived, and by which this type of ware became known in northern Europe. In Holland the town of Delft gave its name to a characteristic blue and white ware, cf *delftware*. In Britain, centres of manufacture were set up in London, Bristol, Brislington, Wincanton and Liverpool, cf *marzacotto*; *coperta glaze*.

Malabar *chinoiserie* figures in *porcelain*, holding musical instruments. They usually have grimacing features.

Malling jugs basically globular in shape and glazed with a splashed or mottled *tin glaze*. Probably made in the sixteenth and seventeenth centuries; thought to be the earliest examples of *delftware* in Britain. The first specimen was discovered at West Malling in Kent.

Mandarin (1) eighteenth-century Chinese jar (and European copies) with panels bearing mandarin motifs, usually as a blue and white *under-glaze decoration*, but some of the later copies are in *enamel*; (2) in the USA, a style of decoration with figures.

Mandrel part of a *turner's* lathe; the tapered spindle or axis to which a block of clay or *plaster of Paris* is fixed in readiness for *turning*.

Manganese oxide produces mauves in low-temperature glazes, or in *alkaline glazes*, rich purples, especially if associated with a small quantity of *cobalt oxide*. By contrast, at high temperatures, manganese will give burnt browns. As a painting pigment or body stain it must be used with care as the fluxing power (cf *flux*) of this oxide may cause a glaze to soften locally causing the decoration to run. Managanese oxide plus *red clay* will produce a black *slip*. It is normally used as a dioxide or carbonate.

Mangle type of drier, used in the production of cast ware (cf *casting*) and dipped ware, cf *dipping*. Essentially a form of conveyor in which boards, onto which the *ware* is placed, are attached at each end to a chain which moves in a vertical plane, taking the ware up into a heated zone, over and down to an unloading point on the opposite side, cf *dobbin*.

Mansion house dwarfs see *Callot figures*.

Marble see *calcite*; *whiting*; *calcium oxide*.

Marbled glaze see *tortoiseshell ware*.

Marbling decorative technique using different-coloured slips. Two or more slips of different colours may be poured into a *leather-hard* dish or bowl, swished about and a marbled effect will result. A more controlled pattern may be obtained by first laying in a *lining* slip of one colour, immediately followed by trailing the other colours, either at random or in a definite sequence, the whole is then swished about as before.

Marl   secondary clay containing a naturally blended proportion of calcium in the form of chalk. Sometimes the term is less accurately used to indicate a low-quality fireclay which may contain no calcium.

Martabani   Near-Eastern term for Chinese and other Far-Eastern *celadon* wares; most probably so called after the Burmese port of Martaban, in Pegu, through which it is likely that such wares were exported.

Martabans   large jars of Burmese origin; named after the Burmese port of that name, from which the wares were exported.

Martin ware   nineteenth-century decorative, salt-glazed *stone-ware* (cf *salt glaze*) made by the brothers Wallace, Walter and Edwin Martin. A fourth brother, Charles, looked after the commercial interests of the business. First made in London and later at Southall, to where their studio was subsequently moved (see ills 82, 83).

Marzacotto   *silicate of potash*, prepared by the fusion of calcined wine-lees and sand. According to writings of Piccolpasso, this was used as the basis for Italian *maiolica* glazes, cf *coperta glaze*; *tin glaze*.

Mask lip   the pouring lip of a jug, decorated with a modelled relief mask. As exemplified by many of the *cabbage-leaf jugs* of the eighteenth century (see ill 17).

Mason's ironstone china   see *ironstone china*.

Massicot   see *lead monoxide*.

Master mould   see *block mould*.

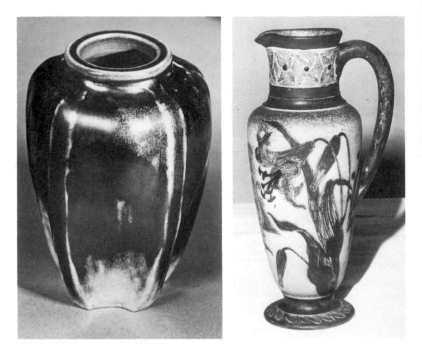

82 (left) Martin-ware gourd vase, stoneware with an iron oxide glaze c 1900-10; 83 (right) Martin-ware jug with incised decoration, dated 1883

Matlatzinca ware   Ancient American, Toltec pottery dating from about the tenth century AD. Made of buff clay and decorated with a red ferruginous pigment, cf *Mazapan ware; fine orange ware; plumbate ware; Coyotlatelco ware.*

Matt glaze   may be achieved by the intentional *devitrification* of a glaze, especially if the composition is rich in *calcium oxide*. The development of such glazes is aided by replacing any lead fluxes with less-strong alternatives. The condition is also encouraged by slow cooling and the presence of *zinc, barium* or *titanium oxides,* cf *opaque glaze; opalescent glaze; satin glaze.*

Maturing   see *ageing.*

Mazapan ware Ancient American, Toltec pottery dating from about the tenth century AD, thought by some authorities to have been the forerunner of *Matlatzinca ware*. Decorated with a red ferruginous pigment on a buff clay, the style of the pattern usually takes the form of parallel wavy lines, cf *Matlatzinca ware*; *fine orange ware*; *plumbate ware*; *Coyotlatelco ware*.

Mechanically-combined water see *water of plasticity*.

Mei ping see *prunus vase*.

Meissner blumen *enamel* painting on English *porcelain*, featuring sprays of idealised flowers, in the style of Meissen, cf *Indianische blumen*; *streu blumen*; *fantasievogel*.

Menninge red-lead oxide, see *lead oxide*. Also known as 'minium'.

Metropolitan ware see *slipware*.

Mezza-maiolica also known as 'alla castellana ware'; mezza-maiolica being the Italian for semi-maiolica, is something of a misnomer in that it has no apparent similarity to *maiolica* other than that both are *earthenware*. The term is used to refer to a coarse, buff ware which is coated with a white *engobe* and decorated by *sgraffito*, supplemented with colours painted in oxides, usually *copper oxide* or *manganese oxide* (see appendix 5).

Mica clay waste *clay* from the *micas* in a *china-clay* mine. It contains a high proportion of mica impurities; sometimes used as a low-grade clay or taken for further purification to extract more china clay.

Micas slightly inclined settling tanks used in the *china-clay* industry for the purification of china clay by means of *elutriation*, in order to remove mica and other fine impurities. Also termed *mica drags* or just *drags*, though strictly speaking these latter refer to a preliminary set of settling tanks, now obsolete but at one time used to remove the coarser impurities before the clay was passed into the micas.

Miletus ware   late fourteenth- and fifteenth-century Turkish wares, named after the town of Miletus where the first pieces were found, but probably made at Isnik. A *red-clay* ware lined with white *slip*, over which the decoration, which may be floral or geometric, is painted in oxides giving blue, green and black under a clear glaze, cf *Rhodian ware*; *Damascus ware*.

Milk skimmer   small saucer-shaped article about four inches in diameter, having a side handle and a perforated base for skimming milk.

Mille fleurs   pattern consisting of a mass of delicate flowers, applied in particular to the enamelled (cf *enamel*) Chinese wares of the Ch'ien Lung period of the Ch'ing dynasty (see appendix 1).

Minium   Latin—'red lead', see *lead oxide*. Also known as 'menninge'.

Mirror black   lustrous black Chinese glaze known as 'wu chin'; K'ang Hsi period of the Ch'ing dynasty (see appendix 1). Coloured by an impure ferruginous ore containing traces of *manganese oxide* and *cobalt oxide,* cf *clair-de-lune*; *peach bloom*; *kingfisher blue*; *peacock blue*; *Nankin yellow*; *Imperial yellow*; *apple green* and *coral red* enamels; *sang-de-boeuf, sang-de-pigeon* and *celadon* revivals of the Sung dynasty.

Mishima   inlaid decoration of Korean origin; dating back to the tenth century in Korea and used by the Chosa potters of the Satsuma princedom from the early seventeenth century. Delicate patterns, often composed of radiating lines, bands and rosettes, are inlaid with white and black clays and glazed with cream or *celadon* glazes. The name is of Japanese origin, by reason that the lines of one of the patterns is similar to some ideographs on almanacs from the town of Mishima, cf *ja katsu*; *namako*; *tessha*; *bekko*.

Miska jug   Hungarian peasant-ware jug in the form of a man with a snake.

Mixing ark   see *ark*.

166

Mizusachi water jar used by the Japanese in the tea ceremony, cf *chaire*; *chawan*; *furidashi*; *futaoki*; *kensui*; *mukozuki*.

Mocca cup small cup used in Europe for serving a strong thick coffee known as mocca.

Mocha decorative technique with a moss-like characteristic, similar in appearance to the Arabian agate stones of that name. An oxide is mixed in a solution of nicotine, made by boiling tobacco in water. Drops of this mixture are applied into wet *slip*, throughout which they spread of their own accord and form a fern-like pattern (see ill 84).

84 Earthenware jug with mocha decoration

Model the solid, three-dimensional interpretation of a design for a shape, from which the *block mould* is made. The model is made from clay, *plaster of Paris* or other suitable material and is scaled up proportionately larger than the finished size to compensate for the shrinkage of the *body* during drying and *firing*, cf *mould making* (ill 86).

Modiolus conical-shaped Roman cup with a flared rim.

Modulus of rupture assessment of the strength of a *ceramic* article, whether fired or *greenware*, by determining its transverse breaking strength.

Mohammedan blue   see *asbolite*.

Molochite   trade name for pre-fired *china clay*; used in the preparation of *refractory* bodies, cf *body*; *grog*; *chamotte*.

Monkey   see *jigger and jolley*.

Monteith   bowl for keeping wine glasses cool in water; the rim is deeply scalloped to receive the stems, the feet remaining outside the bowl (see ill 85).

*85   Caughley porcelain monteith, painted in blue c 1772-99
(Victoria & Albert Museum)*

Moonlight lustre   term sometimes applied to a mottled purple and *pink lustre*, cf *oil-spot lustre*.

Moons   small spots of light visible in some early *soft-paste* porcelains when held to the light. Probably due to incomplete dispersion of the *fluxes* in the *paste*. Some Chelsea pieces are noted for this feature.

Moor stone   local Cornish name for *Cornish Stone*, cf *pegmatite*; *Growan stone*.

Mop see *pencil* (ill 94).

Mortar basin-shaped bowl used in conjunction with a pestle for grinding by hand. Such pieces are usually made thick, for strength purposes, of a very fine porcellaneous material known as *mortar body*.

Mortar body fine porcellaneous *stoneware* body of great hardness, used in the manufacture of *mortars* and pestles.

Mosaic surface decoration for floors and walls, made up of small pieces of stone, glass or pottery, sometimes referred to as *tesserae*.

Mother rock of clay common name for *granite*, being the original source of clay prior to decomposition, cf *clay*; *igneous rock*.

Moulded decoration relief decoration, carved or modelled on the *model* and embodied in the mould, so that any such decoration is integral with the piece and reproduced with it at the time of manufacture, cf *sprigged decoration*; *cameo Parian*.

Moulding see *pressing*.

Mould making with the exception of 'sprig' moulds (cf *sprigged decoration*), which are often made of biscuited clay (cf *biscuit*), *working moulds* for *casting*, *pressing* or *jiggering and jolleying* are made of *plaster of Paris*. Most *blocks* and *cases* are also made of plaster, though in recent years some resin plastics have been used. The stages in the preparation of a working mould are: (1) the 'master mould', otherwise known as the *block mould,* is made from the *model*; (2) the *case mould* is made from the *block*; (3) the *working moulds* are made from the *case*.

Mould runner in the days before mechanical conveyor systems and modern drying equipment, moulds were carried between the making shop and *pens* or 'stoves' by a runner, normally a young boy probably with intentions of becoming apprenticed to the maker.

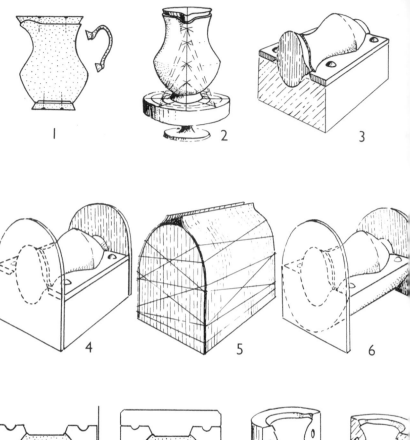

1

2

3

4

5

6

7

8

9

10

Mourning jug *trauerkruge*; German *stoneware* jug, decorated with carved rosettes. Thought to have been made for use at funeral feasts, cf *Rhenish stoneware*.

Moustache cup cup shape popular at the turn of the nineteenth and twentieth centuries, when large moustaches were a fashion. It had a protective ridge which prevented the moustache from entering the drink.

Muffle *refractory* lining to a kiln designed to protect ware from the direct effect of flame, obviating the need to use *saggars*, cf *semi-muffle*; *bag wall*; *baffle*; *kilns*.

Mukozuki small dishes used by the Japanese to take a light meal before the tea ceremony, cf *chaire*; *chawan*; *chatsubo*; *furidashi*; *futaoki*; *kensui*; *mizusachi*.

Muller (1) hand tool for grinding small quantities of raw materials, colour etc. Usually made of glass and shaped like an inverted mushroom. The base is flat, it is used in a rotary action on a glass slab; (2) small mechanical grinder for preparing colour and gold.

Mullite combination of *alumina* and *silica*, $3Al_2O_3 \ 2SiO_2$; formed when *clay* is fired to 1,100°C or thereabouts. The formation of mullite is an essential stage in the *biscuit firing* of *fine earthenware* as it is an important factor to be taken into account to achieve a good glaze *fit*, cf *biscuit firing*; *cristobalite*; *crazing*.

86 (facing page) Sequence of making a block mould for a jug: 1 plaster model with spares attached; 2 striking the centre line; 3, 4 setting-up; 5 cottle in place for running (first part); 6 first part made, model reversed and set-up in readiness to run second part; 7 first two parts cast, model inverted, bottom spare removed, cottle in place to receive plaster for the third part; 8 base (third part) cast, cottle removed; 9 complete block mould with model removed; 10 similar procedure for handle

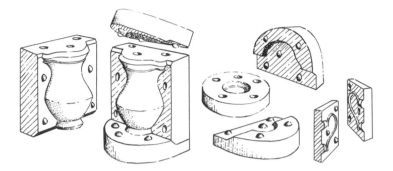

87   Set of cases for jug

Murray-curvex machine   offset printing machine capable of transmitting an image direct onto ware. Developed by Dr G. L. Murray in collaboration with the Spode factory, Stoke-on-Trent, in 1955. An engraved plate is used to provide the image, which is transferred to the ware via a convex dome of gelatine, known as the 'bomb'. The bomb picks up the colour from the engraving and stamps it onto the ware. The technique is particularly suitable for long runs of under-glaze printing. A small version of it is sometimes used for *back stamping*, cf *under-glaze decoration*; *engraved decoration*.

Mutton-fat   Chinese description of certain *stoneware* and *porcelain* glazes which have a smooth, opaque quality, brought about by a high *magnesia* content.

Namako   Japanese reduced (cf *reduction*) *copper-red glaze*, produced by the Chosa potters of the Satsuma princedom in the seventeenth century, after the style of the Chinese Kwangtung *stoneware* glazes. Other Chosa glazes are, *ja katsu, tessha, bekko* and an inlaid decoration called *mishima*.

Nankin   term often used in Staffordshire to describe the inner border of a pattern in oriental style. It is either printed (cf *engraved decoration*), or hand painted on the curved, sloping portion between the rim and the centre of *flatware* and in a corresponding relationship on matching *hollow ware*.

172

Nankin blue blue and white decorated *porcelain* made at Ch'ing-te-Chen for export to Europe and the USA in the eighteenth and early nineteenth centuries. The origin of the well-known 'Willow' pattern and subsequent blue and white transfer wares, cf *blue and white ware*; *transfer decoration*; *under-glaze decoration*.

Nankin yellow golden yellow-brown glaze of the K'ang Hsi period of the Ch'ing dynasty (see appendix 1). Produced by staining the normal white *porcelain* glaze with *iron oxide*. Used as a self-colour glaze or as a *ground* for *famille verte* decoration.

Naples yellow see *antimonate of lead*.

Natch sometimes termed a 'joggle'; device for locating the various adjacent parts of a mould in correct juxtaposition with each other; consisting of a hump of *plaster of Paris* usually hemispherical on one part with a corresponding hollow on the other. Sometimes brass or plastic natches are inserted during the mould making, these have a longer life than those made in the plaster itself and are particularly useful for heavy moulds, cf *mould making* (ill 86); *natch block*; *natch knife*.

Natch block *plaster of Paris* slab containing the hollow impressions of *natches* of various sizes; used by mould makers to obtain clay impressions which may be laid on the *sets* when preparing a *block mould*, cf *natch*; *natch knife*; *mould making*.

Natch knife mould-maker's tool, a knife with a hooked tip for cutting the hollow portion of a natch in a mould, cf *natch*; *natch block*; *mould making*.

Natron Na_2CO_3 $10H_2O$; naturally occurring *sodium carbonate*.

Nepheline syenite K_2O $3Na_2O$ Al_2O_3 $8SiO_2$; felspathic *flux* containing a high proportion of *sodium oxide* and *potassium oxide* which make it a useful replacement for *orthoclase* felspar when a lower melting temperature is required, cf *felspar*.

New rock see *Tabberner's mine rock*.

New stone china   see *stone china*.

Nib   small protuberance on the skirt of a teapot lid, added to prevent the lid slipping while pouring. It is so designed as to catch on the underside of the lid gallery at the rear of the teapot opening.

Nibbed saggar   *saggar* with small internal ridges to support a *bat* which will facilitate more than one layer of ware to be *placed*.

Nickel oxide Ni_2O_3; colouring oxide used to stain glazes, it may also be used as a painting pigment but its *refractory* nature tends to produce dryness if applied too thickly. On its own it will produce drab green-browns to greys; it is normal to use it to modify bright colours. In high-temperature glazes under *reduction* and in the presence of *zinc oxide* some unpredictable yellows or blues may ensue, cf appendix 1.

Night-light   container for a night-light; usually in the form of a cottage, castle, toll-house etc. The windows are often pierced to transmit light, for the same reason they are frequently made of translucent *soft-paste*. Occasionally *lithophane* decoration is used, cf *pastille burner*; *crime cottages*.

Nishiki de   Japanese Satsuma ware; brocaded patterns in gold. Originating towards the end of the eighteenth and greatly used during the nineteenth centuries.

Nitre   see *potassium nitrate*.

Noggin   seventeenth-century English term for a salt-glazed (cf *salt glaze*) *stoneware* shape, possibly a tankard, as imported from Germany. Referred to by Robert Plot in *The Natural History of Oxfordshire* (1677), with reference to John Dwight of Christ Church College, and his discovery of the technique of *Cologne ware*.

Oak-leaf jars   mid fifteenth-century Italian drug jars, decorated all over using a stylised oak-leaf pattern as a background for similarly stylised bird motifs. The pigment used was a slightly raised form of *cobalt oxide*, cf *apothecary jars*.

Ochre   Fe(OH)$_3$; *ferric hydroxide*. A ferruginous earth, see *iron oxide*.

Oeil de perdrix   'partridge-eye decoration'; decorative textured *ground* introduced at Sèvres in the mid-eighteenth century; consisting of numerous small circles of dots in blue with a central black spot. Alternatively in gold dots on a coloured ground.

Oenochoae or oinochoe   Greek jugs or pitchers of varying sizes and shapes, the larger often similar to amphorae, cf *amphora*; some smaller ones have conical bodies and a tall neck. All have a trefoil pouring lip, cf *Greek vases*.

88   Oenochoae

Oil-spot glaze   black, iron glaze of the *tenmoku* type, having small lustrous specks, cf *hare's fur glaze*.

Oil-spot lustre   otherwise known as 'splashed lustre'; pink and purple lustre applied on the fired glaze and spattered with thin oil, causing irregular spots (see ill 89). Fired in a decorating kiln at 750°–800°C. A popular decorative device during the eighteenth century as a *ground* for further decoration or occasionally used on its own. Made at Sunderland, Liverpool, Bristol and in numerous Staffordshire factories, cf *pink lustre*; *liquid lustre*.

Olambrilla   Spanish paving *tile*, somewhat smaller than the conventional tile known as *azulejo*, cf *tablero*; *loseta*; *alfardone*.

89   Pink oil-spot lustre bowl

Old bowl stilt   see *kiln furniture* (ill 62).

Olla   Roman storage jar; sometimes used as a cinerary urn.

Ollio pot   two-handled broth cup; ollio, ollia or olla being a meat and vegetable broth popular in Europe in the eighteenth century.

Olpe   Greek jug, similar in size and usage to the *oenochoe* but without the trefoil pouring lip, cf *Greek vases*.

Once-fired ware   technique in which the *glaze* is applied direct to the *greenware* rather than *biscuit firing* first. The clay and glaze mature together. Much *sanitary ware* and some *hotel wares* are made in this way. Alternatively the term may be used to indicate salt-glazed ware (cf *salt glaze*) or even unglazed ware, cf *green glaze*; *Bristol glaze*; *slip glaze*.

On-glaze decoration   see *enamel*.

Onion pattern   German—'zweibelmuster'; misnomer for an *under-glaze blue and white* painted pattern of stylised peaches and asters, the peaches being mistaken for onions. Of Chinese origin but copied and developed at Meissen (see ill 90) in the mid-eighteenth century and further copied at other centres including Worcester.

176

90 *Meissen, porcelain plate with 'Onion Pattern' decoration painted in blue under-glaze*

Onyx-ware   see *agate.*

Opalescent glaze   milky or cloudy glaze due to refraction, often caused by the presence of bubbles of escaping gases from any volatile materials in the mix. With advancing temperatures this effect will disappear. Opalescence may also be attributed to a mixing of glazes with different refractive indexes, cf *glaze*; *titanium oxide*; *rutile*; *bone ash*; *chun glaze*; *matt glaze*; *satin glaze.*

Opaque glaze   may be achieved by the addition of opacifying agents, such as *tin oxide* or *zircon*, which do not become soluble in the glaze melt. Opacity may also be achieved due to a saturation of one or more oxides so that the latter do not fully melt at the maturing temperature of the glaze. Similarly an under-fired glaze will be opaque or partially opaque. In such cases the glaze will become clear with advancing temperatures. The formation of crystals in a glaze (cf *crystalline glaze*) will produce a degree of opacity, cf *glaze*; *opalescent glaze*; *rutile*; *titanium oxide*; *zinc oxide*; *chun glaze*; *matt glaze*; *satin glaze.*

Open-cast mining obtaining minerals near the surface by removal of *overburden* followed by direct excavation rather than by deep or *shaft mining*.

Open handle the usual type of handle with two points of attachment, as opposed to the *block handle*.

Opening materials materials such as *flint*, *grog*, *sand*, *chamotte* or *molochite*, which may be added to clays if they are too plastic, shrink too much in drying and firing or to facilitate more thorough drying of large pieces, cf *fat clay*; *lean clay*; *short clay*.

Open setting setting or *placing* ware in a kiln without protective *saggars* or *muffles*.

Oriental lowestoft see *Chinese export ware*.

Ornamenting see *sprigged decoration*.

Orthoclase see *felspar*.

Orton cone see *cone*, also appendix 2.

'Oss see *horse* and *'oss off*.

'Oss off method used in *placing bungs* of *saggars* in a kiln so that they will not topple or move during the *firing*. When the bungs of saggars reach the height of ten feet or so, long bricks or *fireclay bats* are placed across the tops to bind them together and to provide a firm base for a fresh stack.

Ovenware *casseroles*, *ramekins* and other such cooking pots and dishes, made of suitably *refractory* materials to withstand oven heat, cf *culinary ware*.

Overburden also known in some localities as 'callow' or *plat*; soil, vegetation and other unwanted materials lying above minerals to be excavated by the *open-cast* method of mining.

Over-glaze decoration see *enamel*.

178

Owl jug jug in the form of an owl, the head of which lifts off to use as a cup; the features are modelled and incised. First made during the sixteenth century in the Tyrol as an archery trophy.

91   Owl jug

Oxidation the presence of ample oxygen in a kiln during *firing*, with the result that complete combustion causes the oxides in glazes to be unaffected and to give their oxide colours (see appendix 5), cf *reduction*.

Ox lip see *cow's lip*.

Oxybaphon see *bell krater*; *Greek vases*.

Ozier pattern relief decoration originating at Meissen in the eighteenth century. There are a number of variations; ordinair ozier, sometimes referred to as the 'Sulkowsky pattern'—a zigzag basket-work pattern; alt ozier, straight basket-work pattern with radiating ribs; altbrandensteinmuster, having radial ribbing and a dotted trellis; neu ozier, basket-work pattern with curved, 'S'-shaped ribs.

Packer tool formerly used in the Dorset *ball-clay* mines, for laying railway tracks on the top of *clay beds*. It has a point at one end for hammering in the wedges between the rails and the sleepers, the other end is flattened for packing the clay firmly beneath the sleepers to make a sound base, cf *tubal* (ill 129).

Paesi decoration *maiolica* patterns depicting landscapes with buildings.

Pagoda jar multiple plant container, made of several diminishing-sized bulb trays set vertically and resembling the roof of a pagoda.

Painted pottery culture ware *ware* of a neolithic race originating in the Kansu region of China towards the upper reaches of the Yellow river. So called on account of the ware being painted with geometric patterns in red and black, which would seem to have some link with similarly decorated early Mediterranean pottery, cf *black pottery culture ware*.

Pai ting see *fen ting*.

Palissy ware sixteenth-century French *earthenware* made by Bernard Palissy and characterised by its decoration in high relief of lifelike animals, reptiles, shells and insects, cf *figuline*.

Pallet board for transporting *ware* within a factory, cf *work board*.

Panathenaic amphora tall *amphora* with accentuated features, eg a narrow *foot* and a tall neck. Filled with oil, it would have been used as a trophy at the Panathenaic games, cf *Greek vases* (ill 47).

Pan hearth see *dry*.

Pan mill *edge-runner* mill in which the pan rotates and the *runners,* two heavy rollers, are free to rotate freely about a horizontal axis, cf *chaser mill*.

Pao shih hung Chinese—'red of precious stones'; a descriptive term for a particular quality of Chinese *copper-red glaze* and under-glaze colour, cf *under-glaze decoration*; *chi hung*; *hsien hung*; *sang-de-boeuf*; *flambé*.

180

Pap warmer English version of a *veilleuse*; shape to contain a night-light or similar source of heat, over which a container for warm drink may be placed to be kept warm; pap being a warm milk drink with some alcoholic liquor, cf *caudle cup*; *posset pot*; *spout pot*.

Parian white, *vitreous* porcellaneous *body*, which, being a *hard*-fired *biscuit*-ware appears similar to the white marble of Paros from whence the name is derived. Introduced in England in the nineteenth century and used extensively for the reproduction of scaled-down replicas of contemporary sculptures (see ill 92 and *statuary porcelain*). Some pieces bear the mark 'Cheverton Sc' or 'Reduced by B. C. Cheverton' (with a date), indicating that the

92 *Copeland Parian figure of Mlle Jenny Lind, 1847. Original sculpture by Joseph Durham, 1842. Reduced by Cheverton, 1847*

scaling down of the model was carried out by the Cheverton mechanical process. The true credit for the invention of Parian is confused by numerous claims, but it is accepted that Copelands were the first to produce it on a commercial scale and to use the name 'Parian' to describe their product. The name soon became a generic term for such wares, but Wedgwood named their version Carrara ware, again after a type of white marble. Mintons were the third major company to manufacture parian though by the time of the Great Exhibition of 1851 there were many other smaller factories making this type of ware.

The early Parian body was in fact a *glassy, soft-paste porcelain*, being made of *china clay, felspar* and *frit*. Later recipes consisted of *china clay* and felspar only with an average composition of one part china clay to two parts felspar, and as such may be considered as a type of true *hard-paste* porcelain. Some of the later bodies did not possess such a fine surface quality, this factor together with the introduction of some *tableware* shapes in parian brought about the need to use a glaze. Sometimes a *smear glaze* was sufficient, but in other cases, low-temperature *lead glazes* were used as is exemplified by the wares produced at the Beleek factory. Glazed Parian was also produced at Worcester and by some of the Staffordshire potteries.

Paris green   green pigment made from *chrome oxide, cobalt oxide* and *zinc oxide*, with *flint, whiting* and *borax*. Suitable for *underglaze decoration* or *maiolica* painting to temperatures up to 1,050°C.

Paris white   see *whiting*.

Parting cup   ceremonial cup, *tyg* or mug used at farewell parties. Usually decorated appropriately.

Parting sand   *sand* used on kiln *bats* to prevent sticking of glazed ware, cf *bat wash*; *placing sand*.

Parting sherd   piece of broken pot used in the seventeenth century for *placing* glazed ware, cf *bitstone*; *stilt*; *parting sand*; *kiln furniture*.

Partridge-eye decoration   see *oeil de perdrix*.

Paste   see *body*.

Pastille burners containers for burning aromatic pastilles; usually in the form of novelty cottages, castles, toll-houses or similar, but not to be confused with *night-lights* or *crime cottages*. Other designs are more to the point by being simple conical containers for the pastilles which are themselves mostly conical in shape. The pastilles are composed of powdered cinnamon, aromatic oils and other perfumed substances of varying kinds, bonded in gum with willow charcoal and moulded into small cones, which when ignited smoulder with a pleasant odour.

Pastries see *setter* (4).

Pâte dure French term for *hard-paste* porcelain.

Patella Roman dish for serving fish. Also a dish for offering up the first fruits to the gods, cf *patina*; *patera*.

Patera Roman bowl similar to the Greek *phiale*, used for the administration of libations.

Pâte-sur-pâte French—'paste on paste'; a very delicate form of *bas-relief* decoration, built up by painting layer upon layer of translucent *slip*, followed by intricate tooling. Usually a *bone-china* technique with a white relief on a coloured *ground*. Where the relief is thin, slight traces of the ground colour show through, imparting the characteristic delicacy. Originating in France at Sèvres and made in England by Solon at Mintons in the late nineteenth century (see ill 93).

Pâte tendre French term for *soft-paste* porcelain.

Patina Roman food dish, cf *patella*; *patera*.

Paver see *chert stone*.

Peach bloom pink glaze of the K'ang Hsi period of the Ch'ing dynasty (see appendix 1); characterised by occasional red or green flecks due to a variation in the degree to which the *copper oxide* content of the glaze has been reduced, cf *reduction*; *clair-de-lune*; *kingfisher blue*; *peacock blue*; *Nankin yellow*; *mirror black*; *coral red* and *apple green* enamels; *sang-de-boeuf*, *sang-de-pigeon* and *celadon* revivals of the Sung dynasty.

93 Minton pâte-sur-pâte vase by M. L. Solon, entitled 'The Toy Seller'. Dated 1899.

Peacock-blue glaze rich turquoise 'lead silicate' glaze (cf *lead glaze*) on *porcelain* of the K'ang Hsi period of the Ch'ing dynasty (see appendix 1), cf *peach bloom*; *clair-de-lune*; *kingfisher blue*; *Nankin yellow*; *mirror black*; *coral red*; *apple green*; *sang-de-boeuf* and *celadon* revivals of the Sung dynasty.

Peacock decoration otherwise known as the 'peacock-feather' pattern. An all-over pattern composed of an overlapping peacock-feather motif, popular on some fifteenth-century Italian maiolica. 'Peacock' pattern is also the name of a nineteenth-century Spode pattern, a copy of a popular Chinese Ch'ien Lung pattern of the Ch'ing dynasty (see appendix 1).

Peacock jar Dutch *drug jar*, the decoration of which contains a peacock in the painted scrollwork *cartouch* surrounding the inscription of contents.

Peacock scale see *scale pattern*.

Pearl ash see *potassium carbonate*.

Pearl ware late eighteenth- and early nineteenth-century white or bluish-white *earthenware*, introduced by Wedgwood and subsequently copied by others; similar to *creamware* but whitened by increasing the proportions of *flint* and *china clay*, a trace of *cobalt oxide* was also added to induce the effect of whiteness. Decorated under a clear glaze by painting or engraved transfer, cf *under-glaze decoration*. A similar effect may be obtained by using creamware but with a slightly blue-tinted glaze which makes the finished product look white or very pale grey.

Peasant ware jugs, bottles, basins and other such utilitarian articles, hand made by small rural workshops usually in country districts. The pieces made by such potters were intended for local or near local use, sometimes being sold at the weekly markets. Most potteries of this kind are no longer in existence or have turned their attention to the tourist trade with an inevitable change in the style of output, cf *studio pottery*.

Pebble mill   see *ball mill.*

Pebble ware   see *agate.*

Peeling   glaze fault, see *shivering.*

Pegging   sealing the joints of a *rush foot* to the base of a pressed dish, using a wooden peg-like tool. A technique still in use at the Spode factory in Stoke-on-Trent. The term also applies similarly for making firm the joints of handles, cf *pressing.*

Pegmatite   felspathic rock containing mainly *felspar* and *silica,* the latter in the form of *quartz.* It is a useful source of felspar in glazes and is often thought to be interchangeable with it, but this is not so because of the variable composition from batch to batch. Potters' millers usually prepare mixed batches in order to obtain a more consistent product. There are deposits in Cornwall which are commonly known as 'Cornish stone', 'Cornwall stone', 'China stone', 'stone' or more locally as 'moor stone' or 'Growan stone'. The Chinese used a similar material for their early *hard-paste* porcelains, this they called *petuntse* or 'petuntze'. Like felspar it is a useful *flux* for high-temperature glazes, in fact it may be considered as a naturally occurring frit, for it contains all the basic ingredients of a *glaze.* It will melt and form a glaze at *stoneware* temperatures, requiring only slight modifications to suit particular circumstances. For example, the following is a simple recipe for a clear stoneware glaze firing between 1,250°C and 1,300°C: Cornish stone, 85 per cent; whiting, 15 per cent.

Pelike   Greek amphora with a low-bellied shape, cf *Greek vases* (ill 47).

Pencil   pottery-decorator's term for a 'brush'. Made of camel hair in a variety of shapes and sizes, each devised for a specific purpose: 'tracers' for drawing thin lines; 'shaders' for infilling areas of flat colour; 'liners' for making thin lines around an article using a *banding wheel.* Similarly 'banders' are for making broader bands around a piece, 'dusters', 'leafers', 'mops' etc. Many of the shapes are known by slightly different names from one factory to

186

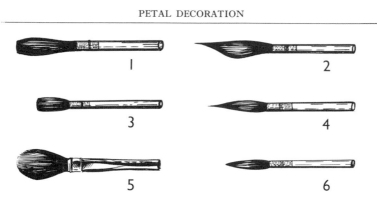

94 *Pottery-painter's pencils: 1 shader; 2 cut liner; 3 bander; 4 tracer; 5 mop; 6 leafer*

another, also over the years some names have fallen into disuse, for instance sometimes a *cut liner* is known as a *slant liner* or simply a *liner*. Much also depends upon the traditions passed down through families of decorators, or upon the particular preferences of an individual head paintress and the terms which she may pass on to her apprentices (see ill 94).

Pencilled decoration   hand-painted decoration composed of fine lines, executed with a 'tracer', a fine brush known in the pottery trade as a *pencil* (see ill 94), cf *black-pencilled decoration*.

Pencilling   (1) see *pencilled decoration*; (2) final finishing of dry clayware, using a brush and water, prior to *biscuit firing*. The brush is useful for difficult corners such as the joins of handles and fittings. A soft sponge may be used for larger open surfaces, cf *fettling*; *towing*; *scrapping*.

Pennsylvania Dutch   Dutch- and German-influenced wares made in Pennsylvania, sometimes confused with *gawdy Dutch*.

Pens   *stillage* racks; particularly applicable in some factories in relation to the storage of moulds for drying, also known as 'stoves'.

Petal decoration   simple relief decoration on *leather-hard* ware in which pellets of plastic clay are applied with a pressing, smearing action so that part is left upstanding and part is smoothed into the contour of the piece. Conventionally applied in bands or rosettes; to be found on some Roman and medieval wares.

Petalite Li_2O Al_2O_3 $8SiO_2$; source of lithium in glazes, cf *lithium carbonate*; *lepidolite*.

Petit feu   French—'little fire'; low-temperature firing, in the range 750°C–900°C, for enamel colours, cf *enamels*.

Petuntse   Chinese kaolinic material similar to 'Cornish stone'; essential to the manufacture of *hard-paste* porcelain. The derivation is, 'pai tun tze', meaning, little white bricks; descriptive of the blocks into which this material was moulded or cut after preparation in readiness for dispatch to the potters, cf *pegmatite*.

Pew group   figure group of two or three persons seated on a high-backed bench or pew. The detailed modelling is usually picked out either in relief or by use of different-coloured clays, or both. Made in Staffordshire during the eighteenth century, in salt-glazed ware (cf *salt glaze*) or lead-glazed *earthenware*, cf *lead glaze*.

Pharmacy jar   see *apothecary jar*.

95   18th-century Staffordshire salt-glazed pew group

Phialle Greek shape; a shallow dish used for drinking or for pouring libations, cf *Greek vases*.

Philistine ware thirteenth- and twelfth-century BC Palestinian wares with painted decoration in brown and black *slip*; showing a strong Mediterranean influence in style.

Photolitho printing by lithographic-transfer process in which the artist's original design is transmitted to the plate by a photographic process, cf *lithography*; *transfer decoration*.

Pie-crust ware imitation pastry-cases made in buff, brown or *cane ware* bodies (see ill 96), lavishly decorated in relief by moulding, impressing and 'sprigging' (cf *sprigged decoration*) after the manner of the pastry originals. Originated by Wedgwood in the 1790s following the flour tax imposed during the Napoleonic wars, causing the disappearance of the large fruit, meat or game pies popular in England at the time. Later a heat-resisting cane ware, sometimes referred to as 'ironstone cane ware', was intro-

96 *Cane ware covered pie-dish (pie-crust ware) c 1795 (Gilbert Strachan collection)*

duced and probably represents the first use of decorative oven-to-tableware, cf *culinary ware*; *ovenware*.

Pierced decoration   pattern cut right through the *leather-hard* body to produce a tracery-like effect (see ill 97). Popular in England in the late-eighteenth and the nineteenth centuries. If very finely cut the technique may be combined with a suitably stiff but transparent glaze used to infill the fret (see ill 46), cf *transparency decoration*; *rice pattern*. Not to be confused with *lacework* or *broderie ware*.

97   *Worcester Parian plinth, decorated by piercing*

Piggin   pottery ladle, used in conjunction with *tygs* and *posset pots*.

Pig-skin pitting   small surface blisters appearing on the surface of *vitreous* ware, caused by air bubbles entrapped in the clay as a result of inadequate preparation.

Pilaertjes   seventeenth-century tiled feature depicting decorative pillars; placed on either side of the large open fireplaces of the time, and used to replace and represent the stone pillars formerly used to support the smoke hood.

Pilgrim bottle   otherwise known as a 'costrel', *beutelflasche* or 'krause'; flask to contain liquid refreshment for the traveller. Usually a flattened shape so that it may be worn comfortably at the hip, suspended from the belt or from the shoulder by a cord attached to two small loops on either side of the neck of the bottle.

Pillar crank   *kiln furniture* for supporting *flatware* in the *glost* kiln. Comprising three pillars with holes to receive triangular *pins*, cf *kiln furniture* (ill 62).

Pill slab   eighteenth-century apothecary ware; a flat slab of *delftware*, used as a work surface for making up pills. Those most commonly still surviving are often decorated with the arms of the Apothecaries' Company and were probably originally only used for display purposes in the manner of a trade sign (see ill 98), cf *apothecary jars*.

98   Tin-glazed earthenware pill-slab, decorated with the arms of the Apothecaries' Company and the City of London c 1690 (Victoria & Albert Museum)

191

Pin small *refractory* bar, having a triangular section similar to a *saddle*, used in conjunction with *pillar cranks* to support *flatware* in the *glost* kiln, cf *kiln furniture* (ill 62).

Pinched pottery hand-built technique in which a ball of plastic clay is pinched out with the fingers and thumb to form a basic bowl shape. This may be further extended by pinching small pieces of clay onto the rim until the required shape is achieved.

Pinholing or pitting (1) *glaze* fault; small craters or 'dimples' in the surface of glazed ware, caused by gases escaping through the molten glaze as it cools, at a time in the *firing* cycle when the glaze has become too stiff to heal over. If the cause is in the glaze itself, the usual remedy is to *soak*. If the fault arises from entrapped air or mineral impurities in the *biscuit*, improved *body* preparation is required; (2) *mould-making* fault, see *blowing*.

Pink lustre *liquid lustre* for 'on-glaze' decoration, prepared from a mixture of gold chloride and tin chloride suspended in a tarry medium. One part of gold to five parts of tin produces the usual pink tint, but a more purple hue will result if the proportion of tin is reduced to four parts. Alternatively, similar results can be obtained by diluting *gold* lustre with *bismuth sub-nitrate*. Usually

99   *19th-century pink lustre, Sunderland jug with engraved-transfer decoration*

painted over *whiteware* or 'tin-glazed' (cf *tin glaze*) ware but it is also found on *redwares* when the effect is as copper. Often used to support and embellish engraved *transfer decoration*, typical of which are the early nineteenth-century Sunderland wares. Also used on its own, sometimes as a mottled ground known as *oil-spot lustre*.

Pink scale   see *scale pattern*.

Pinte   small seventeenth-century *Rhenish stoneware*, salt-glazed tankard, cf *salt glaze*; *Rhenish stoneware* (ill 115).

Pint weight   see *slop weight*.

Pip   (1) item of *kiln furniture*, a small conical-shaped *spur* used for *placing glost* ware, cf *kiln furniture* (ill 62); (2) unit of measurement on a Bullers ring gauge, cf *Bullers ring*.

Pipe clay   white-burning *ball clay*, of the type used to manufacture clay tobacco pipes.

Pipkin   small *ovenware* cooking dish suitable for sauces, usually with two *lug* handles, but sometimes with a single handle similar to a saucepan or large *ramekin*.

Pisano   sixteenth-century Spanish tile decorated in the *maiolica* style.

Pitcher   (1) large *earthenware* jug or water pot; (2) fired and broken *biscuit* ware, may be used to make *grog* or *chamotte*; (3) mould-maker's tool, see *chucker*; (4) presser's tool, a shaped piece of clay, preferably of a *vitreous* type, used in the same manner as a *kidney palette*, and similar in use to a *presser's rubber* (see ills 105, 106), cf *pressing*; *potter's horn*.

Pitchering   smoothing the surface of a 'press-moulded' article with a specially shaped clay tool called a *pitcher* (see ill 105), cf *pressing*.

Pitcher mould   mould made of *soft*-fired *biscuit*. Used in place of *plaster of Paris* when heavy wear resistance is required, eg *sprig* *moulds*, where the mould is subjected to constant *pressing*, scraping with metal tools, and drying.

Pithos   Greek shape; a large storage jar with a narrow base and a short, wide neck, it also had a number of small loops around the shoulder through which a lifting cord may be passed. Designed to be half buried in the earth in order to keep its contents of food or drink cool, cf *Greek vases* (ill 47).

Pitting   see *pinholing*.

Placer   pottery worker who sets ware in *saggars* or who places ware in the kiln ready to be fired, cf *cod placer*; *setter*.

Placing   packing ware into a kiln in readiness for *firing* (see ill 100), also known as *setting-in*, cf *setting*; *saggar*; *bung*; *'oss*.

100   *Placing saggars in a bottle oven*

Placing sand   fine, clean *silica* sand used for placing *earthenware flatware* in the *biscuit* kiln. The term is also loosely used, somewhat incorrectly, to refer to the powdered *alumina* essential for bedding *bone china* flatware to prevent warping. Prior to the use of alumina, *flint* was used for bedding bone china.

Plaster of Paris   calcined *gypsum*; crude forms of plaster, originating from calcined gypsum, had been known for centuries but the term 'plaster of Paris' was the name given in England to the very fine variety produced from the deposits at Montmartre, near Paris, in the eighteenth century. When heated to 150°C, gypsum loses its water of crystallisation. When remixed with water it will set into a hard mass. There are numerous types of plaster, each with varying characteristics, eg degrees of hardness, fineness, porosity, setting times etc. Each prepared for a specific use, ie pottery, medical, dental, building etc, cf *blending*; appendix 4.

Plat   term used locally in Cornwall to mean *overburden*, otherwise known as 'callow' in some districts.

Platinum lustre   see *silver lustre*.

Platter   oval or round meat dish, a term used in the USA in particular, cf *achette*.

Plucked ware   chipped *ware*; blemishes on feet and rims caused by faulty *placing* of *stilts*, glaze running over stilts, glaze too thick or the use of stilts on some types of vitreous ware for which a *dry foot* technique may be preferable.

Plumbate ware   ancient Central-American pottery of the Post-Classical period (980–1521); probably contemporary with *Fine Orange ware*, plumbate ware is distinctive by its lustrous finish, being made of a fusible clay. The name, which is a misnomer, is derived from the erroneous suggestion that some form of *lead oxide* may have been mixed with the clay to cause it to fuse, cf *body*. Decoration is carried out with incised line as opposed to the painted characteristics of other Toltec wares of this period.

Pochoir French—'stencilled decoration'; the term is also applied to a technique using perforated pattern to obtain a pounced outline, which is subsequently filled in by hand painting—'décor à pochoir', cf *pounced decoration*; *poncif*.

Pocked glaze uneven melting of a glaze, due to inadequate grinding and mixing of raw materials.

Pocket clay variety of refractory clay found in pockets within limestone formations, eg near Bakewell in Derbyshire.

Poge see *pug*.

Poncif, spons, or sponse perforated pattern used to transfer a dotted outline of a design to the ware by *pouncing*, cf *pochoir*; *pounced decoration*.

Porcelain *hard-paste*; 'true' porcelain similar in characteristics and composition to the original Chinese paste, being composed of *china clay* (*kaolin*) and 'Cornish stone' (*pegmatite*). *Biscuit fired* in the region of 900°C and *glost* at 1,350°C–1,500°C, when it becomes a very hard *vitreous* and translucent white material, highly aesthetic and practical. The term seems to have first been used to describe decorative wares made of shell or mother of pearl, likewise it became used to describe many other articles with a similar pearly sheen including the imported wares from China in the sixteenth century. It was also used at first in relation to Italian tin-glazed *maiolica*, but gradually the term has become restricted to its present use in describing hard, vitreous, translucent wares. Porcelain was unknown to European potters prior to the importation of the Chinese wares. Their early attempts to copy the technique led to numerous alternatives, similar in outward appearance but technically dissimilar in composition.

Such alternatives, or artificial porcelains, are known as *soft-paste*. *Hard-paste* was not achieved in Europe until early in the eighteenth century, when Bottger succeeded in its manufacture at Meissen. This was followed later in the century in France, at Sèvres, and in Scandinavia. Meanwhile, Cookworthy had discovered the deposits of china clay in Cornwall, about 1747, but hard-paste was made only at Plymouth, later to be transferred to Bristol, and subsequently, by sale of patent, to New Hall. The most outstanding English contribution to the development of porcelain is in the field of *bone china*; most other porcelains in England, with the exception of technical or scientific porcelain and the products of a few craft potters, are soft-pastes of one type or another, cf *glassy porcelain*; *felspar porcelain*; *soapstone porcelain*.

Porringer small breakfast bowl, often with two *lug handles*, used for serving cereal or porridge, cf *bagyne cup*.

Posset pot two-handled cup with a cover; used for serving posset, a hot beverage made of milk, curdled with ale or wine and flavoured with spices. Early examples are in *slipware* or *delftware* and may have a feeding spout, sometimes known as 'spout cups' (see ill 101). Synonymous with a *caudle cup* to some extent, up to the mid-eighteenth century, when the latter term seems to have been preferred for the more fashionable and lavishly decorated *soft-paste* pieces, cf *caudle cup*; *skinker*; *sallibube cup*; *wassell cup*.

101   18th-century English slipware posset pot

Pot (1) generic term for any item of pottery; (2) seventeenth- and eighteenth-century measure; a vessel containing one quart, cf *gallonier*; *pottle pot*; *little pot*.

Potash see *potassium oxide*.

197

Potassium carbonate K_2CO_3, otherwise known as 'pearl ash'; a soluble form of potassium used in the manufacture of some *frits*, cf *potassium oxide*.

Potassium nitrate KNO_3, otherwise known as 'nitre'; a very soluble form of potassium, used in the manufacture of some *frits*, cf *potassium oxide*.

Potassium oxide K_2O, otherwise known as 'potash'; a powerful *flux* useful in glazes when a brilliant colour response is required, cf *glaze*. In *stoneware* glazes it may be introduced as 'orthoclase' *felspar*, this being the only naturally occurring insoluble form of potash. It is also available in the form of *vegetable ashes*, but their composition varies greatly and as such are not suitable for industrial purposes. Nevertheless they can be the source of some of the most rewarding glazes for the craftsman and it is certain that many of the finest Chinese glazes were of this type, cf *ash*; *ash glazes*. In low-temperature glazes potash is used in a 'fritted' form, cf *frit*. It is very similar in characteristics to *sodium oxide*, in fact the two are often used together. Of the two, potassium oxide has a slightly lower coefficient of expansion, but both are relatively high so that *crazing* may be a hazard if used in too great a proportion.

Pot-bank   Staffordshire name for a pottery. The term 'bank' on its own was often used to indicate a yard or other open space on a pottery.

Potiche   vase of Chinese or Japanese origin, having a full, generous body shape, a narrow neck and two handles. Somewhat similar to the Greek *amphora*, cf *Chinese shapes* (ill 23).

Pot lids   nineteenth-century pictorial lids for small jars used for marketing food pastes, in particular fish paste from Pegwell Bay in Kent, which locality is featured in many of the designs. Bear grease, a hair dressing, was sold in jars with pictures of performing bears on the lids. Other subjects include portraits, military scenes, Shakespearean characters, sports, London views etc (see

198

*102   Pratt-ware pot lids, the centre lid depicts a portrait of the
Duke of Wellington*

ill 102). The decorative technique made use of engraved, under-
glaze, transfer printing (cf *transfer decoration*), but is outstanding
in that the designs are multi-coloured, each colour being applied
to the ware separately, using an accurate method of registration.
The first colours to be applied were usually fully stippled tones,
the final engraving being the main outline in sepia. The technique
was brought to an advanced state of perfection by Jesse Austin,
engraver to F. & R. Pratt of Fenton, which firm produced the
greatest amount of this type of ware, cf *Pratt ware*.

Pot-pouri   French—'rotten pot'; container for scented prepara-
tions of dried petals, herbs etc. Such pieces usually have a pierced
cover to allow the fragrance to pass into the atmosphere, cf *pierced
decoration.*

Pot-sherd   a piece of broken pottery.

Potteries collective name for the region in Staffordshire now comprising the City of Stoke-on-Trent. This was formed as the County Borough of Stoke-on-Trent in 1910 by the federation of the six towns, Tunstall, Burslem, Hanley, Stoke-upon-Trent, Fenton and Longton (listing in order north west to south east). Arnold Bennett in his novels refers to these as the five towns, omitting Fenton.

Potter's horn otherwise known as a 'kidney'; a kidney-shaped steel or rubber, formerly made of horn, used by a *presser* for smoothing a *bat* of clay over a mould. Horn was also used to make other tools of various types and uses; long slender tools, probably made from ribs, were fashioned in such a manner as to facilitate the sealing of otherwise inaccessible seams of a moulded piece, cf *kidney palette*; *cow's lip*; *pitcher*; *diddler*; *tommy stick*; *presser's rubber*.

Pottery term sometimes used to denote *wares* made of *soft*-fired *earthenware*, often unglazed and coarse as opposed to *fine* white earthenware; also used in a much looser sense to include most domestic and decorative wares, cf *whiteware*.

Pottle pot seventeenth- and eighteenth-century measure; a pot containing half a gallon, cf *gallonier*; *pot*; *little pot*.

Pounced decoration decorative technique in which the outline of the design is transmitted to the *ware* by means of a perforated pattern or 'spons' which is dusted with lamp black or similar distinctive powder of a non-metallic nature so that staining will not result during the *firing*. The spons may be of paper, or for long runs on *hollow ware* it was customary at one time for them to be made of very thin sheets of lead which could be moulded to the shape of the article. The dusting powder may be applied from a bag or a sifter called a *pounce pot*.

Pounce pot container for the black powder used in *pounced decoration*.

Pouring method of *glaze* application in which the glaze is poured into and over the *biscuit*, cf *dipping*; *spraying*.

Pouring lip the short open spout of a jug as opposed to the long tubular type of a tea-pot.

Powder blue or soufflé blue speckled blue *ground*—known by the Chinese as 'ch'ui ch'ing'—'blown blue', on account of its method of application. Finely powdered *cobalt oxide* is blown onto the ware through a tube, the end of which is covered with a piece of gauze which acts as a filter to effect an even dispersion. Originally used alongside other ground colours and in conjunction with panels of *famille verte* enamels during the K'ang Hsi period of the Ch'ing dynasty (see appendix 1); copied at numerous European factories, notably Worcester, Caughley, Bow and Lowestoft, cf *asbolite*; *smalts*.

The present-day method of producing the powder-blue effect is to apply the colour to the ware with a broad brush, an oily medium being used. When the colour has become slightly tacky it is dabbed with a wet sponge. This method is still in use at the Spode factory in Stoke-on-Trent and other Staffordshire potteries.

Pratt ware (1) collective name for a type of late eighteenth- and early nineteenth-century *earthenware* decorated in a distinctive range of under-glaze colours (cf *under-glaze decoration*), including a dull orange, pale yellow, dull greens, blue and a mauve-brown. So termed on account of the fact that Felix Pratt of Fenton, Staffordshire (see *Potteries*) was considered to be the most outstanding of the makers of this type of ware; (2) collective term for a type of nineteenth-century earthenware decorated with under-glaze prints, noteworthy for the multi-colour technique achieved by superimposing successive engraved transfers upon each other, and which was brought to an advanced state of perfection by the company of F. & R. Pratt (see ill 103). The method was extensively used for the decoration of *pot lids* (see ill 102), but *tablewares* and commemorative ware bearing portraits of such personalities as Nelson, Hardy and the Duke of Wellington were also produced.

*103   Pratt-ware, earthenware dinner plate with a colour
printed centre and yellow border*

Presser   craftsman employed in the making of *ware* by the press-
moulded method; cf *pressing*.

Presser's rubber   piece of rubber used by a presser for smoothing the surface of an article being made in a *press mould*; cf *cow's
lip*; *kidney palette*; *pitcher*; *diddler*; *potter's horn*.

Pressing or press moulding   method of shaping plastic clay
over or into a mould (see ills 104-9). Still in use at the Spode
factory for the production of irregular-shaped dishes, otherwise
the technique is now mainly used by the *heavy clay* industries
or craft potters. Prior to the invention of *casting* and the *jigger
and jolley,* pressing was a principal method of manufacture alongside *throwing*. To make a dish, a bat of clay of even thickness is
pressed over a *hump mould*. To make hollow ware, a *chum* may be
used to pre-form the bat before inserting into the hollow mould;
an article may be pressed in two halves and joined together by
locating the two parts of the mould; the seams being smoothed
over from the inside, cf *pitchering*; *tommy stick*; *potter's horn*;
kidney palette; *presser's rubber*; *cow's lip*; *diddler*; *luting*; *pegging*.

202

104 (above) Pressing; laying the clay bat on to the plaster mould; 105 (below) Pressing; pitchering the bottom of the dish by smoothing the clay across the mould with a fired clay pitcher

106 (above) Pressing the clay to the contour of the mould with a sponge, at the same time lifting the bat to allow any air to escape; 107 (below) Feeding a roll of clay around the footer mould in the first stage of forming a foot

108 (above) Fastening the clay roll to the dish and the footer mould with firm finger pressure. The scrap is subsequently removed and the external surface smoothed with a sponge and rubber; 109 (below) Having removed the footer mould, the inside of the foot is smoothed and the internal joint sealed

The presser works on a turntable known as a *whirler*. It is but a short historical development from the whirler to a turntable driven at a constant speed and used in conjunction with specially shaped forming tools, the principle of the *jigger and jolley* (ill 60).

Press mould   mould specifically designed for production by the *pressing* method.

Primary clay   sometimes termed 'residual clay'; *clay* which is found in its place of origin, ie on the site of the parent felspathic rock. In particular *china clay*, of all clays the most closely to approximate *clay substance*, cf *secondary clay*.

Printed decoration   various claims are made as to the origin of the first *transfer decoration* on pottery; it is certain that Robert Hancock's designs were in production at Worcester by 1757, and other evidence would seem to indicate that the first experiments were made in 1753 at Battersea, and that from this source Hancock took the technique first to Bow and then to Worcester. The first prints were made from engraved plates and applied by using a tissue paper transfer *on-glaze* (cf *engraved decoration*), mainly in black, red or lilac. Underglaze colours followed within a few years during the 1760s, first at Worcester and Caughley but brought to a peak by Spode in the early 1780s. Thus began a tradition of engraving for which Spode and the succeeding company of W. T. Copeland & Sons have become renowned. The popularity of this type of decoration throughout the nineteenth century gave rise to a profusion of *blue and white wares,* particularly after the Chinese style – *chinoiserie,* by most Staffordshire potters including Minton, Wedgwood, Enoch Wood and Stephenson among the most well known, hence the alternative term, *Staffordshire blue*. Pink, green, sepia, purple, lilac, and black prints complemented those in blue. After 1830 multi-colour engraved-transfer prints were developed by Collins and Reynolds of Hanley, and by F. & R. Pratt of Fenton, cf *Pratt ware*; *Potteries*. A variation of the engraved technique, known as *bat printing*, in which a gelatine pad is used as the intermediary between the engraving and the ware, was developed in the 1780s, being introduced into England from Europe about 1760. It would seem that this process was taken up by a number of factories. Flights of Worcester used it but greater advantage was taken of it by the Staffordshire firms of Adams (Cobridge), Baddeley (Shelton), Mintons (Stoke-on-Trent) and Spode (Stoke-on-Trent), the latter using the method for printing gold. Other potteries using the technique were those of Swansea and the Herculaneum factory (Liverpool).

Engraved transfers are still used by the industry in the style of earlier times and as a means of producing pattern guidelines for paintresses, but the major source of printed decoration on *tableware* is now produced by means of *lithography* or *silk-screen*. These two alternative printing techniques have developed to such an extent that *ceramic* transfer-printing has itself become a major complementary industry in Stoke-on-Trent. Silk-screen printing, with its advantages of low cost and relatively simple equipment, has developed greatly in recent years, being easily undertaken by small concerns and individual potters. Apart from the production of *enamel* transfers, *in-glaze* prints are also produced. Printing direct onto *biscuit* or *glost* is possible and particularly suited to the decoration of tiles; cf *engraved decoration*; *lithography*; *Murray-Curvex machine*; *screen-printed decoration*; *bat printing*; *Pratt ware*; *pot lids*; *blue and white ware*.

Printer's bit   small piece of *kiln furniture*; a *refractory* spacing-piece placed between decorated articles in the *enamels* kiln.

Profile setter   see *setter*.

Prop (1) item of kiln furniture upon which *refractory bats* are placed to form shelves in a kiln, cf *kiln furniture* (ill 62); (2) pieces of clay used to keep figures straight during the *biscuit firing,* particularly necessary in the production of *bone-china* figures. The equivalent to *pastries* used in a similar manner for unusually shaped articles of *hollow ware*; the pieces of clay used are of the same *body* as the figure and are placed loosely to support the weaker parts, eg beneath extended arms or legs; underneath the belly of an animal etc, cf *setter*.

Proto-porcelain   greyish porcellaneous *stoneware*, composed of similar kaolinic materials to *hard-paste*, but not fired to such a high temperature with the result that it is not translucent, cf *porcelain*; *kaolin*; *china clay*.

Prunus vase or mei ping   Chinese *porcelain* vase with a squat body and a narrow neck; intended to hold a single spray of prunus blossom, cf *Chinese shapes* (ill 23).

Psykter   Greek shape; a wine cooler, sometimes in the form of a strange mushroom shape, otherwise similar to a normal *amphora*. The psykter was filled with very cold water and immersed in a *krater* of wine. An alternative form has a double shell and a spout protruding from the inner shape. The space between the two parts served to insulate the wine contained in the inner part from the warmth of the sun, cf *Greek vases* (ill 47).

Pug   (1) loam *clay* or brick earth prepared ready for use; (2) spiked tool formerly used in the Dorset *ball-clay* mines for lifting the balls of clay. A similar tool is known in some localities as a *poge,* cf *tubal*; *dubber* (ill 129); (3) abbreviation of *pug mill.*

Pug mill   machine used for preparing *clay* in the plastic state (see ill 110). It consists of a tapered barrel in which a shaft bearing inclined blades rotates, mixing the clay and forcing it out through a tapered orifice at the narrow end. Some of the more effective machines incorporate augers in line with the mixing blades to improve the compression and flow of the clay. Superior designs include a vacuum chamber which de-airs the clay in readiness for immediate use on plastic-making machinery, cf *wedging*; *kneading*.

Pull and dust   method of applying *enamel engraved transfer decoration* in which an otherwise weak colour is supplemented by an additional dusting of powdered colour; see *engraved decoration*.

Pulle   German salt-glazed jug, (cf *salt glaze*), having a spherical body and a short neck, cf *Rhenish stoneware*.

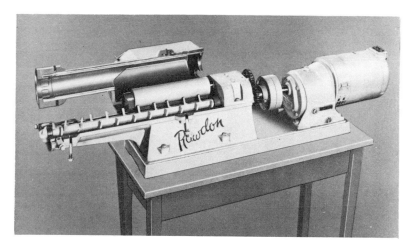

110   Pug mill designed and produced by Rawdon Ltd for studio workshop use

Pulled handle   craft method of making a handle in which a pear-shaped piece of clay is elongated, in a manner somewhat reminiscent of an elephant's trunk, by lubricating with water and pulling out between the fingers until the required shape and size is obtained. A most suitable and appropriate technique to be used in conjunction with thrown ware of an individual nature, cf *dod handle; interlaced handle; foliated scroll-handle; open handle; block handle.*

Punch   see *knocker.*

Purple iron oxide Fe_2O_3, ferric iron; see *iron oxide.*

Purple of cassius   purple colour formed by blending gold chloride with tin chloride. When mixed with suitable *ceramic* fluxes (cf *flux*), it is the basis of most purples, crimsons, the finer quality pinks and some *rose colours* used in *enamel* decoration. It is also the basis of some *pink lustres.*

Putti   cupids without wings, as occur sometimes in Italian *maiolica* painting. Cupids with wings being known as *amorini* or *amoretti.*

Puzzle jug eighteenth-century English novelty shape, popular in the taverns of the time as the basis for a wager. The necks of these jugs are heavily pierced so that to drink from them in the normal manner will surely cause spillage. The secret of draining, and thereby the means of winning a wager, lies in the fact that the rim and handle are hollow, so that if all but one of the openings at the rim are sealed with the fingers, the contents may be sucked through the remaining opening by way of the handle and rim (see ill 111).

111   Bristol   tin-glazed earthenware puzzle jug c 1750 (Victoria & Albert Museum)

Pyrometer device for measuring the temperature in a kiln, or any other situation where a thermometer cannot be used. As opposed to *pyroscopes*, which are temperature indicators visible through spy-holes, pyrometers require additional equipment either in the form of an electrical meter suitably calibrated to read in degrees, or a scale to measure shrinkages in body material, ie *Bullers rings*, which are strictly pyrometers capable of measuring *heat-work* (temperature × time). One of the earliest forms of this type of pyrometer was invented by Josiah Wedgwood for which he was elected a member of the Royal Society in 1783. The most usual interpretation of the term applies to an instrument comprising a thermocouple and a galvanometer. The former is made up of two dissimilar conductors, eg platinum/rhodium; chromel/alumel, housed in a protective *refractory* tube. When heated in contact, a very small electric current is generated, this is measured on a galvanometer. As the voltage increases in proportion to the rise in temperature, the galvanometer may be calibrated to read in degrees centigrade rather than in volts, cf *pyroscope*; *cone*; *Holdcroft bar*; *Bullers ring*.

Pyroscope   visual indicator of kiln temperature or more accurately *heat-work* (temperature × time); made of similar materials to those used in the preparation of pottery bodies and glazes (cf *body*; *glaze*) and as such are an accurate guide to the state of the *ware* being fired, cf *cones*; *Holdcroft bar*; *Bullers ring*; *pyrometer*.

Pyxis   Greek shape; small, round, lidded box for containing toilet requisites, trinkets, jewellery etc, cf *Greek vases* (ill 47).

Quartière   French term indicating the division of a pattern into equal portions, probably originating at Rouen. On *flatware* it usually took the form of radiating panels; on *hollow ware* the divisions were in vertical panels. Also known as 'rayonnant', cf *quartieri*.

Quartieri   Italian term for the division of a pattern into reserves or panels with a firm line of demarcation.

Quartz SiO_2; see *silica*.

Quartz fritware   see *Egyptian paste*.

Queen's ware   see *creamware*.

211

Quintal flower horn   fan-shaped flower container; also known as a *finger vase* (see ill 112).

112   Quintal flower horn or finger vase

Rabesche   style of decoration in the Arabesque tradition, composed of interlaced foliage, cf *rabeschi*.

Rabeschi   Italian—'Arabesques'; contemporary term for the sixteenth-century style of Italian *maiolica* decoration, especially that of Venice after the style of Veneto-Oriental metalwork.

Raddle   otherwise known as 'ruddle' or 'reddle'. A highly ferruginous earth used as a colourant. Also used at one time to transfer a designer's drawing to a litho stone or plate, when it was dusted onto paper and used rather after the manner of carbon paper.

Raised enamel   see *jewelled decoration*.

Raised gold   gilding on a relief pattern applied in *raised paste*. Best results are obtained with the use of *burnished gold*, the pattern being emphasised on account of the upstanding portions becoming more brightly burnished than the lower areas which escape the full action of the burnishing stone, cf *gilding*; *acid gold*; *raised paste*; *blood stone*; *agate*.

Raised paste   relief method of decorating *bone china*; the pattern is built up on the glazed *whiteware*, using an *enamel* paste applied in layers with a brush and finally perfected by *cutting-up* with a sharp tool. The paste is *hardened-on* at enamel temperature, subsequently gilded and fired again to fuse the gold.

Raku very *soft earthenware* based upon a Japanese tradition which stems from the sixteenth century (see ill 113). Its peculiar characteristics lie in its method of manufacture, especially that of glazing. After a very soft *biscuit firing* the glaze is applied, allowed to dry, usually on the warm kiln, and then placed directly into the kiln which has already reached a dull-red heat. After a short while the glaze will be seen to melt, the piece is then removed with tongs and allowed to cool, as it does so the glaze colour is gradually revealed. Alternatively the piece may be quenched in a variety of solutions or vegetable matter to induce staining. So called after a line of Japanese potters, the first of whom was Chojiro, though some authorities claim that the first ware of this kind was in fact made by his wife who it is thought was the potter and not Chojiro. The name Raku—meaning 'pleasure', 'enjoyment' or 'happiness'— was adopted by Chojiro's son Jokei, the second of the line, after the ruler Hideyoshi had presented a seal to him bearing such an inscription in memory of Chojiro. This line of potters remains unbroken—the present head, Kichizaemon Raku, being the fourteenth.

113   Red raku tea-bowl

Pieces are crude by western standards but with considerable aesthetic significance to the Japanese and connoisseur, especially in terms of accidental flaws and imperfections, most of which stem from the unique method of making. For example the inevitable glaze blemish left by the tongs as the piece is removed from the kiln, may take on considerable significance, as do other accidental glaze effects. Such pieces became highly acclaimed by the early Japanese tea masters, who often gave individual names to pieces and were themselves probably more influential upon the ceramic style than the potters themselves, expressing a preference for this type of ware over the more sophisticated imported wares of China and Korea. Consequently so much raku output was taken up by the demands of the tea ceremony that to a ̄great extent the two have become identified together.

Its spontaneity of manufacture and finish has attracted numerous western potters in Europe and the USA, many of whom now make raku ware as an art form in its own right, cf *akaraku*; *kuroraku*; *kochi*; *to-no-tsuchi*; *juraku-zuchi*; *hino-oka*; *chawan*; *chaire*; *chatsubo*; *furidashi*; *futaoki*; *kensui*; *mizusachi*; *mukozuki*.

Ramekin or Ramequin   small saucepan-like *ovenware* dish, usually with a single protruding handle, but also without handles. Used for baking and serving individual dishes of baked egg, sometimes with cheese and spices etc.

Raw glaze   glaze made up entirely of raw materials, none of which are in a fritted form; ie as opposed to a *frit*. Sometimes the term is used erroneously to mean a glaze applied over unfired clay, cf *green glaze*.

Rayonnant   see *quartière*.

Rearing   *setting* of *flatware* on its edge in the kiln; as opposed to *dottling* (horizontally).

Réchaud   French—'food warmer'; originally, in the eighteenth century, made of *porcelain* or *faience* and used in conjunction with a small burner known as a *veilleuse*.

Red clay ferruginous clay, heavily stained, in its natural state, with red *iron oxide* in a very finely divided form. The basis of English seventeenth- and eighteenth-century *slipware*; extensively used at one time for the manufacture of the popular brown tea-pots; mainly used today by craft potters.

Reddle see *raddle*.

Red-figure painting see under *black-figure painting* and *red-figure vase*.

Red-figure vase Greek vase decorated with figure motifs in red on a black *ground*, cf *black-figure painting*; *Greek vases*.

Red-gloss pottery otherwise known as 'Samian ware', on account of its Hellenistic origins, possibly at Samos; most widespread of Roman pottery having a smooth, shiny surface achieved by dipping the ware into a *slip* of fine siliceous clay of the *illite* type, and fired in an oxidising fire, cf *oxidation*; *terra sigillata*.

Red iron oxide Fe_2O_3, ferric oxide; see *iron oxide*.

Red lead Pb_3O_4, see *lead oxide*, also known as 'minium' or 'menninge'.

Red scale see *scale pattern*.

Red stoneware originating in China at Yi-hsing in the sixteenth century, much being teaware and as such found its way to Europe along with shipments of tea in the early seventeenth century. At first the Chinese wares were erroneously classified alongside the quite different but contemporary imported red 'buccaro' or *boccaro* ware from South America. Hence the somewhat confusing term *boccaro*, occasionally applied to Chinese red *stonewares*. European copies of Chinese tea-pot forms were first made by the Dutch, but the hard red *body*, at first thought to be a type of *hard-paste*, was not reproduced until the 1670s when two Dutch potters, the brothers Elers, started to make similar un-glazed red stoneware tea-pots in Staffordshire (see ill 114). John Dwight of Fulham also claimed to have knowledge of the then

215

114 Red stoneware tea-caddy and tea-pot, Elers ware c 1690. Mug, unglazed red stoneware, Elers or John Dwight (Victoria & Albert Museum)

secret of red stoneware, in fact he brought a lawsuit against the Elers brothers for having infringed his patent. Dwight is more famous for his salt-glazed ware (cf *salt glaze*), otherwise known as *Cologne ware*; in the field of red stoneware, the contribution of Elers is more significant.

Suitable clays for making both white *hard-paste* and, so called, 'red porcelain' were discovered by Bottger in Germany in the early 1700s, so followed the manufacture of red stoneware at Meissen. The Meissen body is finer and denser than that of Staffordshire, the former lending itself admirably to the *cut-glass* style of decoration. Gradually the technique spread throughout the European continent and in England where it was made by most major factories, and many smaller ones, throughout the eighteenth century. Wedgwood was making his own researches and in the 1760s produced a variety of red stoneware which he called 'rosso antico'. The Chinese believed that tea made in red-ware was superior to that made in white porcelain. This, and possibly the confusion over the alleged qualities of buccaro ware, led to a similar opinion in England which seems to have persisted with regard to the well-known brown earthenware tea-pots of more recent times.

Reduction opposite to *oxidation*; a kiln atmosphere starved of oxygen so that the colouring oxides in the glazes and bodies are forced to give up some of their oxygen content, thereby having a marked effect upon the resultant colours obtained (see appendix 5). The condition may be achieved in open or *semi-muffle* kilns, using combustible fuels, by restricting the air intake at the burners or fire-mouth. A partial closure of the flue damper will also contribute. Electric kilns with wire elements are not suitable for reducing atmospheres as this shortens element life, but those fitted with silicon carbide elements are suitable, and most studio kilns designed with these also incorporate a purge burner for this purpose, cf *kilns*.

The most common use of reduction techniques is in connection with high-temperature glazes, *celadon, tenmoku,* and *copper red* are all of this type. Reduction of *earthenware* glazes containing *lead oxide* should be avoided. Low-temperature *alkaline glazes* containing metallic salts may be reduced to obtain *lustre* finishes. Lustre painting in the *Hispano-Moresque* style is carried out on similar glazes containing tin to give opacity, cf *lustre glazes*; *celadon*; *tenmoku*; *copper-red glazes*.

Redware *earthenware* or *stoneware* in which a highly ferruginous *red clay* is the principal constituent, cf *slipware*; *red stoneware*; *red-gloss pottery*; *terra sigillata*; *boccaro*.

Refractory (1) ability to withstand high temperature; (2) abbreviated term sometimes used to refer to a piece of *kiln furniture* or other such item made from refractory materials.

Refractory clay that capable of withstanding high temperatures without distortion or fracture. Suitable for use in the construction of kilns, manufacture of *kiln furniture*, scientific apparatus etc.

Relief paste see *raised paste*.

Residual clay alternative term for *primary clay*.

Resist method of decorating pottery at most stages of manufacture, eg on *leather-hard* clay in conjunction with *slip*; on *biscuit* ware as a *glaze* resist; on the unfired glaze with decoration in the *maiolica* technique; for these methods the usual resist medium is melted candle wax, diluted with paraffin and used hot. Alternatively, emulsified wax resists are available from potters' materials suppliers. On *glost* ware a resist of vermilion water-colour in sugar syrup may be used with groundlayed enamels (cf *groundlay*) or *liquid lustres*. In this process the resist is allowed to dry before coating with groundlay *size* or lustre. After application, and when the latter is itself dry, the whole piece is immersed in tepid water which dissolves the sugar causing the unwanted colour to lift away. The water-colour is used as an indication only, vermilion being chosen as it is a vegetable colour which will not leave a permanent stain, cf *stencilled decoration*.

Retch   fault caused by the lateral stretching of a piece of *clay* beyond its tolerance of plasticity, appearing as a number of cracks. It usually occurs when a *bat* of clay is pressed over or into a mould which may have an over-acute radius. The fault normally shows up in the clay state, but it can also become apparent after *biscuit firing*, even if the cracks have been smoothed over during the making.

Rhenish stoneware   salt-glazed stoneware (cf *salt glaze*) made in the Rhineland, having modest origins in the Middle Ages and developing into a distinctive, rugged, ornate style by the seventeenth century. Many of the shapes, influenced by the wine trade, fall into broad categories and are heavily decorated with relief (see ill 115). Made at Cologne, Seigburg and Westerwald.

Rhodian ware   misnomer for a group of sixteenth and seventeenth-century Turkish ceramics (pottery and tiles), made at Isnik but at one time erroneously thought to have been made in Rhodes, on account of some early finds of the ware at Lindos. A *soft*-fired *earthenware*, it is outstanding for the use of a bright-red pigment in addition to the more usual blues, greens, turquoise and black—the latter being used as an outline to the flowing and well-balanced foliate patterns, executed in a particularly successful blend of naturalistic and stylised interpretations, under a clear glaze, cf *Damascus ware*; *Miletus ware*.

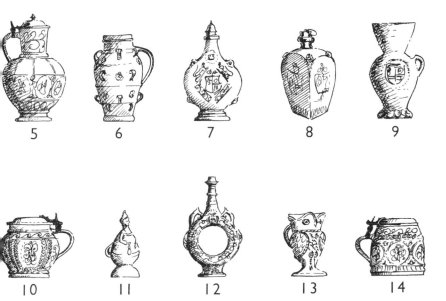

115 *Rhenish stoneware: 1 Bartmannskrug or Bellarmine;*
2 Jakobakanne; 3 Schnabelkanne or Schnabelkrug;
4 Schnelle; 5 Steinzenkrug; 6 Ringelkrug; 7 Beute-
flasche or Krause; 8 Schraubflasche; 9 Trichterbecher;
10 Pinte or Kanne; 11 Sturzbecher; 12 Ringkrug or
Ringflasche; 13 Eulenkrug; 14 Humpen

Rhyton   Greek shape; a cup in the form of a drinking horn modelled after an animal's head (see ill 116), cf *Greek vases*.

116   Rhyton

Rib   (1) throwing tool, made of wood, slate, horn, fired clay or rubber; shaped as a template to aid the *thrower* in the production of particular contours. At one time made of animal bone, a rib itself would provide a useful, long, curved *former* for smoothing the surface of a slender, curved shape; (2) relief-moulding encompassing a shape, formed in a mould or by the use of a throwing rib.

Rice pattern   *pierced decoration* in which the pattern is built up of small shapes about the size and shape of rice grains, filled with glaze to form *transparencies*. Found on Chinese *porcelain* of the Ch'ien Lung and succeeding periods of the Ch'ing dynasty (see appendix 1). Probably influenced by the transparency-decorated wares of Persia dating to the twelfth century, cf *Gombroon ware*.

Rigget or riggot   waste channel to receive excess clay in a press mould for a handle (see ill 117).

Ring   see *setter*.

Ringelkrug   see *Rhenish stoneware* (ill 115).

Ringeloor decoration   term used in relation to a *slip* and *sgraffito* technique used on Dutch tiles of the nineteenth century.

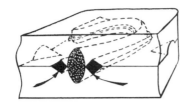

117   Rigget or riggot (arrowed)

Ringkrug   see *Rhenish stoneware* (ill 115).

Rise   see *washing shaft*.

Robin's-egg glaze   opaque, blue-green *glaze* with a pink fleck. One of a number of Chinese self-colour glazes of the Ch'ien Lung period of the Ch'ing dynasty (see appendix 1). Some of the other colours being a continuation of the K'ang Hsi range, eg *clair-de-lune, sang-de-boeuf* etc.

Rockingham glaze   purplish-brown *lead glaze*, containing *iron oxide* and *manganese oxide*. Used extensively during the late eighteenth and nineteenth centuries by various manufacturers in England including the Rockingham pottery where it originated about 1790. It was used on both red and white wares, teaware and other *tablewares* including *Cadogan tea-pots*. Besides imparting a characteristic purple sheen, the manganese also contributed towards the tendency of such glazes to run, thereby showing a variation of tone, lighter on ridges and darker in crevices and towards the foot. The term is also used in the USA in reference to similarly glazed American pottery.

Roller making machine   modern equivalent of the *jigger and jolley*, the template being replaced by a heated, revolving roller profile, which both spreads and shapes the clay. The rate of production is very high, and, according to the shape, may be automated.

Roman kiln   see *kiln*.

Rose colour   pink *enamel* colour obtained from gold chloride, cf *famille rose*.

Rose du Barry   see *rose Pompadour.*

Rose Pompadour   pink *enamel ground,* one of a series of *ground* colours developed at Vincennes and Sèvres during the eighteenth century. Named after Louis XV's favourite mistress, Madame Pompadour, a powerful influence behind the Sèvres factory and who particularly liked this colour. Sometimes referred to as *rose du Barry,* after Madame du Barry, another keen patron of Sèvres, cf *bleu céleste; bleu de roi; gros bleu; vert pomme; jaune jonquille; oeil de perdrix; caillouté; vermicule; jewelled decoration.*

Rosso antico   Wedgwood's name for his dry *red stoneware* after the manner of that produced by Elers.

Rouge d'or   ruby-red *enamel* pigment made from *purple of Cassius.*

Rouge flambé   see *flambé glaze.*

Royal blue   see *bleu de roi.*

Rubber   (1) see *presser's rubber;* also *cow's lip;* (2) see *gold rubber.*

Rubber-stamp decoration   see *stamping.*

Rubbing-up   setting *flatware* in *placing sand* or *alumina* in readiness for the *biscuit* kiln. After inserting a small quantity of sand between each article, handfuls are drawn up the sides of the *bung* so that the remaining spaces between the rims are filled to give extra support.

Ruby-backed dish   Chinese *porcelain flatware* of the Yung Cheng period of the Ch'ing dynasty (see appendix 1); decorated with intricate painted patterns of figures, flowers, insects, birds etc, and often with ornate diaper border repeats, but characterised by the backs of the pieces which are coated with a ruby *enamel,* cf *seven borders dish.*

Ruckling   see *crawling.*

Ruddle   see *raddle.*

Runner (1) stone block, usually Derbyshire *chert stone*, formerly used in the milling of *flint*. It was pushed round the pan (cf *pan mill*) by the sweep arms causing it to slide over the *pavers*, the flint being ground between the two. Superseded in modern mills by heavy rollers; (2) see *mould runner*.

Running (1) glaze fault in which the glaze runs down the ware often causing it to stick to the kiln shelf, due to (a) too much *flux* or, conversely, too little *silica* and/or *alumina* (cf *glaze*); (b) over-firing; (2) pouring a mix of *plaster of Paris*; (3) in mould making, a day's work; (4) in modelling, to form the model of a plate or dish from wet plaster, using a rotating profile. Alternatively the profile may be held firm in a *monkey* and the plaster rotated on a *whirler*. Otherwise known as *cutting a plate*.

Rush foot simple 'foot-ring' (cf *foot*) made in a drop-out *press mould* to fit a pressed dish, cf *pressing*; *pegging*.

Rutile ore of *titanium oxide* and *iron oxide*; otherwise known as *break-up* on account of its property of causing mottled or broken effects in glazes when used in conjunction with other colouring oxides. On its own it gives fawn to brown and tends to make for opacity. It may be used in glazes as a source of titanium so long as the iron content does not interfere with the colour quality required (see appendix 5).

Saddle item of *kiln furniture*; a *refractory* bar of triangular section, made in various sizes, cf *kiln furniture* (ill 62).

Saggar *fireclay* box in which *ware* is *placed* as a protection from the direct action of flames and kiln gases during firing. Extensively used when 'bottle ovens' (cf *kilns*) were the normal means of firing. Since the advent of the electric kiln and those using cleaner fuels, *open setting* has become more predominant. Saggars may be oval, round or rectangular with rounded corners; 'slab built' (cf *slab building*) from *refractory* fireclay. The derivation of the term is thought possibly to be a corruption of 'safe-guard', cf *saggar-maker's bottom-knocker*; *bung*; *placing*; *shrager*.

Saggar-maker's bottom-knocker saggar-maker's assistant, possibly an apprentice, whose job it is to beat out *bats* of *fireclay*, about one inch thick, suitable to make the walls and bottoms of *saggars*.

Saint porchaire ware see *Henri Deux ware*.

Saliera 'salt cellar', a container for salt, cf *trencher salt*.

Sallibube cup seventeenth-century term for a cup similar to a *posset pot* or 'spout-pot'. Possibly later known as a 'sillabub' or *syllabub cup*, by which name a slightly varied shape is also known, cf *spout-pot*; *caudle cup*; *posset pot*; *wassell cup*; *skinker*.

Salmon scale see *scale pattern*.

118 Doulton brown and buff salt-glazed stoneware tea-pot with sprigged decoration

224

Salt glaze 'once-fired' (cf *once-fired ware*) technique in which common salt is introduced into the kiln when the *firing* is well advanced. Salt, *sodium chloride*, vapourises at temperatures in the region of 1,100°C, the sodium (being a *flux*) combines with *silica* on the surface of the *clay*, forming a thin, hard *glaze* often with a characteristic orange-peel texture (see ill 12). In the process, hydrochloric acid is given off and escapes as a gas. Glaze quality can be improved by the addition of *borax* with the salt, in proportion of about one of borax to four of salt, when a thicker, full-bodied glaze will result. Colour is directly influenced by the clay—moderate to high content of *iron oxide* gives various degrees of brown; low iron content produces pale buff if oxidised, or grey if reduced, cf *oxidation*; *reduction*. Other colours may be obtained by using *cobalt oxide* or *copper oxide* (see appendix 5).

The technique was pioneered in Germany during the fifteenth, sixteenth and seventeenth centuries, with important centres of manufacture at Cologne (later removed to Frechen), Seigburg and Raeren with other, smaller factories related to the Rhenish wine trade. Early pieces were brown, characteristically solid Germanic shapes, with the familiar orange-peel textured glaze, often decorated heavily in relief. Towards the end of the sixteenth century a blue-grey firing clay with cobalt blue decoration was introduced at Raeren. Much of this Rhenish ware, especially the wine bottles known in England as *bellarmines* or 'greybeards' on account of the bearded mask embossed on the neck, found its way to England with the imported wine. English attempts to copy these so-called *Cologne wares*, also known as 'Tiger ware', began some time in the early seventeenth century. A patent for its manufacture was granted by Charles II in 1622 to two Dutch potters, Rous and Cullyn, but it was not until Dwight's patent in 1671 that English salt-glaze began in earnest.

Then followed, throughout the seventeenth and eighteenth centuries, an important and formative era in the history of English pottery. There were factories in London, Nottingham and in Staffordshire where the principal developments took place. Much domestic ware was produced in the familiar brown clay oft𝓇 n

119 Staffordshire salt-glazed stoneware tankard with sprigged relief decoration

decorated with white clay *sprigged decoration*, of which the products of Doulton are perhaps among the most well known (see ills 118,119). The use of Devon and Dorset *ball clays* gave rise to the development of white salt-glazed ware, which was later improved by the addition of calcined *flint*. This, together with advancements in potting technique, first by *pressing* into moulds and later *casting* (introduced in the 1740s), brought about greater refinement and delicacy including decoration in enamels, cf *enamel*. Other pieces bore intricate relief modelling, such decoration usually being contained within the mould so that the embossed effect (cf *embossing*) was created simultaneously with the manufacture of the piece. Such items often closely resembled contemporary silverware. By contrast, the figure models of the time were beautifully simple and stylised, so much so that it would be difficult to conceive of anything more claylike in its interpretation.

The advent of *creamware* and the development of *soft-paste* and *bone china*, gradually brought about the end of domestic salt-glaze, with the exception of decorative wares by some studio potters, noteworthy among whom were the Martin brothers (cf *Martin ware*) working in London at the turn of the twentieth century. There has been a further revival among a few studio potters in recent years. The most common application of salt-glaze in modern times has been the manufacture of drainpipes and sanitary fittings. However, clean air legislation and the availability of alternative materials has now reduced this to a minimum, cf *Cologne ware*; *bellarmine*; *Rhenish stoneware*; *stoneware*; *scratch blue*; *Littler's blue*.

Same-yaki Japanese—'shark-skin' *glaze*; seventeenth-century Satsuma ware glaze with a shrivelled characteristic; similar to 'dragon-skin' glaze (cf *ja katsu*) but having smaller divisions. A similar glaze was also produced by the Soma potters in the nineteenth century.

Samian ware see *red-gloss pottery*.

Sand most sands consist entirely, or almost entirely, of *silica*, usually in the form of *quartz*. Some may contain varying amounts of other materials such as *iron oxide, zircon, rutile* etc. Therefore, certain varieties are more useful in potting than others, or may be used for different reasons, eg in England, the Staffordshire potters obtain *placing sand* from North Wales, whereas Lynn sand is used for making *frits* and *glazes*. The very fine sand for *burnishing* gold is often a zircon sand from Australia.

Sang-de-boeuf glaze French—'ox blood' *glaze*; a *copper-red glaze* of the *flambé* type, originating in China during the K'ang Hsi period of the Ch'ing dynasty (see appendix 1), repeated in later dynasties and copied in the western world on decorative and studio wares. Copper glazes are among the most difficult to reduce (cf *reduction*) and especially to maintain consistent results from kiln to kiln. For this reason, in addition to the obvious beauty of the best examples, such glazes are held in high esteem by the connoisseur. Slight variations in the degree of reduction, or of the firing sequence are likely to produce quite different results ranging from delicate strawberry reds and those with a distinct purple fleck, to those of an equally unpleasant liver quality; hence

227

the numerous alternative names for what are basically similar glazes, eg 'sang-de-pigeon'; 'strawberry red'; *chi hung: hsien hung*; *lang yao*; *pao shih hung*. Such red glazes often contain a proportion of *tin oxide*; the best results being obtained on iron-free bodies and in kilns which do not contain other wares made of iron-bearing clay, or with iron glazes, cf *iron oxide*. There is some evidence to suppose that wood fuels favour good copper reduction, cf *ash*; *ash glaze*. This is possibly due to the relatively clean nature of this fuel and partly to the effect of the alkaline wood ash passing amongst the ware along with the gases of combustion. It is also thought that the natural sequence of alternate *oxidation* and *reduction*, caused by the stoking, is particularly helpful to copper reduction. Unlike iron glazes (cf *celadon*), reduced copper glazes often benefit from a short period of oxidation for about the last fifty degrees before the maximum temperature is reached, cf *copper-red glaze*; *flambé*; *chi hung*; *hsien hung*; *lang yao*; *pao shih hung*.

Sang-de-pigeon   see *sang-de-boeuf*.

Sanitary ware   wash basins, lavatory fittings etc, made of various bodies (cf *body*), including *earthenware*, *fireclay* and *vitreous china*.

San ts'ai   Chinese—'three coloured ware'; *stoneware* and *porcelain* of the Ming dynasty (see appendix 1) with decoration carried out in three colours of *glaze*, chiefly yellow, purple and green. The pattern is delineated, and the colours are prevented from merging by a raised outline. The style continued into the Ch'ing dynasty when it became most popular during the K'ang Hsi period, cf *wu ts'ai*; *cuenca*; *tube lined decoration*.

Saqua ni wei   Fijian water-jar; the shape has a narrow neck and sometimes a small pouring spout set low on the shoulder.

Satin glaze   otherwise referred to as 'vellum glaze'; a semi-*matt glaze* used extensively for wall tiles and by some manufacturers of ornamental *earthenware*. The glaze being matt, is necessarily opaque, such glazes usually containing significant proportions of *tin oxide*, *zinc oxide* and *titanium oxide*.

Scale blue see *scale pattern*.

Scale pattern otherwise known as 'salmon-scale' or 'pink scale'; an all-over pattern resembling fish scales. Origin uncertain but probably Chinese, though it is possible that even the Chinese versions may have been first influenced by European originals or made to order for export. Copied to a limited degree by Meissen but becoming more famous as a Worcester *ground* in the mid-eighteenth century. The most common colour was blue, but the pattern was also carried out in pink, yellow, crimson and brick red. The first method of application was to outline the scales with a brush and shade in the darker areas; later, similar but less distinct versions were achieved by wiping away the lighter areas; some fakes and modern versions are applied as a printed *sheet pattern*.

Scaling see *shivering*.

Scallop or scollop (1) small semi-circular indentation cut at regular intervals around the rim of an article, to give a decorative effect. Formerly cut by hand but nowadays the process is mechanised. Alternatively the scalloping may be formed in the mould; (2) small shallow dish; (3) deep, open serving dish used for salads or vegetables; sometimes with a cover when it is known as a 'covered scollop'. The derivation of each usage has a bearing on the shape of a scallop shell.

Schamotte German equivalent of *chamotte* or *grog*.

Schnabelkanne or schnabelkrug German shape; Seigburg, *salt-glazed stoneware* jug with a long bridge spout, made at the turn of the seventeenth century, cf *Rhenish stoneware* (ill 115).

Schnelle German shape; sixteenth and seventeenth-century Seigburg, *salt-glazed stoneware* tankard; a near-cylindrical shape, heavily decorated in relief and sometimes surmounted with a hinged silver or pewter lid. The latter often having been added in England after importation, cf *Rhenish stoneware* (ill 115).

Schraubflasche German—'screw-flask'; seventeenth-century flask or bottle with a metal screw-stopper; the shape is flattened to make four sides which are made into panels for decoration. Each panel is separated from its neighbour by figured column motifs, the tops and bottoms of each panel being bounded by a rope-like relief. The panel decoration is often carried out in enamel. Made at Kreussen, examples are to be found in both salt-glazed *stoneware* (cf *salt glaze*) and *tin-glazed earthenware*, cf *Rhenish stoneware* (ill 115).

Schwarzlot seventeenth- and eighteenth-century German decoration in black *enamel*, sometimes relieved with red or gold; influenced by a similar Dutch red and gold style. Subject matter usually consists of delicately painted landscapes.

Scodella *stem bowl* with two loop handles.

Scouring process of cleaning fired *biscuit* to remove *sand* or *alumina* used for *placing*. The term is especially applicable when the process is carried out by hand.

Scraper (1) flat, steel-edged tool used for removing surplus printer's colour from a copper plate when printing engraved transfers, cf *engraved decoration*; (2) also known as a *scrapper*, flat-edged tool, often made of spring steel, used in *mould making* to remove excess *plaster of Paris*. Varying in size according to requirements; rectangular or shaped, when it may also be known as a *kidney palette*.

Scrapper see *scraper* (2).

Scrapping in mould-made wares, the removal of excess pieces of scrap clay formed at the edge of the mould or *spare*, cf *bittings*; *bitting edge*; *rigget*.

Scrapping edge otherwise known as a 'bitting edge', see *bittings* (ill 14); *scrapping*.

Scrat or scratch edge relief border pattern for a plate or dish. Comprising irregular incised lines (cf *incised decoration*), radiating outwards for about the outer half inch of the rim. Originally cut or scratched at random in the clayware but later incorporated into the mould. Frequently further embellished with colour or gold (cf *burnished gold*), usually with a solid band at the rim shaded or feathered out towards the inner edge of the scrat.

Scratch blue   decorative technique popular in Staffordshire during the eighteenth century for use on white salt-glazed *stoneware*, cf *salt glaze*. The pattern is first incised into the clayware before firing (cf *incised decoration*), the incised lines are then filled with *cobalt oxide*, any surplus being cleaned off the main surface of the piece so that the design eventually appears as a thin blue line inset into a white clay background.

Screen   (1) see *screen-printed decoration*; (2) alternative term for a *sieve*, also known as a *lawn*.

Screen gold   *gold* lustre specially prepared in a medium suitable for printing by silk-screen, either direct on to ware or as transfers, cf *screen-printed decoration*; *transfer decoration*.

Screen-printed decoration   economic method of pattern reproduction, suitable for application 'under-glaze', 'in-glaze' or 'on-glaze' by transfer or direct to the ware, eg tiles. The pattern is transmitted to a screen of silk or alternatively, man-made fibre, in such a manner that the pigment may pass through the mesh only in those areas corresponding to the image. The advantages of screen-printing are low cost and simplicity of equipment, together with the possibility of multi-colour patterns. Technical developments in recent years in the field of materials and photographic processes have removed many of the former limitations of this technique.

Scroddled ware   term used in the USA for a type of nineteenth-century *agate* ware. A similar term, 'scrodledy', was also used at one time in Staffordshire and with the same meaning, cf *agate*; *lava ware*.

Scrodledy   see *scroddled ware*.

Scum or scumming (1) see *efflorescence*; (2) term used in engraved-transfer printing to describe the residue of colour left on the copper plate after scraping the bulk of the pigment from the surface. This scum is finally removed with a *boss*, but may become apparent on the printed ware, if inefficiently carried out, cf *engraved decoration*; *transfer decoration*.

Scutella Roman drinking cup.

Seat earth sometimes called 'underclay', normally a *fireclay* found immediately below a coal seam; alternatively it may be a siliceous rock known as *ganister*.

Secondary clay 'sedimentary clay'; transported by geological phenomena, notably river and glacial action, away from its original source. As a result of the often long journeys to their sedimentary beds, such clays vary considerably in composition, quality and *firing* characteristics, depending upon whatever other minerals with which they may have become associated. They are usually finer in particle size than *primary clays*, which fact, together with the occasional presence of organic matter, greatly increases their plasticity. All clays other than *kaolin* are secondary clays; *ball clays* are examples of very plastic secondary clays.

Seconds finished *ware* with very slight imperfections, not first quality, cf *firsts*; *lump*; *waster*.

Sedimentary clay see *secondary clay*.

Segar cone see *cone* and appendix 2.

Selenium used in conjunction with *cadmium* to produce low-temperature red glazes and *ceramic* painting pigments.

Semi-muffle partial *refractory* lining to a kiln, such that the ware is protected from the direct impact of flame entering the kiln, but otherwise *open set* so that the gases of combustion are free to flow between the pieces of *ware*, cf *muffle*; *bag wall*; *flash wall*; *kilns*.

Semi-porcelain greatly misused term applied to various partially *vitreous* whitewares, similar to *porcelain* in first outward appearances only. The fired *body* is composed of some particles of fused material whilst others remain porous. There is no strict classification of *body* or *paste* to meet this term, it is more accurately described as a trade term occasionally used to indicate a hard, near-vitreous ware which may be a type of hard-fired *fine* white *earthenware*, or a *stoneware* similar to *ironstone china*. Not to be confused with *proto-porcelain* or *soft-pastes*.

Set bat see *sets*.

Sets flat *bats* made from *plaster of Paris*, shaped to fit the contours of the *model* when making a *block mould*. An *end-set* being the bat placed to form the top or bottom of a mould; these are very often D-shaped, the semi-circular portion forming half of a round mould, as for most hollow *tablewares*, cf *mould making* (ill 86).

Setter any type of *refractory* support to prevent the distortion of *ware* during the *biscuit firing* (see ill 120). Particularly necessary in the manufacture of *bone china*. (1) a refractory tray or box containing *alumina* or *placing sand*, the surface of which has been shaped with a *bedder* so that it will fit the contour of the ware it is intended to support; (2) 'ring', either made of the same *body* as the ware or, for large-scale production, of a refractory material which may be used many times; (3) 'profile setter', a purpose-made fitting, usually of refractory material; shaped to fit irregular rims, feet etc, and used in much the same way as placing alumina; (4) 'pastries'; usually made of the same body as the ware; flat *bats* of clay, with a hole in the centre, made by hand or cast in a mould; laid on the rims of unusually shaped pieces, such as sauceboats, to prevent the rims from becoming crooked during firing.

Setting originally, packing ware in *saggars* ready for the *placer* to take to the kiln. Nowadays, with the greater use of *open setting*, made possible by modern kiln designs and cleaner fuels, the term has become synonymous with *placing*, cf *bedding*.

233

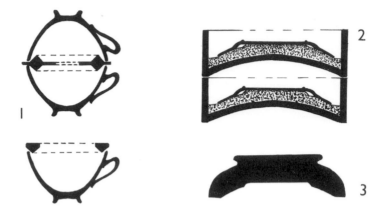

120   1 cup setter ; 2 flatware setter ; 3 bedder

Setting-in   see *placing.*

Settling ark   see *ark.*

Seven-borders dish   name given to some Chinese *porcelain flatware* of the Yung Cheng period of the Ch'ing dynasty (see appendix 1). Such pieces were decorated with intricately painted patterns of figures, flowers, insects, birds etc, and enclosed in ornate diaper border patterns, the latter often being made up of seven different motifs in repeat.

Sgraffito or sgraffiato   from the Italian 'sgraffio'—to scratch. The incising of a pattern through a slip, oxide or other ground colour to reveal the *body*-colour beneath, cf *champlevé.*

Shader   type of pottery-painter's *pencil* or brush, shaped for the purpose of applying graded tones of shading, cf *pencil* (ill 94).

Shaft mining   obtaining minerals which lie too far underground to be obtained by the *open-cast* method. Shafts and underground tunnels, or roadways, have to be excavated at the required depth.

Shagreen   decorative effect attempting to reproduce the quality of the skin of an animal. Used on expensive *fancies*, desk ornaments etc. This consists of black rings of varying sizes on a green background.

234

Shard, sherd or shord   broken and discarded pieces of pottery.

Shark-skin glaze   see *same-yaki*.

Sha t'ai   Chinese—'sandy body'; a grey to buff, and relatively coarse, *stoneware* body, one of two types of *body* used for the Chun wares of the Sung dynasty (see appendix 1), the other, a white *porcelain* body, was called *tz'u t'ai*.

Sheet pattern   all-over pattern or textured *ground* printed as a transfer sheet and from which areas are cut to fit the *ware*. As opposed to a *fit* being prepared for individual shapes.

Sherd   see *shard*.

Shining-black ware   see *Jackfield ware*.

Shino ware   Japanese tea-ceremony ware made at Seto at the turn of the seventeenth century. Characterised by the use of thick *slip* with free brushwork designs of plants, blossoms, grasses etc, in *cobalt oxide* or *iron oxide*, painted on the unfired glaze, cf *chaire*; *chawan*; *chatsubo*; *furidashi*; *kensui*; *mizusachi*; *mukozuki*; *futaoki*; *raku*.

Shivering   glaze fault caused by excessive compression of glaze upon cooling; manifested by thin, sharp slithers of glaze flaking off the fired ware, particularly on rims, ridges and other such vulnerable areas. The exact opposite to *crazing*. Alternatively known as 'scaling' or 'peeling', though the latter is more appropriate to a similar fault in *slips*, cf *glaze*; *cristobalite*.

Shord   Staffordshire dialect spelling for *shard* or 'sherd'.

Shord ruck   Staffordshire term for a heap of broken pots; a heap of *shards* or 'sherds'.

Short clay   otherwise termed *lean clay*; non-plastic clay, unsuitable for modelling, *throwing* or *pressing* without modification by blending with a more plastic material, cf *fat clay*; *ball clay*; *bentonite*; *body*.

Short fired alternative for underfired; ware which has not received a long enough or high enough fire. Not to be confused with *soft* fired which indicates that the ware has been fired at a low temperature intentionally.

Shrager in old Staffordshire dialect, an alternative name for a *saggar*.

Sieve otherwise termed a 'lawn' or 'screen'; equipment for separating the coarser particles or impurities from *slip, glaze* or colour. Normally in the form of a shallow, wooden, cylindrical frame with a base insert made from phosphor-bronze wire mesh, the original sieves were made from silk thread. Usually calibrated as 80s, 100s, 120s, 200s etc, the figures relating to the number of holes per linear inch. Hence sieves of 80–100 mesh, used for slip, are coarser than those of 100–200, used for glaze or colour. This system of calibration is gradually being superseded by metric measurement, the size of the holes being quoted as plus or minus so many microns. Other types of sieves have funnel-shaped metal frames, the smaller varieties of which are used for colour. In mechanically operated processes, sieves of various designs are mounted on vibrator units to replace the manual brushing-through of the material in suspension. Some such sieves are made in the form of a slowly rotating continuous belt which facilitates the constant clearance of waste, *knottings* or 'knockings'.

Sigillata ware see *terra sigillata*.

Silica SiO_2, silicon dioxide. Occurs naturally as *flint, quartz, sand* and as a constituent of many other raw materials. An essential ingredient in all *ceramic* mixes and a prime constituent of *glaze*. Highly *refractory* having a melting temperature in the region of 1,700°C, cf *glaze*; *frit*; *cristobalite*; *mullite*; *crazing*.

Silicon carbide SiC; used in ceramics for the manufacture of high-temperature *kiln furniture*, and for specialised electric kiln elements suitable for use in reducing atmospheres, cf *reduction*; *kilns*.

Silicon ware unglazed *stoneware* made by Doultons at Lambeth in the late nineteenth century. Decorated with coloured clays, applied as *slip*.

Silicosis medical term—'pneumoconiosis'; lung disease caused by the inhalation of *silica* dust. In the past, a very real health hazard in the pottery industry, nowadays minimised by the application of the factory health regulations.

Silk-screen printing see *screen printing*.

Sillimanite Al$_2$SiO; used in the manufacture of high-grade refractories, cf *kiln furniture*; *refractory*.

Silver lustre normally made from platinum, on account of the tendency for silver itself to tarnish. Extensively used in the second half of the nineteenth century as an all-over coating in imitation of contemporary silverware. The earliest, and some of the finest and most valued pieces were made quite early in the century, about 1815–30. In the 1850s John Ridgway & Co produced some such wares using an electro-plating method of application, this proved unsuccessful on account of the low wear resistance of the very thin coating. The period is best remembered for the stencil and resist-decorated pieces, usually on white *earthenware* with a transparent glaze, cf *resist*.

Silver marking fault on finished *bone china* or *porcelain* which becomes apparent during normal domestic use. Minute areas of *glaze*, which have not returned to a smooth surface after the *enamel* kiln, present an abrasive surface to silverware, forks, spoons etc. This causes particles of silver to be removed, forming a black deposit. Pieces affected in this way can be cleaned with a fine powder such as may be recommended by the individual manufacturers of the items concerned. Not to be confused with *spit-out*, another but quite different enamel kiln fault. Silver marking is more of a glaze starvation over a multitude of minute specks not normally visible to the naked eye.

Sinus Roman shape; a large cup.

Sitella or situla Greek shape; container for wine, a small version of a *stamnos* or *kados*, cf *Greek vases* (ill 47).

Size (1) solution normally made from soft soap; used in *mould making* to prevent new *plaster of Paris* sticking to a mould, or *model*; (2) soft soap solution used in engraved-transfer printing to soften the tissue, cf *engraved decoration*; *transfer decoration*; (3) special size made from boiled oil and additives, used to prepare the surface of *glost* ware to receive *on-glaze* transfers or *enamel* colour; (4) term used in the differentiation between actual and trade sizes of various pieces. Especially noticeable in the sizes of plates, often a source of confusion, eg a ten inch plate.

Sizing (1) application of a *size*, whether for *mould making* or decorating; (2) selection of fired ware into batches of comparable size. The sizes of articles can vary due to the degree of *firing* and this can have a detrimental effect upon the fitting of transfer decoration, cf *frit*.

Skaphion fifth-century Greek urinal, boat shaped and used by women, cf *bourdaloue*; *chamber pot*; *coach pot*.

Skillet early three-legged cooking pot, the German *grapen*.

Skinker a *spout-pot*; see *caudle cup*.

Skivet Dorset ball-clay digger's name for a conventional spade, as opposed to a *cutting spade* or a *biddy shovel*.

Skyphos or kotyle Greek shape; a deep cup, flat at the base with a low foot, and having two *lug handles* at the rim, cf *Greek vases* (see ill 47).

Slabber see *tile slabber*.

Slab building hand fabrication from slabs, or *bats*, of *clay* rolled to the required thickness and cut to shape; allowed to stiffen a little to facilitate ease of handling and to avoid collapsing, then luted together using slip as a bond, cf *chamotte*; *grog*; *saggar*.

Slab pot article constructed by the *slab building* method.

Slake in the mixing of *plaster of Paris*, to allow water to penetrate the plaster for a short time prior to *blending*; the action contributes towards the attainment of a smooth mix.

Slant liner otherwise known as a *cut liner* or 'liner', cf *pencil* (see ill 94).

Slip (1) *clay* mixed with water to a creamy consistency, used by craft potters as a decorative medium, cf *slipware*; (2) casting slip (cf *casting*), suspension in water of clay and other such *ceramic* materials as may constitute a particular *body*, aided by the addition of a *deflocculant* which promotes dispersion with minimum water and maintains suspension.

Slip glaze *green glaze* in which a significant proportion of fusible *clay* is used to aid adhesion to the unfired ware.

Slip house department of a pottery works where clay bodies are prepared, cf *body*. The raw materials are first mixed with water to form a slip which is purified and made into plastic clay by removing the water through a *filter press*. This is subsequently made into a homogeneous mass by processing through a *pug mill*.

Slip pan see *sun pan*.

Slip trailing method of decoration using *slip* as a medium, cf *slipware*.

Slipware decoration of red *earthenware* by using coloured *slip* has been traditional in Europe since the seventeenth century and is still continued by some craft potters today. Early pieces were essentially village craft wares, vigorous in style with a freedom of line far outweighing any lack of technical finesse. Some of the earliest English pieces are attributed to the village of Wrotham in Kent, and another early group was made in London, now referred to as 'Metropolitan ware'. Throughout the seventeenth, eighteenth and in some places on into the nineteenth centuries, the technique became widespread in the southern counties, the West Country, South Wales, the Midlands, Derbyshire and Yorkshire. A favourite decorative feature was the use of trailed slip inscriptions or names,

121   Slipware, Toft dish, diameter 19½in

cf *trailer*. Perhaps the most well-known being the *Toft ware* of Staffordshire, so called on account of the frequent use of the names of the Toft family, particularly Thomas Toft and Ralph Toft. It is still a matter of conjecture as to whether the Tofts were patrons or in fact a family of potters, evidence can be interpreted either way. It is certain that the lavishly decorated *chargers* (see ill 121), jugs, *puzzle jugs*, *tygs*, *posset pots* and *loving cups*, presentation cradles, etc which still exist in collections today, were all special pieces and do not represent the day to day utilitarian wares of their time.

The usual slip colours are brown (*red clay* slip), black and a creamy white. Other colours may be achieved by staining white slip with oxides such as *copper oxide* or *cobalt oxide* (see appendix 5), but these seldom attain the aesthetic balance of the traditional colours. Black slip is prepared by staining red clay with an oxide such as *manganese oxide, copper oxide* or *cobalt oxide*. A very satisfactory black slip is made by using 5 per cent of cobalt oxide in 95 per cent of red clay (dry weight).

Slipware decoration may be carried out in a number of recognised methods, eg painting, using a large full-bodied brush—*trailing*; *lining*; *feathering*; *marbling*; *combing*; *resist*; *stencil*; *inlay*; *sgraffito*, cf *barbotine*; *impasto*; *tulip ware*.

Slop mixture of *ceramic* materials in a wet state, ie suspended in water, cf *slop flint*; *slop glaze*; *slop moulding*; *slop stone*; *slop weight*.

Slop flint calcined and powdered flint suspended in water in readiness for inclusion with other slop materials into a mix for a body or glaze.

Slop glaze glaze materials suspended in water, usually with an additive to aid suspension, cf *glaze suspender*; ready for application to ware.

Slop moulding technique of *press moulding* in which a wet, sloppy mixture of *clay* and water is thrown into the mould, smoothed evenly over the whole surface and allowed to dry in a warm atmosphere before releasing. Used extensively for moulding *heavy-clay ware*, eg sanitary and drain fittings. Grogged clay bodies are preferred for this method of production, cf *grog*; *chammotte*.

Slop stone ground 'Cornish stone' (cf *pegmatite*) suspended in water in readiness for mixing with other slop materials to make a *body* or *glaze*.

Slop weight liquid weight of *slip* or *glaze*. Hitherto measured in ounces per pint and therefore known as the 'pint weight'. Now also measured in grammes per litre.

Slow wheel see *wheel*.

Slug piece of prepared *clay*, ready weighed to an amount sufficient to make one piece of ware.

Slurry clay *slop* as it occurs in a rough state in the water tray of a *throwing* wheel or similar plastic-making machinery.

Smalt otherwise known as 'Dumont's blue'; a blue pigment prepared by fusing *cobalt oxide* or *zaffre* with *silica* and a *flux*.

Smaltino Italian term for sixteenth-century blue tin-glazed wares, cf *beretino*; *smalt*; *tin glaze*.

Smear glaze a thin suggestion of a *glaze* transmitted to *vitreous* wares, such as *parian*, as a volatile mist during *firing* (see ill 122). Wares are placed in a *saggar* or full *muffle* kiln (cf *kilns*) together with a crucible of *soft* glaze, alternatively the walls of the saggar may be liberally coated with the glaze. At high temperatures the glaze becomes volatile and transmits a thin deposit on the outer surfaces of the *ware*. If such a piece requires a fuller glaze internally, this would be applied by *dipping* or *pouring* in the usual way before *firing*.

*122   Staffordshire stoneware jug with relief decoration;
smear glazed and banded at the neck with Littler's blue*

Smithum old Staffordshire name for a finely ground ore of lead—*galena* or lead sulphide. This would normally be crushed from a good quality ore known as *bing ore*. Used to dust on to early *slipwares* in order to form a *glaze*, cf *lead oxide*.

Smuiger Dutch fireplace, the smoke hood and back wall of which is faced with tiles, cf *pilaertjes*.

Soak to hold a *firing* at its maximum temperature for a period of time. For glazes, long enough for any bubbles to subside and heal over, thereby avoiding *pinholing*. In a *biscuit firing*, to allow the individual materials to flux and form a homogeneous body, particularly important with *bone china* to permit the bone fluxes (cf *flux*) to yield translucency, cf *loseta*; *alfardone*.

Soapstone see *steatite*.

Soapstone porcelain *soft-paste* porcelain containing *steatite* as a *flux*, with the result that it vitrifies at a relatively low temperature. It possesses a useful *refractory* property in that it is able to withstand boiling water without damage. Made at Bristol, Worcester, Liverpool and Caughley during the eighteenth century.

Socarrat rectangular *tile* made in Barcelona, Valencia and Paterna since the fifteenth century. Used to decorate walls and ceilings, lead glazed (cf *lead glaze*) and bearing motifs of animals or, less frequently, floral patterns.

Soda ash Na_2CO_3; see *sodium carbonate*; *sodium oxide*.

Sodium borate $Na_2B_4O_7$; see *borax*.

Sodium carbonate Na_2CO_3; 'soda ash', source of *sodium oxide* in glazes, cf *glaze*.

Sodium carboxymethylcellulose may be used as a *glaze hardener* in quantities of up to 1 per cent.

Sodium chloride NaCl—common salt; used in the production of salt-glazed ware (cf *salt glaze*), by throwing it on to the fire at temperatures in excess of 1,100°C, when it volatalises, causing the sodium to combine with the *silica* on the surface of the *ware* and thereby forming a *glaze*. In the process, hydrochloric acid is given off and escapes as a gas.

243

Sodium oxide Na$_2$O; used as a *flux* in *glazes* when a brilliant colour response is required, eg *copper oxide* in a glaze containing sodium will produce outstanding blues and turquoise. The famous Persian and *Egyptian blue* wares are of this type. The main source of sodium in glazes is 'soda ash' (*sodium carbonate*). Unfortunately, like most other sources of this material it is water soluble and therefore requires 'fritting' before use, cf *frit*. As with *potassium oxide*, sodium oxide has a high coefficient of expansion causing a severe tendency to craze, cf *crazing*. In contrast to its use as a glaze material, soda ash is used in conjunction with *sodium silicate* as a *deflocculant* in the preparation of 'casting' *slip*.

Sodium silicate Na$_2$O SiO$_2$; otherwise known as *water-glass*. A fused mixture of *sodium oxide* and *silica*. Together with *soda ash* it is used as a *deflocculant* in the preparation of 'casting' *slip*.

Soft low fired, or relatively low fired; also known as 'easy' fired, eg *earthenware* is softer fired than *stoneware*. *Soft-paste* porcelain, by reason of its *frit* content, is capable of being produced at softer temperatures than *hard-paste*.

Soft glaze *glaze* maturing at a low or relatively low temperature. *Earthenware* glazes as opposed to *stoneware* glazes.

Soft-paste various porcellaneous bodies which contain glassy *frits* as fluxes (cf *flux*) which cause the other materials to fuse, often to a degree of translucency, at relatively low temperatures. Originally made in imitation of Chinese *hard-paste*, most such soft-pastes have since become recognised *ceramic* compositions in their own right, eg *glassy porcelain, soapstone porcelain, parian,* cf *bone china; ironstone china; felspar china; stone china; Turner's patent.*

Solid casting see *casting; double casting.*

Solid jasper see *jasper.*

Solitaire set tea service for one person, cf *cabaret.*

Soluble salts usually sulphates or carbonates of 'magnesium', 'sodium', or 'calcium', present in some clays and which appear on the surface of dried ware as a *scum*. A similar deposit may also occur on the surface of fired ware, particularly *redware*, eg bricks, pipes etc, cf *efflorescence*; *weathering*; *barium carbonate*.

Sometsuki   Japanese—*under-glaze decoration* on *porcelain* in blue and white.

Sorting   also known as 'ginnetting'; removal of small blemishes, *stilt* marks etc, from finished *ware* by means of a fine abrasive tool, cf *sorting tool*; *sorting lathe*.

Sorting lathe   otherwise known as a 'ginnetting wheel'; machinery used for *sorting* or 'ginnetting'; usually in the form of a horizontal spindle with various-shaped head fittings, some machines also include adaptation for flexible drives if required.

Sorting tool   chisel-like instrument of iron, used for removing *stilt* marks without the need to use an abrasive tool, cf *sorting*; *sorting lathe*.

Soufflé blue   see *powder blue*.

Souring   see *ageing*.

Spare   an extra piece added to the *model*, which in turn provides an extra section at the opening of the mould, usually the top. This allows for a reserve of *slip* which compensates for the drop in level, due to plaster absorption, during the *casting* period, cf *casting*; *mould making* (ill 86); *bittings*.

Spatterware   eighteenth-century English *blue and white ware*, the *ground* of which is spattered with a brush or sponge, probably in imitation of the Chinese 'blown' or *powder blue*. Reserves were normally left in the ground to contain other painted motifs. Bristol and Liverpool were among the factories which produced such wares.

Specking   fault manifested by specks of colour on finished ware; particularly undesirable on white *tableware*. Caused by contamination in the *clay*, *body*, raw materials or *biscuit ware* by air-borne dust containing particles of *iron oxide* or other colouring oxides;

rusty and dirty equipment; faulty hardening-on (cf *harden-on*), of glaze colour may also be a source of contamination in glazes. *Iron oxide* and *cobalt oxide* are the most likely offenders, the former from metal fittings and equipment, the latter on account of the fact that the smallest particle of this oxide can produce a blue speck in a fired glaze.

Spirit flask nineteenth-century bottle, often slightly flattened and with the upper portion modelled to represent topical characters, political and royal portraits; others were made in the guise of clocks, books, powder horns, animals etc. Made by numerous potters but probably initiated by the Derby pottery of Joseph Bourne, whose wares were made of a buff *stoneware*.

Spit-out fault occurring on decorated ware during the *enamel* firing. Comprising a mass of minute burst bubbles on the surface of the glaze, giving the first impression of fine sugar stuck to the ware. Caused by moisture entering the body between the *glost* and enamel firings, and escaping through the glaze during the enamel fire. Enamel temperatures are not high enough to fuse the glaze so that the blisters remain unhealed. Not a frequent fault on *vitreous* wares.

Splashed lustre see *oil-spot lustre*.

Sponged ornament similar technique to *clouding*, but restricted to selected areas in conjunction with painted motifs, eg birds painted in a background of foliage depicted by sponging. Furthermore, sponging is normally an *under-glaze decoration*, whereas clouding was frequently carried out using coloured glazes.

Spons or sponse see *poncif*.

Spout pot see *caudle cup*; *posset pot*.

Spraying application of *glaze*, colour or *slip* by *aerography*.

Spreader see *batting machine*.

Sprigged decoration *bas-relief* decoration in which shallow *press moulds* are used to reproduce the motifs of a pattern, often

123 (above) Figure making; 124 (below) Ornamenting

247

in the form of a series of figures or classical ornament. Wedgwood *jasper* (see ills 56, 58) and Doulton 'salt-glazed' (cf *salt glaze*) wares (see ills 118, 119) are both well-known examples of this technique. The moulds may be made of *plaster of Paris* for short runs or trial pieces, but it is more usual to use *pitcher* moulds made from *soft* fired *biscuit*.

Alternatively known as 'ornamenting', especially at the Wedgwood factory, this probably stems from one of the two stages in the process. First, the production of the pieces of relief, ie the motifs used to build up the full pattern, this is termed 'figure making' (see ill 123) irrespective of whether the motif is of figure, plant or geometric form; secondly, the actual application of the relief to the ware, known as 'ornamenting' (see ill 124).

Sprig mould   see *sprigged decoration*

Spud   engraved-transfer printer's tool, cf *engraved decoration*; *transfer decoration*; it has a short, wide blade and is used for pressing the colour into the engraved parts of a copper plate. It is especially employed when only a small section of an engraving is to be used, thus saving colour by not spreading it over the entire plate.

Spudgel   wooden scoop with a long handle, used by *ball-clay* diggers to throw water upon the clay as a form of lubrication for the *cutting spade*, to prevent it sticking, cf *tubal* (ill 129).

Spur   item of *kiln furniture*, shaped as a pyramid with concave sides, having one point upwards and three downwards, cf *kiln furniture* (ill 62).

Squatting   collapsing of *ware* in the kiln, due to overfiring, faulty *body* preparation, faulty *placing*, manufacture or design.

Staffordshire blue   see *printed decoration*.

Staffordshire cone   see *cone*, also appendix 2.

Stalk   a solid cone of *clay* centred (cf *centre*) on a thrower's wheel and from which he may make a number of small items, rather than using a separate *slug* for each piece, cf *throwing*.

Stamnos Greek shape; a storage jar, something between an *amphora* and a *kelebe* in shape, cf *Greek vases* (ill 47).

Stamping use of cut rubber stamps as a means of printing repetitive motifs; used as single stamps, in the form of a hand roller or mechanised. Present use of this method is mainly confined to back stamping, cf *back stamp*; *bat printing*; *Murray-curvex machine*; *stamping gold*.

Stamping gold gold *lustre* specially prepared for application by rubber stamp, cf *stamping*; *gold*; *liquid lustre*.

Stamp-mill an obsolete form of mill in which a series of vertical rams were caused to stamp up and down upon the rock mineral, in a similar manner to the action of the manual roadman's rammer.

Starved glaze insufficient *glaze* on finished *ware*, cf *dry edge*.

Statuary porcelain the name first given to the nineteenth-century *soft-paste* used for reproducing figures in the classical style, later called *parian*. Some pastes contained traces of *iron oxide* which produced a popular ivory tone, as opposed to the subsequent whiter domestic parian.

Steatite $3MgO\ 4SiO_2\ H_2O$, hydrous magnesium silicate; otherwise known as 'soapstone', 'talc' or 'French chalk'. Used as a *flux* in low-fired bodies (cf *body*), and in glazes (cf *glaze*) where *magnesium oxide* is required, cf *soapstone porcelain*.

Steingut German equivalent of *fine earthenware*; cf *faience fine*; *terraglia*.

Steinzengkrug see *Rhenish stoneware* (ill 115).

Stem tall *foot*, cf *stem bowl*.

Stem-bowl bowl on a tall *foot*, see *Chinese shapes* (ill 23).

Stencilled decoration form of *resist* decoration, particularly suitable for designs of a precise nature. Cut paper-tissue is a convenient material for craft *slipware*; the paper is moistened and applied to the *leather-hard* clay, a *slip* coating is then poured or sprayed over the design and allowed to set, after which the paper motifs may be lifted to reveal the pattern. Cut paper may also be used *on-glaze* after the manner of some nineteenth-century *lustre* wares; paper patterns are pasted on to the ware using water-soluble paste, the whole is coated with lustre and allowed to dry, the stencils may then be removed with a moist sponge. Alternatively a reverse image may be obtained as follows—the stencil is pasted on to the ware as before, the remaining glazed areas are then coated with wax, the stencil is removed with a moist sponge revealing the unprotected surface of the glaze. When this part of the glaze surface is dry it is coated with lustre, the wax acting as a resist over the other areas. The wax is finally removed with benzine, taking care not to disturb the lustre. Stencils may also be used to mask out a design applied by *aerograph* or spatter, cf *spatterware*; paper or card may be used for short runs or one-offs, a more practicable method for longer runs is to cut a stencil from a thin sheet of lead or other suitably malleable material, which can be formed to fit a particular shape.

Stent   Cornish term for waste stone tipped on the *stent tips* or 'burrows'. Otherwise known as 'blue vein' or 'lode'; veinstone forms part of the waste of a *china clay* mine.

Stent tip   formerly known as a 'burrow', a mound of waste deposit from a *china clay* mine; a familiar sight in the St Austell locality of Cornwall, cf *stent*.

Sticking-up   assembling and joining together the component parts of a piece of ware or *model*, eg spouts, handles, knobs, arms, legs etc, cf *luting*.

Stillage   (1) dry storage for clayware prior to *firing*, cf *pens*; (2) pallet or board used to transport *ware* from the making shop to the dry storage.

Stilt   at one time known as a 'dump'; most common form of *kiln furniture* used to support glazed ware in the kiln, to prevent sticking. Basically a three-armed shape with upward- and downward-facing points at the end of each arm; there are variations in design and size. The term is loosely applied to most other similar items, cf *kiln furniture* (ill 62).

Stipple decoration   see *clouding*; *sponged ornament*; *powder blue*; *spatterware*.

Stirrup cup   tankard for ale or hot punch, used by huntsmen; made in the form of an animal's head, the fox being the most popular, but other subjects include hounds, various breeds of dog, stag, hare and even trout, presumably for the angling fraternity, cf *jagd service*.

Stone   see *pegmatite*.

Stone china   *vitreous whiteware* introduced by Spode in the early nineteenth century, possibly based upon *Turner's patent*, the rights of which may have been bought by Spode from the Turner brothers upon their bankruptcy. It is a plastic *body*, easily fashioned and greyish in colour. Deliberately similar to Chinese hard-paste in appearance, shapes and patterns. In fact some copies of Chinese pieces are difficult to distinguish from the originals. Spode's first stone-china body is believed to have been composed of *ball clay*, *china clay*, *Cornish stone*, *flint* and 'patent ironstone'; the latter probably refers to *Tabberner's mine rock*. A later recipe, known as 'new stone china', did not appear to have contained the ironstone. Stone china is basically similar in composition, but superior in quality and potting to *Mason's ironstone china*. The patent for the latter probably being a greater protection of a clever trade name rather than any special qualities in the composition. The true background to the development of this type of ware is complex and the reader is referred to Leonard Whiter: *Spode: 1733-1833* (1963), cf *ironstone china*; *Turner's patent*; *Tabberner's mine rock*.

Stoneware   very hard, *vitreous*, opaque ware; usually grey, buff or brown in colour, but a class of white stonewares do exist. The name is an apt description of the visual characteristics. *Biscuit* fired in the region of 900°C, *glost* 1,200°C–1,300°C. Alternatively it may be 'once-fired', cf *once-fired ware*. First known in China in the Sung dynasty (see appendix 1), though some authorities claim an earlier date. The predecessor of *hard-paste* porcelain, from which it differs mainly in its lack of translucency. Popular in Europe during the seventeenth and eighteenth centuries, cf *salt glaze*; it is still a favourite medium with craft potters and in the industry for chemical ware and *ovenware*, for which its high strength is a desirable asset. In recent years there has been a marked revival in the field of commercially produced stoneware *tableware*. Many vitrifiable *secondary clays* are excellent natural stoneware material, very plastic and easily worked by conventional plastic-making methods, eg *throwing, jigger and jolley* etc. Alternatively, stoneware bodies may be prepared from *ball clay, flint, felspar* etc.

Stope   Cornish name for the face of a *china-clay* pit; formerly known as a *strake*.

Stove   see *pens*.

Strakes   obsolete Cornish term for the sloping sides, or face of a *china-clay* mine, now known as a *stope*.

Strawberry-red glaze   variation of a Chinese *copper-red glaze*; see *sang-de-boeuf*.

Streu blumen   German—'strewn flowers'; flower patterns painted in a naturalistic style, cf *fantasievogel*; *Indianische blumen*; *Meissner blumen*.

Striking   decorating fault; normally restricted to under-glaze printed wares (cf *printed decoration*) which have been placed too close together in the kiln, causing the colour to 'strike' across from one piece to another. Particularly noticeable on *flatware* when the pattern from the face of one article may be transmitted quite clearly to the back of another. Colours containing *cobalt oxide* or *copper oxide* are especially prone to this fault. The term *flown* blue may also be applicable in this sense but not to be confused with *flow blue*, which is a different and intentional effect.

Strip handle hand-made handle produced from a strip of clay, either wire cut or extruded from a *dod box*, as opposed to being 'pulled' or modelled and cast, cf *casting*; *interlaced handle*; *dod handle*; *foliated scroll handle*; *pulled handle*.

Strontium carbonate $SrCO_3$; *flux* similar in characteristics to *calcium carbonate*, occasionally used as a secondary flux in high-temperature glazes, cf *glaze*.

Stuck ware *wasters* which have stuck to *kiln furniture* or to each other during the *glost* firing. Possible causes—*glaze* too *soft*, careless *placing*, overfiring of glaze.

Studio pottery (1) decorative and utilitarian wares made by individual craftsmen using hand methods as opposed to industrial *tableware*; (2) workshop producing hand-made *ware*.

Sturzbecher German—'tumbler'; *Rhenish stoneware* stem-cup, the handle of which is usually modelled in the form of a figure and is attached underneath the cup, forming the stem, rather after the manner of a handbell. There is no *foot*, so that when the vessel is not in use it is stood upside down on its rim, the figure is then the correct way up, standing on the upturned bell, cf *Rhenish stoneware* (ill 115).

Sucked ware fault occurring on *ware* glazed with volatile glazes, such as those containing *lead oxide*, and which are placed in a kiln too close to porous refractories (cf *refractory*), eg *saggars*. In some circumstances the porosity of the refractories may attract some of the volatile glaze away from the ware, thus leaving it 'starved', cf *starved glaze*. The fault may be prevented by the use of *bat wash*, *open settting*, and the use of less-porous refractories.

Sui yu Chinese—*crackle* glaze.

Sulkowsky pattern see *ozier pattern*.

253

Sulphuring *glaze* fault manifested by a dull bloom apparent on the surface of the finished glaze. Caused by attack from sulphur during the *glost* firing, this may originate from traces in the *clay* itself or in the kiln fuel. Glazes containing *barium oxide* or *calcium oxide* are more susceptible to this fault than *lead glazes*, cf *dulling*.

Sun pan or sun kiln open settling tank for drying water-ground materials, usually stone lined and sometimes divided into several compartments to accommodate successive *charges*. Now obsolete.

Sussex pig drinking vessel in the form of a pig, the body being a jug and the head a detachable cup. Eighteenth- and nineteenth-century traditional wares from Cadborough near Rye in Sussex; still made by the Rye Pottery, cf *Cadborough ware*.

Syllabub cup a small handleless bowl for the serving of syllabub, a sweet, rich dessert cream.

Tabberner's mine rock otherwise known as *little mine rock* or 'new rock'; mineral found in the Staffordshire coal mines in association with ironstone and marl; the name is probably derived from that of the first Tabberner's mine, in which it was discovered by the Turner brothers at the turn of the nineteenth century, and used in their new *body—Turner's patent*. According to the Turner patent (number 2367) it is a siliceous and argillaceous earth with magnesia, lime and water. A description which indicates a *clay* rather than a rock. This view is borne out in that the patent also states that an *earthenware* body may be prepared by using 6–10 parts of the rock to 1 of *flint*; and *porcelain* by using equal parts of rock and *Cornish stone* plus a little *flint*.

Tablero abbreviation for '*azulejo* por tabla'; Spanish—tiles for the ceiling; rectangular, sixteenth-century Spanish tiles used to decorate ceilings. The longer dimension being twice that of the normal tile or *azulejo*, and so designed as to fit between the roof beams, cf *olambrilla*.

Tableware cups, saucers, plates, dishes, and various other such utilitarian pieces specifically made for use at mealtimes, cf *culinary ware*; *tea ware*; *dinner ware*; *studio pottery*.

Take-up amount of *glaze* deposited on a piece of *ware*. This can vary according to the porosity of the ware, time taken to apply, viscosity of the glaze.

Talc see *steatite*.

Tanagra figures small Greek *terracotta* figures dating from the fourth and third centuries BC. Probably used for display in the home or temple to represent certain gods. Some known examples show evidence of having been painted, which is thought likely to have been the case with all originally. The name is derived from the ancient Greek city of Tanagra where some of the first examples were excavated. They are of additional interest to the archaeologist in that they provide an insight into early Greek modes of costume.

Taws or carpet bowls glazed balls used in the Victorian game of carpet bowls; three or four inches in diameter, usually made in *earthenware* and decorated in a variety of ways, including stylised florals, marbling, geometric patterns of concentric or interlinking circles etc. Made at Sunderland and at several potteries in Staffordshire.

Tazza shallow cup on a *stem* foot, after the manner of the Greek *kylix*; derivation Italian.

Tea-bowl Far-Eastern drinking vessel; a bowl-shaped cup without handles, cf *chawan*; *raku*.

Tea-dust glaze *stoneware glaze*; reduced iron green, cf *reduction*, opaque and sometimes with a slight iron fleck, due to crystallisation on cooling. The formation of this type of glaze is favoured by the use of *wood ash* as a *flux*. Originating in the Far East, it is still used by craft potters.

Tea ware *tableware* specifically made for afternoon tea, cf *dinner ware*.

Tenmoku glaze deep, rich black *stoneware glaze* with a characteristic tendency to break to rust where it runs thin on rims, ridges etc. For the best results it should be applied fairly generously, preferably by *pouring* and *dipping*. Originating in the Far East, some of the finest examples are to be found among the Chinese wares of the Sung dynasty (see appendix 1). It is still a favourite glaze with many craft potters today. A typical recipe being *Cornish stone* 85 parts, *whiting* 15 parts, *iron oxide* 10 parts; fired to 1,280°C in a reducing atmosphere (cf *reduction*), cf *tessha glaze*; *hare's-fur glaze*.

Terracotta   Italian—'baked earth'; strictly any fired but unglazed *ware*, more conventionally low fired, porous *earthenware*; not necessarily *red clay* as is often assumed.

Terra de pipa   eighteenth-century Spanish *earthenware*, made at Alcora in imitation of English *creamware*.

Terraglia   Italian equivalent of English *creamware*.

Terra sigillata   (1) 'figured clay'; a term derived from the relief-decorated Roman, *Arretine ware*, much of which was decorated with figure motifs in relief, though other styles of more formal patterns were also used. All were originally inspired by earlier silverware. The ware was made from moulds which also included the relief pattern so that the making and the decoration were carried out at the same time. The term is also sometimes erroneously used to include most other forms of *redware*; (2) R. L. Hobson. 'A Guide to the Islamic Pottery of the Near East' (British Museum collection, 1932), quotes an explanatory note referring to a cup and saucer:

> . . . *terra sigillata*, a peculiar silicious earth from the volcanic island of Lemnos believed to possess medical qualities. It is dug up on the 6th August with religious ceremonies in the presence of the Governor, and the parcels are sealed—hence the name . . . The medicinal clay of Lemnos was known to the Greeks and Romans in classical times. It was taken internally as well as made into pots. In the sixteenth century its vogue was revived in Europe, and the Turks exploited the beds at Lemnos. Similar material, however, was found in Germany, France, Italy, and elsewhere, and was stamped and sold as *terra sigillata*.

Terrine   container for a table delicacy such as pâté de fois gras.

Tesserae   Latin—a cube of wood or stone etc; fragments of fired *clay* or other substances used in the making of *mosaic*.

Tessha glaze   Japanese version of the Chinese *tenmoku glaze*, cf *namako*; *ja katsu*; *bekko*.

Test   term used in connection with *gilding*. A small area of a gold pattern is lightly sanded to try the gold after the firing in order to ensure that it has been correctly fired and fixed to the ware before it is burnished.

Tête-à-tête set   see *cabaret*.

Théière   French—a 'tea-pot'; also used sometimes to indicate a type of *veilleuse* specifically used for drinks.

Thermocouple   see *pyrometer*.

Thimble   small item of *kiln furniture* (see ill 62), used for *placing glost flatware* in a bung.

Thin-casting   see *casting*.

Thorondell   sixteenth- and seventeenth-century Staffordshire term for a large drinking vessel.

Thrower   craftsman who makes pottery by the technique known as *throwing*.

Throwing   traditional method, since ancient times, of shaping plastic clay on a spinning turntable, known as a potter's wheel or throwing wheel, cf *wheel*. At one time a staple process of the potting industry, only replaced in comparatively recent times by more automated mechanical methods. Now rarely used in the industry but still a basic process of craft potters. The technique requires a degree of acquired skill best learnt at first hand from a competent craftsman, although the reader may gain a useful insight from Bernard Leach. *A Potter's Book* (1940); Dora Billington. *The Technique of Pottery* (1962) or one of the numerous other craft publications.

Thwacking beating *leather-hard* clay into a final shape, more often referred to simply as 'beating'. The technique was used at one time to shape curved roof tiles over a wooden *former* block. It also applies to converting a 'thrown' (cf *throwing*) pot into a square or flattened shape, cf *blocking*.

Tigel or tigele Anglo-Saxon word meaning an article made of *clay*, eg a pot, tile or brick. A possible origin of the terms *tyg* and *tile*.

Tiger glaze also known as 'egg and spinach glaze'; a multi-coloured *glaze* consisting of green and yellow or orange splodges. Not to be confused with *tiger ware*.

Tiger ware alternative English name for *Rhenish stoneware*, also known as *Cologne ware*, cf *salt glaze*.

Tile possible corruption of *tigel* which in turn is derived from the Latin 'tegula'—cover. Normally a flat slab of fired clay for cladding walls, floors, pavements, ceilings, drains etc. In the USA the term is sometimes extended to include land drains, hollow building-blocks, partitions etc.

Tile crank see *crank*.

Tile slabber craftsman who fixes *ceramic* tiles specifically for fireplaces when they are bonded to a cast concrete slab prior to installing.

Till see *boulder clay*.

Tincal or tinkal from the Malayan—'tingkal'; an impure form of *borax*, little used on account of the unpredictable effects of impurities.

Tin enamel (1) 'tin-glazed ware' (cf *tin glaze*) decorated *in-glaze* with oxides or similar prepared colours, cf *maiolica*; *delftware*; (2) see *tin glaze*.

Tin glaze sometimes referred to as 'tin enamel'; *glaze* made opaque and white due to the presence of *tin oxide*; used as a basis for *maiolica* and *delftware*; normally an *earthenware* glaze but tin oxide can be used at high temperatures also, cf *marzacotto*; *opaque glaze*.

Tinja large spherical-shaped Spanish jar, used for water, wine or oil.

Tin Oxide SnO$_2$; the most effective of *glaze* opacifiers which also gives a clear white. The basis of *maiolica, delftware* and similar tin-glazed wares, cf *opaque glaze*.

Tin-vanadium yellow yellow *glaze* stain or *ceramic* painting pigment; prepared by calcining (cf *calcine*) a mixture of vanadium and tin at a temperature in the region of 1,000°C.

Titanium oxide TiO$_2$; occurs as *anatase, rutile* or *brookite*; an opacifier in glazes giving a creamy-white quality when oxidised. In a reducing atmosphere (cf *reduction*) it tends to produce an opalescent white, breaking to blue where it is thick. Like rutile, it also helps to develop broken, mottled effects when used in conjunction with other colouring oxides, cf *opaque glaze*; *opalescent glaze*.

Toby jug generic name for numerous variations of a tankard design based upon the form of a seated figure, dressed in a long coat, knee breeches, buckled shoes, tricorn hat etc, often holding a foaming tankard of ale in one hand and a churchwarden pipe in the other (see ill 125). The original subject—Toby Fillpot—a notorious drinker, is depicted in a mezzotint illustration to the drinking song, 'The Brown Jug' by the Rev Francis Fawkes, published in 1761. Subsequent variations are based upon characters with similar notorious drinking habits, eg sailor jugs, a planter, the squire, Martha Gunn and others. Later examples turned to historical, military and naval characters. Modern examples generally copy the original figure with the tricorn hat, but these are usually of little interest, being produced for the novelty market and of doubtful aesthetic merit. Toby jugs were made during the eighteenth and nineteenth centuries by numerous Staffordshire potters, but those made by Ralph Wood are probably among the most well known. Early pieces were made in *earthenware* and decorated with coloured glazes, or a transparent *glaze* stained locally with *cobalt oxide, copper oxide, manganese oxide* and *iron oxide* (see appendix 5). Later pieces were decorated in *enamel,* some glazed in the treacly brown style of Rockingham ware (cf *Rockingham glaze*) others made of salt-glazed ware (cf *salt glaze)* and even *bone china.*

125   Toby jug

Toft ware   seventeenth-century English *slipware*, particularly large *chargers* with trailed (cf *trailing*) and painted decoration, and bearing the names of Thomas, Ralph or occasionally, James Toft. Opinion is still divided as to whether these pieces were made for or by the Toft family. Evidence is not conclusive either way, but it is known that a family of that name did reside in North Staffordshire at the time in question, cf *slipware* (ill 121).

Toki   type of high-fired Japanese *ware.*

Tommy stick   stick to which is attached a piece of felt; used by a *presser* for smoothing the seams or joints of two parts of a *hollow ware* pressing, especially useful when the shape in question has a narrow neck such as will not admit the presser's hand, cf *cow's lip*; *presser's rubber*; *diddler*; *kidney palette*; *pitcher*.

Tong clay English *fireclay* associated with the coal seams of Yorkshire.

To-No-Tsuchi Japanese—a form of *lead carbonate* used for making some *raku* glazes, cf *hino-oka*.

Top-hat kiln see *kilns*.

Tortoiseshell ware multi-coloured *earthenware* made in imitation of the tortoise-shell (see ill 126); an effect obtained by staining *lead-glazed* wares with colourants such as *copper oxide*, *cobalt oxide*, *manganese oxide* and *iron oxide* (see appendix 5). These stains were applied by dusting or dabbing with a wet sponge onto the unfired lead glaze, or on the *biscuit* before glazing.

126   Staffordshire tortoiseshell ware tea-pot c 1750 (Victoria & Albert Museum)

Made in quantity during the second half of the eighteenth and into the early nineteenth centuries, by numerous potters but the most well known of these is Whieldon—in fact such wares are frequently erroneously referred to as 'Whieldon ware' irrespective of their true manufacturer, cf *clouding, sponged ornament, dabber.*

T'o T'ai Chinese—'body-less'; term used to describe the extremely thin Chinese *eggshell porcelain.*

Towing use of tow (coarse hemp) to effect the smoothing of dry clayware, to remove any rough edges or seam marks prior to *biscuit firing.* Particularly applicable to the edges and rims of *flatware,* cf *fettling; scrapping; pencilling.*

Tracer decorating brush or *pencil* used by gilders and decorators in the *tableware* industry for the application of *gold* or *enamel,* cf *pencil* (ill 94); *pencilled decoration; black pencilled decoration.*

Trailer tool for *trailing* slip decoration, comprising a container for the *slip* and a nozzle through which thin or thick lines (according to the size of the nozzle) may be drawn onto the ware. There are several types of trailer, the most common today have a flexible reservoir bag with a glass or metal nozzle. Otherwise the reservoir may be a metal or clay container sealed except for the outlet for the nozzle at one end, and a small hole at the other used for filling and controlling the flow of the slip. The control is effected by placing the thumb or finger over the hole, lifting the thumb to let in air will allow the contents to flow. Sometimes porcupine quills are used to make nozzles.

Trailing decorative *slipware* technique in which linear patterns are applied using a *trailer. Slip* may be trailed direct onto the clay or for better results into a wet slip lining, cf *feathering; combing; marbling; sgraffito; slipware; barbotine decoration.*

Transfer decoration indirect method of printed decoration in which the pattern is obtained from an engraving, lithograph or silk-screen print on transfer paper, from which it is applied to the ware by one of three methods:

262

127 (above) Transfer decoration—pulling a print; 128 (below) Transfer decoration—rubbing down

(1) using tissue paper to carry a sticky engraved (see ill 127) or screen-printed image which is immediately rubbed, face downwards (see ill 128), on to the *biscuit ware* for *under-glaze decoration,* or on to an unfired glaze, incorporating a special *hardener,* for *in-glaze* decoration; (2) using a double paper, trade term 'duplex', comprising a tissue supported by a stiffer backing paper to facilitate ease of handling during the lithographic or silk-screen process. The image is printed on the tissue and coated with a protective *size.* To apply to the ware, the tissue is stripped off the backing paper and the image offered face downwards to the ware which has previously been prepared with a tacky litho *size.* The tissue is finally removed with a damp, soapy sponge; (3) wet-slide transfer, using a single sheet paper, trade term 'simplex', of a fairly stiff nature to facilitate printing by lithography or silk-screen. The paper is coated with water-soluble gum and a film on which the image is printed; the whole is finally coated with a protective *cover-coat.* When immersed in water the gum dissolves, allowing the image, sandwiched between the two protective films, to slide away from the backing paper, cf *printed decoration; lithography; screen-printed decoration; engraved decoration; blue and white wares.*

Transmutation glaze   that in which the components, especially those governing colour, are changed as a result of variations in kiln atmosphere, eg *celadon* and *copper-red glazes,* cf *oxidation; reduction.*

Transparencies   decoration by piercing and infilling with glaze; cf *rice pattern; pierced decoration; Gombroon ware* (ill 46).

Trauerkruge   German — *mourning jug;* seventeenth-century Freiberg *stoneware,* decorated in relief with bands and rosettes emphasised in white and black enamel, cf *Rhenish stoneware.*

Treader   protective attachment for a clay-digger's boot; formerly used in the Dorset *ball-clay* mines, it is a metal plate, shaped to fit under the arch of a boot and held in place by lacing, cf *tubal; packer; spudgel; cutting spade; graft; pug; biddy shovel; skivet; beater.*

Treading primitive method of *kneading* clay; the potter supports himself by his hands from an overhead beam and treads the *clay* with his bare heels.

Trek linear outline to a painted design; particularly applicable to Dutch tile painting. Usually carried out in a blue-grey pigment made from *cobalt oxide* and *manganese oxide*, cf *trekker*; *kap*; *dieper*.

Trekker Dutch tile-painter's brush; fine-pointed and intended for drawing the outlines of a pattern, cf *trek*; *dieper*; *kap*.

Trembleuse saucer saucer with a more than usually firm recess into which the *foot* of the cup fits. Made for ease of the sick and infirm.

Trencher salt shallow container for small quantities of salt at table. Introduced at the time when salt was an expensive commodity, before the present known deposits were found in various parts of the world. Trencher salts are usually found in services of *Chinese export ware,* cf *saliera*.

Trent-kiln see *kilns*.

Trichterbecher sixteenth- and seventeenth-century *Rhenish stoneware* cup with a funnel-shaped mouth. Made at various centres but particularly at Seigburg, cf *Rhenish stoneware* (ill 115).

Trofei in Italian ceramics, decoration in which the subject matter is based upon arms and armour.

Trompe l'oeil highly realistic form of painted decoration in which the subject matter appears deceivingly real. A form of decorative art conspicuous in virtuosity rather than aesthetic merit.

Trough see *dry*.

Truite French—'spotted'; term used by the French for the smaller type of *crackle* otherwise known as *fish-roe crackle*.

Trulla Roman basin; also the term for a ladle.

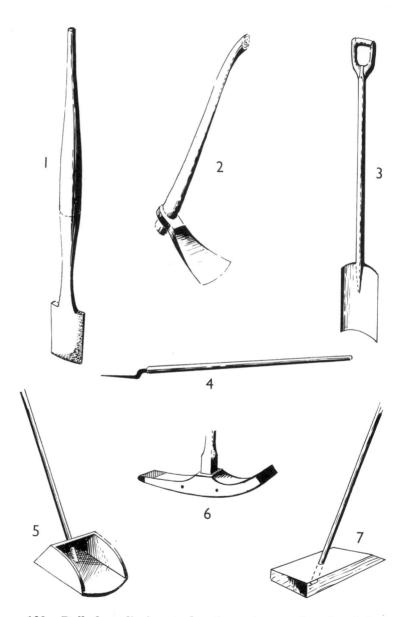

129 Ball-clay digging tools: 1 cutting spade; 2 tubal; 3 graft; 4 pug; 5 spudgel; 6 packer; 7 beater

Tubal also sometimes spelt 'tuball'; Dorset *ball-clay* digger's tool (see ill 129); somewhat similar to an adze and used to make the horizontal cut after the vertical cut had been made with the *cutting spade*. In Dorset, it is thought that a corruption of this term may have been the origin of the term *ball clay*, cf *ball clay*; *pug*; *cutting spade*; *graft*; *biddy shovel*; *skivet*; *spudgel*; *beater*; *packer*; *treader*.

Tube lining decorative technique in which the design is defined by a thin *slip* outline. The areas enclosed are subsequently flooded with coloured glazes, the slip acting as a barrier to prevent the colours merging. Application may be on the *greenware* and biscuit fired, or on the *biscuit* in which case a highly silicious slip is used and 'hardened-on' (cf *harden-on*) before the glazes are

130   Tube lining on an architectural plaque at the Carter Tiles factory, Poole, Dorset

*131 Earthenware bowl with tube-lined decoration infilled
with glazes in blue and yellow. Designed by W. Moorcroft as part of the 'Florian' range produced by Mackintyre & Co c 1900*

applied. The method is particularly suited to the decoration of
wall-tiles and murals, as exemplified in recent years by Carter
Tiles of Poole (see ill 130). Tube lining has also been used for the
decoration of plates and *hollow ware* by numerous potters in the
early twentieth century in the art nouveau style, prominent among
which are the designs by J. W. Wadsworth and L. F. Solon for
Mintons and W. Moorcroft for Mackintyre and Co (see ill 131).
A subsequent and cheaper alternative technique for mass-produced

cast pieces makes use of a raised pattern outline which is cast in the mould at the time of making, cf *cuenca*; *san ts'ai*.

Tudor greenware   English post-medieval *ware* distinctive by its green-coloured *lead glaze*, smoother and better-controlled than earlier pieces; a great deal of this type of ware was made in Surrey.

Tulip ware   in the USA—term used to describe seventeenth- and eighteenth-century *slipware* decorated with designs of stylised tulips, usually carried out in the *sgraffito* method.

Tunnel kiln   see *kilns*.

Tureen   round or oval covered dish, an item of *tableware* used for serving soup, sauce or sometimes vegetables.

Turner   craftsman who completes the shaping of a piece by *turning*.

Turner's patent   patent number 2367, taken out in 1800 and appertaining to the use of a certain stone (or stones) known as *Tabberner's mine rock*, 'little rock' or 'new rock', together with *flint* and *Cornish stone* in the production of a white *body*, itself known as 'Turner's patent' (short for 'Turner's patent body'), cf *stone china*.

Turning   (1) preparation of a solid *model* for *casting*—from clay or *plaster of Paris* by turning on a lathe; (2) completing the shape of a pot by means of paring down the sides and cutting the *foot-ring*. This is carried out in the *leather-hard* state, either on a lathe using a *chum* or *chuck*, or by inverting on a *wheel*, cf *engine turning*.

T'u ting   see *fen ting*.

Twaddle degrees   °Tw; system of calibrating the specific gravity of a liquid; applicable to ceramics in the preparation of *slip* for *casting* and *glazes*. Named after William Twaddle who made a hydrometer to the appropriate scale.

Twiffler   late eighteenth- and nineteenth-century term for a plate or dish, five to six inches in diameter, with a slightly raised rim, suitable for cereal or pudding.

Tyg sixteenth- and seventeenth-century beaker with two or more handles. The derivation of the term may be *tigel*.

132   English Cistercian-ware tyg

Tz'u Chinese term referring to *porcelain* and *stoneware*, not specifically distinguishing between the two but applicable to all *hard, vitreous* bodies, cf *body*; *paste*.

Tz'u T'ai Chinese *porcelain* body; one of two bodies used in the manufacture of the Chun wares of the Sung dynasty (see appendix 1), the other, a coarser *stoneware*, was called *sha t'ai*— 'sandy body', cf *body*.

Unaker American felspathic material, cf *felspar*; mentioned in the 1744 application by the Bow factory for a patent to manufacture *porcelain*, in which a North American *clay*, known locally by the Cherokee Indians as 'unaker', was to be used.

Underclay see *seat earth*.

Under-glaze decoration application of decoration to the *biscuit* ware before glazing; subsequently covered with a transparent *glaze* which affords a high degree of protection. Colours are restricted to those which will withstand the firing temperature of the glaze, therefore offering a relatively limited range compared with *enamel* colour. Nevertheless a considerable choice of specially prepared colours is available from potters' suppliers. Alternatively, the craftsman may blend his own palette from various oxides

270

(see appendix 5). Application may be by hand painting or printing, cf *printed decoration*. In either case, water or oil media may be used. If oil is used it will be necessary to *harden-on* the pattern prior to glazing. If water is used, a small addition of gum or synthetic hardener (cf *alginates*; *dextrine*) will prevent the design running when the glaze is applied. Alternatively it may prove practical to decorate in the dry clay state, in which case the *biscuit firing* will also serve to harden-on the decoration, cf *printed decoration*; *transfer decoration*; *blue and white wares*; *engraved decoration*; *bat printing*; *Murray-curvex machine*; *screen-printed decoration*.

Unity formula   method of comparing the basic characteristics of different glazes, cf *glaze*. In each case the proportion of *flux*, in molecules, is reduced to one, this provides the constant factor by which comparison is possible. The calculations involved are basically those of converting the amounts of materials, such as *felspar*, *flint*, *stone* etc in the recipe, into their respective molecular proportions in a formula. This is necessary as glazes cannot be compared in terms of recipes. After comparison and appropriate adjustment if required, the reverse calculations have to be undertaken to obtain a recipe. Glazes cannot be prepared direct from the formula (see appendix 3).

Updraught kiln   see *kilns*.

Uranium oxide U_3O_8; used in low-temperature glazes to give yellows or orange in *lead glazes* (see appendix 5).

Urceus or Urceolus   small Roman jug similar to the Greek *oenochoe*.

Urn   burial container for funerary ashes; the modern equivalent being known as a casket.

Urna   Roman water jar, similar to the Greek *hydria*.

Ushabti figure   Egyptian *fritware* tomb figures dating from about 1500–1300 BC. Shaped like mummies and made from simple moulds; buried with the dead to aid them in the after life.

133   Egyptian ushabti figure

Vanadium oxide V_2O_3; usually prepared with *tin oxide* to make a yellow pigment or glaze stain, cf *tin-vanadium yellow* (see appendix 5).

Vapour glaze   glaze caused by vapour deposit in the kiln during firing, cf *glaze*; *salt glaze*; *smear glaze*.

Vasi puerperali   see *accouchment set*.

Vegetable ash   see *ash*.

Veilleuse   French—'veiller', to keep a night vigil; originally a veilleuse was any form of night-light but it became used as a food or drink warmer. To be precise, a food warmer was known as a *réchaud*, and the variation for drink sometimes referred to as a *théière*. The normal accepted interpretation is a composite shape comprising a hollow cylindrical base which contains a burner, this is surmounted by a bowl, cup or *spout pot* (as appropriate) in which the food or drink to be kept warm is contained, cf *pap warmer*; *caudle cup*; *posset pot*.

Vellum glaze   see *satin glaze*.

Vermiculé or vermiculated decoration   one of a series of *grounds* developed at Sèvres during the eighteenth century, subsequently copied at Worcester, Chelsea, Bow, Derby and other English factories. Consisting of wavy lines, interconnecting like meandering water courses. Usually in *gold* on a coloured ground, cf *caillouté*; *oeil de perdrix*; *jewelled decoration*; *gros bleu*; *bleu de roi*; *bleu céleste*; *rose Pompadour*; *vert pomme*; *jaune jonquille*.

Vermiculite form of mica which has been expanded under heat and which is used as an insulation material in the construction of kilns, especially modern electric kilns.

Vert anglais or **vert pré** grass-green *ground* used at Sèvres in the late-eighteenth century.

Vert foncée rich olive-green *ground* developed in England during the early nineteenth century, following the style of Sèvres.

Vert pomme French—*apple green*; one of a series of coloured and textured *grounds* developed at Sèvres in the eighteenth century, cf *bleu céleste*; *bleu de roi*; *gros bleu*; *rose Pompadour*; *jaune jonquille*; *oeil de perdrix*; *caillouté*; *jewelled decoration*; *vermiculé*.

Vert pré see *vert anglais*.

Victoria green see *chrome oxide*.

Vieux Paris Parisian *porcelain*, not identified by the marks of any particular factory, nevertheless known by collectors to have been made in Paris during the eighteenth century.

Vitreous Latin—'vitreus', glassy; applied to a ceramic *body* or *paste* which has a very low porosity as a result of a high degree of vitrification, caused by high temperatures and/or the presence of a *flux* in the body mix, cf *stoneware*; *porcelain*; *soft-paste*.

Volute krater Greek shape; a type of *krater* distinguished by two handles shaped after the volutes of an Ionic column (see ill 134), cf *Greek vases* (ill 47).

Wa Chinese term meaning *earthenware*, cf *yao*; *tz'u*.

Wad (1) roll of plastic *clay*, placed between the *saggars* in a *bung* to seal the contents from the effect of the gases of combustion.

Essential in the days of coal-fired *bottle ovens*; otherwise used as a means of providing a firm, even bedding for *kiln furniture*; (2) see *black wad*.

134   Volute krater with red-figure decoration

Wad box   see *dod box*.

Wad clay   inferior *clay* to which *grog* is usually added, used to make *wads* or for *clamin*.

Wall pocket   flower container, having one flat side to facilitate wall attachment.

Wan   Chinese—'bowl'.

Ware   pottery of any kind and in any stage of manufacture.

Wash banding   application of a broad band of thin colour; usually in *enamel* and normally as part of a decorative scheme rather than complete in itself.

Washer   operative formerly employed in a *china-clay* mine; he was responsible for seeing that the *strakes* were maintained in a state of efficiency so that an even flow of water continued, cf *dubber*.

Washing shaft or rise   vertical shaft used in the old *china-clay* mines into which the *buttonhole launder* was inserted and through which the raw china clay in suspension in water was excavated by pumping. Now obsolete.

Wassell cup   alternative English seventeenth-century name for a *spout pot*; also known as a *posset pot, caudle cup* or *skinker*.

Waster   unsaleable defective ware. *Biscuit* or *refractory* wasters are often ground to make *grog*, cf *shard*; *lump*; *seconds*; *firsts*.

Water-glass   trade name for *sodium silicate*.

Water of formation   chemically combined water; ie that combined with *clay substance* at the time of formation from the original granite *mother rock of clay*, cf *clay*.

Water of plasticity   sometimes referred to as 'mechanically combined water'; that added to the *clay* to produce a plastic mass, cf *interlayer water*; *water of formation*.

Water-smoking   early stages in a *biscuit firing*—up to about 250°C—during which the *water of plasticity* is slowly driven off. In the days of coal-fired *bottle ovens* the fires were damped down during this stage in order to restrict the rate of temperature rise, this caused the emission of considerable quantities of smoke (compare ills 135, 136). It was this condition which caused the characteristic pollution at one time so prevalent in the *Potteries*. Many of the older buildings, notably the churches of the area, are still blackened to this day.

Weathering   deliberate exposure of *clay* to the elements; after successive periods of sun, rain and frost, together with regular turning of the *clay bed*, plasticity is greatly improved and many undesirable impurities, such as *soluble salts* are washed away, cf *ageing*.

Wedging   (1) hand method of preparing plastic *clay*, still preferred by craft potters but in the industry replaced by mechanisation, particularly in the form of the de-airing *pug mill*. A large lump of clay is repeatedly thrown onto a firm bench. Between throws, the clay is cut through with a wire and rejoined in a

135 (above) Water smoking, a view of Longton, Stoke-on-Trent, in the days of the bottle oven; 136 (below) The same view as ill 135, taken in more recent times

different orientation—the object being to exclude air and to constitute a more homogeneous mass (see ill 137); (2) fault in tile making in which one edge is thinner than another; (3) fault in tile making in which one edge is shorter than another, usually caused by uneven firing.

276

137 Wedging

Welsh ware apparent misnomer for some rectangular or oval dishes, made in *slipware* and decorated with parallel *trailing* and *feathering*. Made at Isleworth and other London centres in the early nineteenth century.

Welt the part of a mould which forms the rim or edge of an article, cf *bitting edge*; *bittings*; *spare*.

Wet pan a variety of *edge-runner mill* used for wet grinding non-plastic materials.

Wheel the principle of the potter's wheel dates back to the beginnings of recorded history. No individual culture can be identified with its invention, though the general consensus of opinion, based upon archaeological evidence to date, favours the probability of the Near East. It most likely began as a simple turntable, the *slow wheel*, to aid the making of hand-built and coiled pots. It is but a short step forward to using a heavy turntable capable of retaining momentum, or the use of a separate flywheel and shaft supporting a wheel head at a more convenient height. Kick wheels with a mechanical linkage to a foot treadle came later, but even these and the modern motorised versions all retain the same basic principle, which probably represents one of man's simplest and most satisfactory aids to creativity (see ill 138), cf *throwing*; *turning*.

Whirler (1) simple turntable, normally comprising a *plaster of Paris* head cast on a spindle and set in a socket bearing. Of general use in a pottery but particularly by modellers, mould makers and casters, cf *whirlering*; (2) warped *flatware* such that will not stand firm on its foot-ring; also known as *dishing*, cf *bowing*.

Whirlering rotating a mould on a *whirler* while it is being filled with *slip*, cf *casting*. This is sometimes found to be beneficial especially for taller pieces of *hollow ware*; it helps the slip to flow into any small recesses and may reduce any tendency towards *wreathing*.

White dirt clay dust, fragments from *fettling* and *towing*; *alumina* used for *placing* or other such materials left on the *ware* after *biscuit firing* so that they cause spoiling of the glazed ware, cf *crawling*.

138 *(facing page) Types of throwing wheel: 1 slow wheel (Malayan type); 2 early Chinese wheel, momentum achieved by whirling with a stick inserted into notch on rim of wheel head; 3 Indian wheel, momentum achieved by whirling with a stick inserted into notch on rim of large flywheel; 4 continental kick-wheel, momentum achieved by kicking action of thrower's foot directly on to large flywheel; 5 conventional kick-wheel in present-day use, incorporating treadle and crank principle; 6 early Staffordshire wheel, driven by rope pulley from a large flywheel turned by thrower's assistant; 7 popular modern power-wheel, often used by small studios and schools; 8 modern friction-cone driven power-wheel, a well-proven design favoured by many craftsmen*

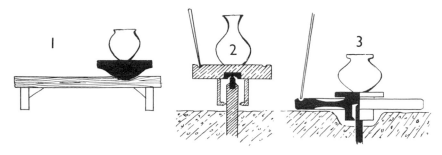

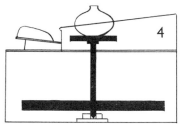

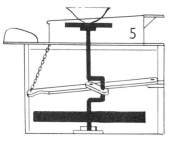

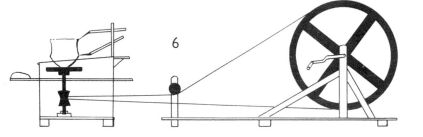

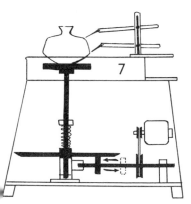

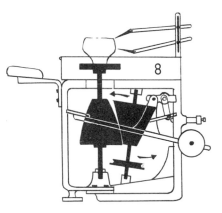

White-hard   clayware dried and ready for *biscuit firing*.

White lead $2PbCO_3. Pb(OH)_2$; see *lead carbonate*.

Whiteware   (1) all pottery made of a white firing *body* or *paste*, especially *tableware*; (2) white tableware in the *glost* state but before decorating.

Whiting $CaCO_3$; sometimes referred to as 'Paris white'; a material manufactured by grinding *calcite*-bearing rocks such as *limestone, chalk* or marble and used in glazes as a source of *calcium oxide*.

Wicket   the bricked-up entrance of a kiln, cf *clamin*.

Witherite $BaCO_3$; natural form of *barium carbonate*, deposits of which are to be found in north-eastern England, Germany and the USA, cf *barytes*.

Window dip   partial sideways immersion of a pot in *slip* or *glaze* so that the shape of the piece itself dictates the shape of the panel thus formed. Sometimes used as a decoration in its own right or as a *ground* for further pattern.

Winning   excavation of clay; otherwise known as *getting*.

Wollastonite $CaSiO_3$, calcium metasilicate; occasionally used in some 'bodies' (cf *body*) and glazes as a source of *calcium oxide* and *silica*. Natural deposits are found in Finland, Russia and the USA, cf *glaze*.

Wood ash   see *ash*.

Wool-drag or **wool-mark**   decorating fault occurring in *ground-laying* if the cotton wool is allowed to touch the oil before the latter has fully absorbed the powdered colour. More likely to happen if the colour is applied too vigorously or before the oil has reached the correct degree of tackiness.

Worcester shape   term used in the trade and by collectors to indicate a cylindrical cup, similar to a *can* but with a rounded base.

280

Work board plank of wood, used to carry ware from one part of a factory to another. Now largely replaced by modern conveyor systems. Up until the 1950s it was a common sight in the *Potteries* to see workmen carrying loads of ware on such boards balanced on their shoulders and sometimes on their heads (see ill 139), cf *palette*.

139 Ware being carried off on work boards

Working mould mould made from a *case mould* and which is used in the actual production of the ware. The working life of these moulds is limited, varying according to the type of *ware* and *body* in use. In a factory producing an average *fine* white *earthenware*, approximately thirty pieces may be cast from each mould before the *face* begins to deteriorate beyond acceptable limits. Moulds for *pressing* may have a longer life providing they are not subjected to harsh physical treatment. Mould makers in a factory are kept busy constantly replacing used working moulds and as such constitute a more vital part of the production chain than is some-times realised.

Wreathing (1) *casting* fault manifested by an uneven, curtain-like deposit on the inside of a piece, cf *whirlering*; (2) uneven deposit of *glaze*.

Wu Chin glaze see *mirror black*.

Wu Ts'ai Chinese—'five-colour decoration'; something of a misnomer for the polychrome decoration of the Ming and succeeding dynasties (see appendix 1), carried out in *soft enamel*-like glazes on *biscuit* porcelain or as *on-glaze*. It does not follow that five colours were always used at one time. The colours avail-able were several yellows and greens, turquoise, brownish-mauve, red and a rust-brown used for outlining. The latter may have been a resist pigment used after the manner of *cuerda seca*, cf *san ts'ai*.

Yaki Japanese – (1) kiln; (2) any form of pottery, the equivalent of the Chinese *yao*, or the English *ware*.

Yang Ts'ai Chinese—'foreign colours'; descriptive term used for a particular quality of *rose colour* used during the Yung Cheng period of the Ch'ing dynasty (see appendix 1); presumably re-lating to the colours used on export *porcelain* for Europe, cf *juan ts'ai*; *Chinese export ware*.

Yao Chinese term meaning any form of pottery, the equivalent of the English *ware* or the Japanese *yaki*.

Yao Pien Chinese term for *ware* glazed with a *transmutation glaze*, cf *celadon*; *copper-red glaze*.

Ya Shou Pei Chinese—'press hand cup'; shallow, broad-rimmed cup or bowl with a small *foot*: intended to be held in the palm of the hand. Very delicate and thinly potted in white *porcelain*; usually decorated with a pattern in white *slip*, which shows through as a delicate shading against the translucency of the remainder. Made during the Yung Lo period of the Ming dynasty (see appendix 1).

Yellow ochre $Fe(OH)_3$, ferric hydroxide; a ferruginous earth; cf *iron oxide*.

Yellow scale   see *scale pattern*.

Yen Yen vase   Chinese shape; a tall baluster (cf *baluster vase* or *jug*) shape with a high neck and flared mouth.

Ying Ch'ing   Chinese—'misty blue'; pale blue *celadon* glazed ware.

Zaffre   early, crude form of *cobalt oxide*, prepared by roasting cobalt ore to extract the main impurities, sulphur and arsenic. A further preparation was also made by fusing the zaffre with *potassium carbonate* or another such *flux*, even glass sometimes, the resultant product is known as *smalt*.

Zinc oxide ZnO; useful as a secondary *flux* in some glazes (cf *glaze*) when it may impart smoothness and colour response if used in moderation. If used in excess it can be troublesome, causing dryness or even *crawling*. As it may have a marked effect upon colouring oxides, it should be used with caution in relation to *under-glaze decoration*.

Zircon $ZrSiO_4$, zirconium silicate; a highly *refractory* opacifier in glazes, though not so effective in this role as *tin oxide*. Used in the manufacture of refractories, cf *refractory*. It occurs naturally as a beach sand in south Australia. The finer grading of this sand is used as a *burnishing* sand for *gold*, cf *burnished gold*; *opaque glaze*.

APPENDICES

1 CHINESE DYNASTIES

Hsia 2205–1766 BC
Shang or Yin 1766–1122 BC
Chou 1122–249 BC
Ch'in 249–207 BC
Han 206BC–AD 220
The Six Dynasties 220–589:
    Western Chin ⎱ 265–317
    Eastern Chin ⎰ 317–420
    Liu Sung 420–479
    Northern Wei 386–636
    Ch'i 479–502
    Liang 502–557
    Ch'en 557–589
Sui 589–618
T'ang 618–906
Five Dynasties 907–960
Sung 960–1279
Yuan 1280–1368
Ming 1368–1644:
    Hung Wu, Chu Yuan or T'sai 1368–1398
    Chien Wen or Yun Wen 1399–1402
    Yung Lo 1403–1424
    Jen Tsung, Hung Hsi or Kao Chih 1425
    Hsuan Te or Chun Chi 1426–1435
    Cheng T'ung 1436–1449

Ming—*continued*
    Ching T'ai 1450–1457
    T'ien Shun 1457–1464
    Ch'eng Hua or Chien Shen 1465–1487
    Hung Chih or Yu T'ang 1488–1505
    Cheng Te or Hon Chao 1506–1521
    Chia Ching or Hon Tsung 1522–1566
    Lung Ch'ing 1567–1572
    Wan Li or Yi Chun 1573–1619
    T'ai Ch'ang or Ch'ang Lo 1620
    T'ien Chi or Yu Chiao 1621–1627
    Ch'ung Cheng or Yu Chien 1628–1643
Ch'ing 1644–1912:
    Shun Chih 1644–1661
    K'ang Hsi 1662–1722
    Yung Cheng 1723–1735
    Ch'ien Lung 1736-1795
    Chia Ch'ing 1796–1820
    Tao Kuang 1821–1850
    Hsien Feng 1851–1861
    T'ung Chih 1862–1874
    Kuang Hsu 1875–1908
    Hsuan T'ung 1909–1912
Chinese Republic 1912

Note: Slight variations in some dates may be found from one authority to another, particularly in the early dynasties.

2 COMPARATIVE PYROSCOPE TEMPERATURES

Table of selected useful temperatures and approximate indication by *cones*, *Holdcroft bars* and *Bullers rings* (subject to relative *heat work*)

°C	STAFFS CONES	SEGER CONES	ORTON CONES	HOLDCROFT BARS	BULLERS RINGS
600	022	022		1	
650	021	021	020	2	
700				4	
720			018		
750	016	016			
770			017		
815	014	014a			
855	012	012a			
900	010	010a			
905			011	12	
950			08	15	
960	07	07a		16	1
990			07		
1,000	05	05a		19	5
1,015			06		
1,020	04	04a			
1,060	02	02a	04	21	
1,065					15
1,080	01	01a		22	
1,100	1	1a		23	20
1,115			03		
1,140	3	3a		25	
1,200	6	6a		26	35
1,205			5		
1,250	8	8	7	27	
1,280	9	9		28	
1,285			9		
1,300	10	10		29	
1,305			10		
1,350	12	12	13	31	
1,490			18	36	
1,500	18	18			

3 GLAZE UNITY FORMULA TABLE

Table of molecular proportions of *silica*, *flux* and *alumina* in glazes relative to approximate melting temperatures, cf *unity formula*

KILN TEMPERATURE °C	STAFFS CONE	FLUX MOLECULAR PROPORTION	ALUMINA MOLECULAR PROPORTION	SILICA MOLECULAR PROPORTION
900	010	1	.085–.325	1.060–2.350
1,000	05	1	.100–.390	1.200–2.825
1,050	03–02	1	.100–.450	1.375–3.150
1,100	1	1	.150–.500	1.600–3.500
1,200	6	1	.275–.650	2.400–4.700
1,250	8	1	.375–.750	3.000–5.750
1,300	10	1	.500–.900	4.000–7.200
1,400	13–14	1	.800–1.25	7.200–11.30

4 PLASTER MIXING TABLE

CASTING MOULDS PLASTER (LB)	WATER (PT)	JOLLEY MOULDS PLASTER (LB)
$1\frac{3}{4}$	1	$1\frac{3}{4}$
$3\frac{1}{2}$	2	$3\frac{3}{4}$
5	3	$5\frac{1}{2}$
$6\frac{3}{4}$	4	$7\frac{1}{2}$
$8\frac{1}{2}$	5	$9\frac{1}{4}$
$10\frac{1}{4}$	6	11
12	7	13
$13\frac{1}{2}$	8	$14\frac{3}{4}$
$15\frac{1}{4}$	9	$16\frac{3}{4}$
17	10	$18\frac{1}{2}$
$18\frac{3}{4}$	11	$20\frac{1}{4}$
$20\frac{1}{2}$	12	$22\frac{1}{4}$
22	13	24
$23\frac{3}{4}$	14	26
$25\frac{1}{2}$	15	$27\frac{3}{4}$
$27\frac{1}{4}$	16	$29\frac{1}{2}$
29	17	$31\frac{1}{2}$
$30\frac{1}{2}$	18	$33\frac{1}{4}$
$32\frac{1}{4}$	19	$35\frac{1}{4}$
34	20	37

5 CERAMIC COLOUR GUIDE

Note : The quantities in parentheses indicate approximate percentages for the use in glazes, or for use as a guide to the proportions used in mixing painting pigments

COLOUR	MINERALS oxidised fire	MINERALS reduced fire	REMARKS
Black	iron (10) cobalt (2)		hard and soft glazes
	iron (10) copper (5) and/or cobalt (1)		may also be reduced in high-temperature glazes
	iron (8) cobalt (1) manganese (3)		
		iron (10)	stoneware and porcelain—tenmoku
Blue	cobalt (0.5) pale cobalt (1) dark		hard and soft glazes. Similar results oxidised or reduced. May be harsh on its own—best blended with other oxides
	copper (1) to (2) in sodium glazes		Egyptian and Persian blues
		iron (1) in felspathic glazes containing potash	celadons of the Chun type. Best results from wood firing
Browns		iron (8)	applied very thinly
	iron (1) straw iron (2) tan iron (4) medium iron (6) dark		hard and soft glazes
	manganese (2) iron (2)		hard and soft glazes
	manganese (2) chrome (2)		glazes containing zinc
	rutile (5) tan to fawn		opaque, useful as the first glaze of a double dip
	rutile (6)		inclined towards opacity

287

COLOUR	MINERALS oxidised fire	MINERALS reduced fire	REMARKS
Browns			inclined towards
	manganese (3)		opacity
	rutile (4) nickel (2)		
Gold	gold lustre		on-glaze
Green	copper (2) pale copper (4) dark		hard and soft glazes
	copper (2) iron (2)		warm green, hard and soft glazes
	copper (2) manganese (2)		
		iron (1) pale iron(2) dark	stoneware and porcelain—celadon
	chrome(2)		dull green, sometimes known as Victoria green
Grey	nickel (2) grey/brown	nickel (1) grey or grey/brown	colour and quality varies with type of glaze. Usually combined with other oxides, hard and soft glazes
	iron chromate (2)		hard and soft glazes
		nickel (1) cobalt (0.5)	stoneware and porcelain—grey/blue
		iron (1) tin (5)	stoneware and porcelain
Mauve	manganese (4)		hard and soft glazes may be made more blue by adding cobalt (0.5)
Orange	selenium cadmium		prepared stain, low temperatures only
	uranium		in low-temperature lead glazes
Pink	chrome tin		prepared stain low temperatures, but can sometimes be effective on some hard glazes

COLOUR	MINERALS oxidised fire	MINERALS reduced fire	REMARKS
	purple of Cassius (lustre)		on-glaze lustre
Red	selenium		prepared stain, low
	cadmium		temperatures
		copper (0.5)	hard and soft glazes—flambé, sang-de-boeuf, etc
Turquoise	copper (1)–(3) in alkaline glazes		soft-fired glazes, rich in soda or borax. Tendency to craze. Persian turquoise type
	copper (1)–(2) cobalt (0.5)		hard and soft glazes, best results in low-fired alkaline glazes
White	tin (10)		hard and soft glazes, more usual as a soft glaze for maiolica, opaque
	titanium (10)		off-white/cream hard-fired glazes. Tendency to mottle
		titanium (10)	tendency towards opalescence
	zircon (15)		refractory
Yellow	antimonate of lead (10)–(15)		soft-fired glazes. Naples yellow painting pigment
	vanadium		prepared stain
	uranium (2)–(7)		hard-fired glazes, best over relatively iron-free bodies

BIBLIOGRAPHY

Adams, P. J. *Geology and Ceramics* (Geological Survey Museum, 1961)

Amis, P. *Journal of Ceramics*, no 2 (1968)

Bemrose, G. *19th Century English Pottery and Porcelain* (1952)

Berendsen, Anne. *Tiles, A General History* (1967)

Billington, Dora M. *The Technique of Pottery* (1962)

Burton, William. *Porcelain, Its Nature, Art and Manufacture* (1906)

Bushnell, G. H. S. and Digby, Adrian. *Ancient American Pottery* (1955)

Charleston, Robert J. *Roman Pottery* (1955)

——. *World Ceramics* (1968)

Clarke, H. G. *Under-glaze Colour Picture Prints in Staffordshire Pottery (Th* *Centenary Pot Lid Book)* (1949)

——. *Under-glaze Colour Picture Prints in Staffordshire Pottery (The Pictorial Po* *Lid Book)* (1955)

Copeland, T. Robert. *Cheddleton Flint Mill and the History of Pottery Millin* *1726–1900* (1969)

Cox, Warren E. *The Book of Pottery and Porcelain* (1953)

Coysh, A. W. *Blue and White Transfer Ware 1780–1840* (1970)

Dodd, A. E. *Dictionary of Ceramics* (1949)

Dugas, C. *Greek Pottery* (1926)

Evans, I. O. *Observer's Book of Geology* (1971)

Fisher, S. W. *The Decoration of English Porcelain* (1954)

Folson, S. *Handbook of Greek Pottery* (1967)

Frank, Ann. *Chinese Blue and White* (1970)

Garner, F. H. *English Delftware* (1948)

Godden, Geoffrey A. *British Pottery and Porcelain* (1963)

——. *An Illustrated Encyclopaedia of British Pottery and Porcelain* (1966)

——. *Lowestoft Porcelain* (1969)

——. *Caughley and Worcester Porcelains 1775–1800* (1969)

Gray, Basil. *Early Chinese Pottery and Porcelain* (1963)

Green, David. *Understanding Pottery Glazes* (1963)

Haggar, Reginald G. *The Concise Encyclopaedia of Continental Pottery an* *Porcelain* (1960)

Hobson, R. L. *British Museum Handbook of the Pottery and Porcelain of the Far East* (1932)
——. *A Guide to the Islamic Pottery of the Near East* (British Museum collection, 1932)
Honey, W. B. *Ceramic Art of China and other Countries of the Far East* (1945)
——. *The Art of the Potter* (1946)
——. *English Pottery and Porcelain* (1947)
——. *German Porcelain* (1947)
——. *Corean Porcelain* (1947)
——. *French Porcelain of the 18th Century* (1950)
——. *European Ceramic Art* (1952)
Howard, G. E. *Early English Drug Jars* (1931)
Howe, J. Allen. *Geological Museum Handbook to the Collection of Kaolin, China Clay and China Stone* (1914)
Jenner, J. S. P. and Kent, D. T. N. *Ceramics* (1962)
Jenyns, Soame. *Ming Pottery and Porcelain* (1963)
——. *Japanese Pottery* (1965)
Jewit, L. *Ceramic Art of Great Britain* (1878)
Lane, A. *Style in Pottery* (1948)
——. *Greek Pottery* (1953)
——. *Early Islamic Pottery* (1957)
Leach, Bernard. *A Potter's Book* (1940)
Lewis, G. *A Collector's History of English Pottery* (1969)
Mankowitz, W. *Wedgwood* (1953)
—— and Haggar, R. G. *The Concise Encyclopaedia of English Pottery and Porcelain* (1963)
Mikami, Tsugio. *The Art of Japanese Ceramics* (English edition) (1972)
Morley-Fletcher, Hugo. *Investing in Pottery and Porcelain* (1968)
Mountford, A. R. *Journal of Ceramics*, no 3 (1970)
——. *The Illustrated Guide to Staffordshire Salt-glazed Stoneware* (1971)
—— and Celoria, F. *Journal of Ceramics*, no 1 (1968)
Pike Bros and Fayle Co Ltd. *The Clay Mines of Dorset 1760–1960* (1960)
Rackham, Bernard. *A Key to Pottery and Glass* (1940)
——. *Italian Maiolica* (1952)
——. *Medieval English Pottery* (1958)
Rhodes, Daniel. *Clay and Glazes for the Potter* (1957)
Rosenthal, Ernst. *Pottery and Ceramics* (1949)
Searle, A. B. *Encyclopaedia of the Ceramic Industries* (1930)
——. *The Glazer's Book* (1948)
Shinn, Charles and Dorrie. *The Illustrated Guide to Victorian Parian China* (1971)
Singer, Dr Felix and German, Dr W. L. *Ceramic Glazes* (1960)
Solon, M. L. *The Art of the Old English Potter* (1891)

Solon, M. L. *A Brief History of Old English Porcelain* (1903)

Van Shoick, Emily C. (ed). *Ceramic Glossary* (1963)

Watney, Bernard. *English Blue and White Porcelain of the Eighteenth Century* (1963)

Whiter, Leonard. *Spode: History of the Family, Factory and Wares 1733–183.* (1963)

Wills, Geoffrey. *English Pottery and Porcelain* (1969)

Wykes-Joyce, M. *7000 Years of Pottery and Porcelain* (1958)

ACKNOWLEDGEMENTS

I wish to express my sincere appreciation to my many friends for all their encouragement and help towards the production of this book, especially those who so generously entrusted me with pieces from their private collections and which now appear among the photographic plates.

I am particularly indebted to Philip Wadsworth, Robert Copeland and John Austin, the latter of Virginia, USA, for their invaluable guidance and advice concerning the manuscript.

Thanks are also due to: Bournemouth Municipal Central Reference Library; British Ceramic Research Association; Carter Tiles (Poole) Ltd; English China Clays Ltd, St Austell and Wareham; E. W. Good & Co (Longton) Ltd; Minton Ltd; The Borough of Poole Central Reference Library; Poole Pottery Ltd; Rawden Ltd; Riddett & Adams Smith, Antique and Fine Art Auctioneers, Bournemouth; Spode Ltd; the City of Stoke-on-Trent Central Reference Library; Victoria & Albert Museum, Photographic Department; Josiah Wedgwood and Sons Ltd.

The photographs in this volume are reproduced by kind permission of the following:

H. K. Bowen: ills 93, 104–9, 137
British Ceramic Research Association: ills 135, 136
Camera & (Wilmslow) Ltd: ill 40
Robert Copeland: ills 39, 51, 59
English China Clays Ltd: ills 7, 22
Gordon McLoish: ill 130
John Martin (Staffs) Ltd: ills 100, 127, 128
Norman May's Studio, Malvern, Worcestershire: ills 84, 92, 97, 113
Riddett & Adams Smith, Bournemouth: ills 79, 83
Philip Smith: ills 12, 25, 31, 54, 58, 78, 80, 82, 89, 102, 103, 118, 119, 122
Spode Ltd, Stoke-on-Trent: ills 5, 96
Victoria & Albert Museum: ills 1, 13, 15, 17, 20, 41, 46, 49, 53, 55, 61, 81, 85, 98, 111, 114, 126
Josiah Wedgwood and Sons Ltd: ills 38, 56, 123, 124

CLASSIFIED LIST OF ENTRIES

TYPES AND STYLES OF WARE

accouchment set
acid-proof ware
adobe
agate
aka
akaraku
alla castallana
alla porcelana
ao
armorial ware
Arretine ware

bacile amatori
bamboo ware
basalt
basket ware
Batavian ware
beaker ware
biscuit
biscuit figure
black-figure vase
black pottery culture ware
blanc de chine
bleu persan
blue and white ware
blue-dash charger
boccaro
bone china

brinjal
brocaded Imari
buccaro

cabbage-leaf jug
Cadborough ware
cailloutages
Callot figures
cals noirs
Cambrian argil
cameo parian
cane ware
Carrara ware
cauliflower ware
chalk body
chamotte
chemical ware
chiang t'ai
china
china trade porcelain
Chinese export ware
chinoiserie
Cistercian ware
clobbered ware
Cologne ware
coppa d'amore
corded ware
coyotlatelco ware

creamware
crockery
crouch ware
culinary ware

Damascus ware
delft dore
delft noire
delftware
dinner ware
dipylon
dragon lustre
drug jar
dry body
dry-edge figure
duck-egg porcelain
Dutch

earthenware
egg-shell porcelain
Egyptian black
Egyptian paste
escudelles ab orelles
Etruscan ware

faience
faience d'oiron
faience fine
faience Japonée
faience parlante
faience patronymiques
fairings
fairyland lustre
famille jaune
famille noire
famille rose
famille verte
fancies
fayence
felspar china
felspar porcelain
fen ting

fine
fine earthenware
fine orange ware
firsts
flat ware
flint-enamelled ware
flint-porslin
fritted porcelain
fritware

Gabri ware
gallyware
gardenware
garnitures de chiminée
gawdy ware
glassy porcelain
glost
Gombroon ware
granite ware
Greek vases
greenware
grès
greybeard
guelder rose vase

habaner ware
hafner ware
hard
hard-paste
heavy-clay ware
Henri Deux ware
Hispano-Moresque ware
historical blue
hollow ware
hotel ware

ichotero
Imari
ironstone china
istoriato

Jackfield ware

Jacobite ware
jagd service
jasper
Jesuit china
jet ware
Joseph jug

kameoka
kast-stel
kitchenware
kochi
kuroraku

lakabi
laqabi ware
lava ware
leather-hard
loza fina
lump

maiolica
malabars
Malling jug
mandarin
mansion house dwarfs
martabani
Martin ware
Mason's ironstone
matlatzinca
mazapan
Metropolitan ware
mezza-maiolica
Miletus ware

Nankin blue
nishiki de

oak-leaf jar
once-fired ware
onyx ware
oriental Lowestoft
ovenware

painted pottery culture ware
pai ting
Palissy ware
Parian
parting cup
pâte dure
pâte tendre
peacock jar
pearl ware
pebble ware
Pennsylvania dutch
pew group
pharmacy jars
Philistine ware
pie-crust ware
pinched pottery
plumbate ware
porcelain
pot
pot lids
pottery
Pratt ware
proto-porcelain

quartz fritware
Queen's ware

raku
red-figure vase
red-gloss pottery
red stoneware
redware
Rhenish stoneware
Rhodian ware
rosso antico
ruby-backed dish

Saint Porchaire ware
salt glaze
Samian
sanitary ware
san ts'ai

scroddled ware
scrodledy
seconds
semi-porcelain
seven-borders dish
shard, sherd or shord
sha t'ai
shining-black ware
shino ware
sigillata ware
silicon ware
slab pot
slipware
smaltino
soapstone porcelain
soft-paste
solid jasper
spatterware
statuary porcelain
steingut
stone china
stoneware
studio pottery
Sussex pig

tableware
Tanagra figures
tea ware
terracotta
terra de pipa
terraglia

terra sigillata
tiger ware
tin enamels
Toby jug
Toft ware
toki
tortoiseshell ware
t'o t'ai
Tudor greenware
tulip ware
Turner's patent
t'u ting
tz'u
tz' t'ai

ushabti figures

vieux Paris
vitreous

wa
ware
waster
Welsh ware
white-hard
whiteware

yaki
yao
yao pien
yellow ware

DECORATIVE STYLES AND TECHNIQUES

acid etch
acid gold
ackey
aerography
agate
ailes de mouches
akaji-kinga

alla porcelana
amorini or amoretti
an-hua
antikzierat
apple-green
Arabian lustre
arista

banding
barbeaux
barbotine
bas relief
basse-taille
bat printing
beading
berittino
Berlin transparency
bianco-sopra-bianco
black-figure painting
black-pencilled decoration
blanc fixe
bleu céleste
bleu de roi
bleu lapis
bleu persan
bleu royal
blown blue
blue and white ware
blue lustre
blue-scale pattern
bocage
brandenstein pattern
brocaded Imari
broderie ware
brown gold
burnishing

caillouté
camaieu
cameo parian
cameo relief
candeliere
cantharides lustre
Canton blue
carquois
cartouche
cash pattern
Cassius purple
cauliflower ware
celeste blue

cerquate
chambrelan
chamois lustre
chamotte
champlevé
Chantilly sprig
chatironné
chiaro-oscuro
chi hung
ch'ui ch'ing
clobbered ware
clobbering
cloisonné
clouding
cold colours
combing
coperta glaze
coppa d'amour
coral red
cording or cord-mark decoration
corne
crab's-foot crackle
crackle
cuenca
cuerda seca
cut-glass decoration
cut-glaze decoration
cutting-up

decal
decalcomania
décor à la corne
décor aux cinq bouquets
delft dore
delft noire
dentil
Derby blue
Deutsche blumen
devil's work
dontil
dotted green
double glaze

dragon lustre
dry blue
Dumont's blue

émaillé sur bisque
émaux ombrants
embossing
embossment
enamel
enamel painting
encaustic
engine turning
English pink
engobe
engraved decoration

faience d'oiron
fairyland lustre
famille jaune
famille noire
famille rose
famille verte
fan hung
fantasievogel
Fazackerley colours
feathering
ferronerie
figuline
figure making
fish-roe crackle
fit
flashing
flash lustre
fleurs chatironnées
fleurs fines
fleurs Indes
flow blue
fluting
foglie
fruti

gilding
gold

grease-spot pattern
grisaille
gros bleu
ground
groundlay
guelder rose vase
gurtfurchen
gutbrennblau

hakeme
harden-on
hausemaler
Henri Deux ware
Hispano-Moresque
historical blue
hsien hung

Imari
impasto
impressed decoration
Indian floweers
Indianische blumen
in-glaze decoration
incised decoration
inlay
intaglio printing
iridium oxide
istoriato
itokiri

Japanned colour
Japans
jasper dip
jaune jonquille
jewelled decoration
Joseph jug
juan ts'ai

Kakiemon
kap
kinran-de
knocking-on
kuei kung

lace-work
lacquers
lajvardina
lakabi
lambrequin
lange liszen
lapis-lazuli
laqabi
laubengrupen
lava ware
Limoges enamels
ling lung
lining
liquid lustre
lithography
lithophane
Littler's blue
long Elizas
lustre

madreperla
maiolica
mandarin
marbling
Meissner blumen
mille fleurs
mishima
mocha
Mohammedan blue
moonlight lustre
mosaic
moulded decoration
Murray-curvex process

Nankin
Nankin blue
Nankin yellow
Naples yellow

oak-leaf jar
oeil de perdrix
oil-spot lustre

on-glaze decoration
onion pattern
onyx
ornamenting
over-glaze decoration
ozier pattern

paesi decoration
Palissy ware
Paris green
partridge-eye
pâte-sur-pâte
peacock decoration
peacock scale
peacock jar
pebble ware
pencilling
pencilled decoration
pettle decoration
petit feu
photolitho
pierced decoration
pink lustre
pink scale
platinum lustre
pochoir
poncif or spons
pounced decoration
powder blue
Pratt ware
printed decoration
pull and dust
putti

quartière
quartieri

rabesche
rabeschi
raised enamel
raised gold
raised paste

rayonnant
red-figure painting
red-scale
resist
rib
rice pattern
ringeloor decoration
rose colour
rose du Barry
rose Pompadour
rouge d'or
rouge flambé
royal blue
rubber-stamp decoration
ruby-backed dish

salmon scale
san ts'ai
scale blue
scale pattern
scallop or scollop
schamotte
schwarzlot
scrat
scratch blue
scratch edge
screen-printed decoration
scroddled ware
scrodledy
seven-borders dish
sgraffito
shagreen
sheet pattern
silk-screen printing
silver lustre
slip trailing
slipware
smaltino
solid jasper
sometsuke
soufflé blue
spatterware

splashed lustre
sponged ornament
spons
spraying
sprigged decoration
Staffordshire blue
stamping
stencilled decoration
stipple
streu blumen
Sulkowsky pattern

test
tin enamels
tin-vanadium yellow
tortoiseshell ware
trailing
transfer decoration
transparencies
trek
trofei
trompe l'oeil
truite
tube lining
tulip ware

under-glaze decoration

vermiculé or vermiculated decoration
vert anglais
vert foncée
vert pomme
vert pré
Victoria green

wash banding
window-dip
wu ts'ai

yang ts'ai
yellow scale

SHAPES

accouchment set
acetabula
achette
ai vakariri
alabastron
albarello
alcarraza
alfardone
amphora
aquamanile
arbour group
aryballos
askos
asparagus holder
azulejo

bacile
bacino
bagyne cup
baluster vase or jug
barber's bowl
barbman
bartmannskrug
beaker
bear jug
bellarmine
bell krater
benitor
beutelflasche
biberon
bishop bowl
bleeding bowl
block handle
boetja
bombentopf
bonbonnieres
botijo
bourdaloue
bowl-tile
bread crock

bromias
brush jar

cabaret
cabbage-leaf jug
cachala
cachemire
cachepot
Cadogan tea-pot
cadus
calix
Callot figures
calyx krater
can
canopic jar
cantaros
carboy
carpet bowls
casserole
catinus
caudle cup
celebe
chaire
chaki
chamber pot
charger
chatsubo
chawan
chicken-brick
Chinese shapes
clapmutsen
coach pot
column krater
comport
costrel
coup
coupe
cow creamer
crabstock handle
crater

crime cottages
crock
crock pie
cup
cupboard set
cup-stand
cylix

d'alva bottle
dinos
dod handle
double-gourd vase
double-interlaced handle
drillingsbecher
drug jar

enhalskrug
epergne
Essex jug
etui
eulenkrug
ewer

finger vase
flower-brick
foliated scroll handle
foot
frog mug
fuddling cup
furidashi
futaoki

gallipot
gallonier
garnitures de cheminée
gaulus
ginger jar
goat and bee jug
godet
goglet
gorgelet
granary urn

grapen
Greek vases
greybeard
gurglet
guttus

hand and cup vase
head cup
hill jar
humpen
hydria

interlaced handle

Jacqueline
jagd service
jakobakanne
jardinière

kachel
kados or kadiscos
kalpis
kantharos
kast-stel
kathos or kyathos
kelebe
kensui
keros
kitu
klapmutsen
kobishi
kothon
kotyle
krater
kreuse
kugeltopf
kylix

lebes
lebes gamikos
lekanis
lekethos

little pot
longbeard
loseta
loutrophorous
loving cup
lug handle

malabars
Malling jug
mansion house dwarfs
Martabans
mask lip
mei ping
milk skimmer
miska jug
mizusachi
mocca cup
modiolus
monteith
mortar
mourning jug
moustache cup
mukozuki

nib
night-light
noggin

oak-leaf jar
oenochoe or oinochoe
olambrilla
olla
ollio pot
olpe
open handle
owl jug
oxybaphon

pagoda jar
panathenaic amphora
pap warmer
parting cup

pastille burners
patella
patera
patina
pelike
pew group
pharmacy jars
phaille
piggin
pilgrim bottle
pill slab
pinte
pipkin
pitcher
pithos
platter
porringer
posset pot
pot
potiche
pot lid
pot-pouri
pottle-pot
pouring lip
prunus vase
psykter
pulle
pulled handle
puzzle jug
pyxis

quintal

ramekin
réchaud
rhyton
ringelkrug
ringkrug
rush foot

saliera
sallibube pot

saqua ni wei
scallop or scollop
schnabelkrug or schnabelkanne
schnell
schraubflasche
scodella
scutella
sinus
sitella or situla
skaphion
skillet
skinker
skyphos
socarrat
solitaire set
spirit flask
spout-pot
stamnos
steinzengkrug
stem
stem-bowl
stirrup cup
strip handle
sturzbecher
Sussex pig
syllabub cup

Tanagra figures
taws
tazza
tea-bowl
terrine

tête-à-tête set
théière
thorondell
tinja
Toby jug
trauerkruge
trembleuse saucer
trencher salt
trichterbecher
trulla
tureen
twiffler
tyg

urceus or urceolus
urn
urna
ushabti figures

vasi puerperali
veilleuse
volute krater

wall-pocket
wan
wassel cup
Worcester shape

ya shou pei
yen yen vase

GLAZES, TYPES AND TECHNIQUES

alkaline
ash
aventurine

bekko
break-up
Bristol

calcareous
celadon
chi hung
Chun
clair-de-lune
columbine
coperta

copper celadon
copper red
crystalline

double
dragon-skin

egg and spinach
Egyptian blue
enamel

felspathic
flambé
flash lustre
flint-enamelled ware
fond écaille
frit

glaze
glaze-fit
green-glaze

hare's-fur
hsien hung

Imperial yellow

ja katsu

ki
kingfisher blue
kuro
kwaart

lakabi
lang yao
laqabi
lead bisilicate
lead boro-silicate
lead
leadless glaze
low-solubility
lustre

marbled
Martabani
matt
mirror black
mutton-fat

namako
Nankin yellow

oil-spot
once-fired ware
opalescent
opaque

pao shih hung
peach bloom
peacock blue

raw glaze
robin's-egg
Rockingham
rouge flambé

salt glaze
same-yaki
sang-de-boeuf
sang-de-pigeon
satin
shark-skin
slip glaze
slop
smaltino
smear
soft
strawberry red
sui yu

tea-dust
tenmoku
tessha
tiger glaze
tin

tin enamel
transmutation glaze

vapour
vellum

wu chin

yao ping
ying ch'ing

MATERIALS

ackey
adobe
aeolian clay
agglomerate clay
alabaster
Albany clay
albite
alginates
alluvial clay
alumina
aluminium oxide
amakusa
amboy clay
anatase
Anglo-gum
aniseed (oil of)
anorthite
antimonate of lead
antimony
argil
Armenian bole
asbolite
ash
ash marl
aubergine purple

ball clay
barium carbonate
barium oxide
barium sulphate
barium sulphide
barytes
basalt

bat-wash
bauxite
bentonite
best gold
bing ore
bismuth sub-nitrate
black ash
black iron oxide
black wad
blue lustre
blue vein
body
body stain
bone ash
bone china
borax
boric oxide
boulder clay
boulder flint
break-up
bright gold
Bristol blue
British gum
bronze lustre
brookite
brown gold
burnished gold

cadmium oxide
calcite
calcium carbonate
calcium fluoride
calcium metasilicate
calcium oxide

307

calcium phosphate
calc-spa
callow
cantharides lustre
Canton blue
carrageen moss
Carrara ware
Cassius purple
caulk stone
chalk
chalk body
chalk flint
chamois lustre
chamotte
Chert stone or Cherts
china
china clay
china stone
Chinese blue
chrome oxide
clay
clay substance
cloam
coalad flint
cobalt oxide
colcothar
cold colours
colemanite
colluvial clay
conglomerate clay
copper carbonate
copper oxide
corafin
Cornish stone or Cornwall stone
cover-coat
cristobalite
crocus martis
cryolite
cullet
cupric oxide
cuprous oxide
cutty clay

deflocculant
Derby blue
dolomite
dry blue
dry body
duck-egg porcelain
Dumont's blue

earthenware
Egyptian paste
enamels
English pink
engobe

fan hung
fat clay
fat oil
Fazackerley colours
felspar
felspar china
felspar porcelain
fennel
ferric oxide
ferrous oxide
filter-cake
fireclay
flint
flow blue
flow powder
fluorspar
flux
French chalk
frit
funori

galena
ganister
glassy porcelain
glaze hardener
glaze suspender
gold
gosu

grog
grout
Growan stone
gum Arabic
gum tragacanth
gypsum

haematite
hardener
hard-paste
heavy spa
hino-oka
hua shih
hydrofluoric acid

Iceland spar
igneous rock
illite
illmanite
iridium oxide
Irish moss
iron oxide
ironstone china

Japanned colour
jasper
juan ts'ai
juraku-zuchi

kaolin
kidney ore
kiln wash

labradorite
lavender (oil of)
lead antimonate
lead bisilicate
lead carbonate
lead chromate
lead monosilicate
lead monoxide
lead oxide

lead sesquisilicate
lead sulphide
lean clay
lepidolite
lime
limestone
liquid lustre
litharge
lithium carbonate
little mine rock
Littler's blue

madreperla
magnesia
magnesium oxide
magnesite
magnetic iron
magnetite
magnus
manganese oxide
marble
marl
marzacotto
massicot
mennigne
mica clay
minium
Mohammedan blue
molochite
moor stone
mortar body
mother rock of clay
mullite

Naples yellow
natron
nephaline syenite
new rock
new stone china
nickel oxide
nitre

ochre
opening materials
orthoclase

Parian
Paris green
Paris white
parting sand
paste
pâte dure
pearl ash
pegmatite
petalite
petuntse
pipe clay
pitcher
placing sand
plaster of Paris
platinum lustre
pocket clay
porcelain
potash
potassium carbonate
potassium nitrate
potassium oxide
powder blue
primary clay
proto-porcelain
pug
purple iron oxide
purple of Cassius
putnam clay

quartz

raddle or reddle
raised enamel
raised paste
raku
red clay
reddle
red iron oxide

red lead
red stoneware
refractory clay
relief paste
residual clay
resist
rose colour
rosso antico
rouge d'or
ruddle
rutile

sand
schamotte
screen gold
seat-earth
secondary clay
sedimentary clay
selenium
semi-porcelain
sha t'ai
short clay
silica
silicon carbide
silimanite
silver lustre
size
slip
slop
slop flint
slop stone
slug
slurry
smalts
smithum
soapstone
soapstone porcelain
soda ash
sodium borate
sodium carbonate
sodium carboxymethylcellulose
sodium chloride

sodium oxide
sodium silicate
soft-paste
soufflé blue
stamping gold
statuary porcelain (body)
steatite
stent
stone
stone china
stoneware
strontium carbonate

Tabberner's mine rock
talc
terracotta
terra sigillata
till
tincal
tin oxide
tin-vanadium yellow
titanium oxide
tong clay
to-no-tsuchi

Turner's patent

unaker
under-clay
uranium oxide

vanadium oxide
vegetable ash
vermiculite

wad clay
water-glass
white lead
whiting
witherite
wollastonite
wood ash
yang ts'ai
yellow ochre

zaffre
zinc oxide

zircon

MATERIALS PREPARATION

ageing
air drying

banking
blending
blunge
burrow
buttonhole launder

calcine
charge

de-air
deflocculant
drags

dry

elutriation

filter cake
filter press
flow chart

getting

kneading
knockings
knottings

launder

magnetic purification
maturing
mechanically combined water
micas

open-cast mining

pan hearth
pint weight

rise

shaft mining
slake
slip house
slip pan
slop

slop weight
slug
slurry
souring
stent
stent tip
stope
strakes

treading
trough

washing shaft
weathering
wedging
winning

MAKING PROCESSES

aerography
agate
ageing
air drying

balling
basket ware
batting-out
biscuit firing
bitting edge
bittings
blending
blocking
bocage
bone edge
boxing
bung
bunging-up
burning

cameo Parian
carrying-off

case mould
casting
centre
clamin or claming
clothing
coiling
cord-throwing
cutting a plate

deflocculant
dégourdi
demi-grand feu
dipping
dottling
double casting
draw
dressing
dry-edge figure
dry foot
dry pressing
dust pressing

easy fire
engine turning
extrusion

facing-up
fettling
firing
flow chart

ginnetting
giving
glaze
glaze-fit
grand feu
green-hard

handling
harden-on
heat-work
hollow casting
hump
hygroscopic water

itokiri

jasper dip
jigger and jolley

kap
knocking-on

laubengrupen
leather-hard
lining
luting

model
moulding
mould making

once-fired ware
onyx

open setting
'oss-off
oxidation

pebble ware
pegging
pencilling
petit feu
pinched pottery
pitcher mould
placing
pouring
pressing
press moulding
pull and dust

rearing
reduction
rigget or riggot
rubbing-up
running

salt glaze
scouring
scrapping
scroddled ware
scrodledy
setting
sizing
slab building
slake
slop moulding
slug
soak
soft
solid casting
solid jasper
sorting
spare
spraying
stalk
sticking-up

take-up
throwing
thwacking
towing
turning

unity formula

water-smoking
welt
whirlering
white-hard
working mould

EQUIPMENT, TOOLS, MACHINERY ETC

ark

backstone
baffle
bag wall
ball mill
bad bench
band or bont
bander
banding wheel
bar crusher
bat
batter
batting machine
beater
bedder
biddy shovel
bitstone
bitting edge
blank
block mould
blood stone
blow hole
blunger
bolting cloth
bont
bosch
bottle oven
bowl-pin
brushes
Bullers ring

bung
buttonhole launder

cage mill
case mould
chaser mill
Chert stone
chock
chuck
chucker
chum
clamin or claming
clamp
clean ark
climbing kiln
clot
clouder
cockspur
cone
cottle
cow's lip
crank
cutter
cutting spade

dabber
damper
diddler
dieper
dirty ark
dobbin

314

dod
dod box
dot
drag
drift
dry
dry-pan
dubber
dump
duster

edge-runner mill
embossing wheel
end set
energy regulator

filter cloth
filter press
flash wall
footer
former
frit kiln

ginnetting wheel
gold rubber
graft
greenhouse
ground-hog kiln

hanging arms
hammer mill
hatchel
head pins
heat fuse
Holdcroft bar
horizontal kiln
horn
horse ('oss)
hoval
hump mould

jar mill

jaw crusher
jigger and jolley
joggle
jolley

kidney palette
kidney stone
kilns
kiln furniture
knocker or knocker-out

launder
lawn
leafer
liner
linhay

mandrel
mangle
master mould
micas
mixing ark
monkey
mop
muffle
muller
Murray-curvex machine

natch
natch block
natch knife
nibbed saggar

old bowl stilt
Orton cone
'oss
ox lip

packer
pallet
pan hearth
pan mill

parting sherd
pastries
paver
pebble mill
pencils
pens
pillar crank
pin
pip
pitcher
pitcher mould
placing sand
poge
poncif
potter's horn
pounce pot
presser's rubber
press mould
printer's bit
profile setter
prop
pug
pug mill
punch
pyrometer
pyroscope

refractory
rib
rigget or riggot
ring
rise
roller machine
Roman kiln
rubber
runner
rush foot

saddle
saggar
scraper
scrapper

scrapping edge
screen
Segar cone
semi-muffle
set bat
sets
setter
settling ark
shader
shrager
sieve
silicon carbide (elements)
skivet
slip house
slip pan
slow wheel
sorting lathe
sorting tool
spare
spreader
sprig mould
spud
spudgel
spur
Staffordshire cone
stamp-mill
stillage
stove
sun pan

thermocouple
thimble
tile crank
tommy stick
top-hat kiln
tracer
trailer
treader
trekker
Trent kiln
trough
tubal

tunnel kiln

updraught kiln

wad box
washing shaft
welt

wet pan
wheel
whirler
wicket
work board
working mould

yaki

FAULTS

alligator's teeth

balling
black cores
blebbing
blibbing
blistering
bloating
blotching
blowing
blushing
bowing
bulging
bursting

casting spot
chattering
chittering
crawling
crazing
crocodile's teeth
crowsfoot
crystalline glaze
curtain glaze

devitrification
dimples
dishing
dog's teeth
drag
dragon's teeth

droppers
dry edge
dulling
dunting

efflorescence

flashing
fled
flown
frizzling

humper

ironing

kiln white
knocked glaze

livering

peeling
pig-skin pitting
pinholing
pitting
plucked ware
pocked glaze

retch
ruckling
running

scaling
scumming
shivering
short fired
silver marking
soluble salts
specking
spit-out
squatting
starved glaze

striking
stuck ware
sucked ware
sulphuring

wedging
whirler
white dirt
wool-drag
wreathing

ARCHITECTURAL APPLICATIONS

alfardone
alicatados
aliceras
azulejo

bacino
bowl-tile

cachala

grout

hafner ware

kachel
kachelenoven
kap

lajvardina

loseta

mosaic

olambrilla

pilaertjes
pisano

ringeloor decoration

slabber
smuiger
socarrat

tablero
tesserae
tile
tile slabber
tube lining

MISCELLANEOUS

back stamp
bad bench
baffle
bag wall
bander

bank
bat
batch
biscuit
bittings

318

black-hard
blank
blow hole
bocage
body
bone edge
bung
burrow

Callot figures
callow
ceramic
chambrelan
charge
clamin or claming
clay bed
cobbler
cod placer
crate-man
crock
crockery

demi-grand feu
devitrification
dry
dry foot

easy fire

face
filter cake
fire
firsts
flashing
flow chart
foot

ganister
getting
giving
glost
grand feu
greenhouse

hanging arms
hard
hausemaler
heat-work
hump
hygroscopic water

interlayer water
itokiri

kap

laubengrupen
linhay
lump

mechanically combined water
model
modulus of rupture
moons
mould runner

open-cast mining
overburden
oxidation

petit feu
pip
placer
plat
pot
pot-bank
pot-sherd
potteries
pottery
presser

reduction
refractory
rigget or riggot
rise
runner

running

saggar-maker's bottom-knocker
scrapping edge
seat earth
seconds
shaft mining
shard, sherd or shord
shord ruck
shrager
silicosis
size
sizing
slabber
slip house
slop
slop weight
slug
slurry
soft
spare
stalk
stem
stent
stent tip
stillage
stope

strakes
studio pottery
syllabub

take-up
thrower
tigel
tile slabber
turner
Twaddle degrees

unity formula

vitreous

wad
ware
washer
waster
water of formation
water of plasticity
welt
winning

yaki